PIONEER
OF THE
AZUSA STREET
REVIVAL
Sect of Fanatics Is
Breaking Loose.

WILLIAM J. SEYMOUR

PIONEER

OF THE AZUSA STREET REVIVAL

VINSON SYNAN &
CHARLES R. FOX, JR.

BRIDGE LOGOS

Alachua, Florida 32615

Bridge-Logos
Alachua FL 32615 USA

William J. Seymour: Pioneer of the Azusa Street Revival
By Vinson Synan and Charles R. Fox, Jr.

Edited by Harold J. Chadwick

Printed in the United States of America.

Library of Congress Catalog Card Number 2011945734
International Standard Book Number 978-0-88270-848-5

Unless otherwise indicated, all Scripture verses are from the King James Version (KJV) of the Bible.

BP 12-05-16

Dedications

CHARLES R. FOX, JR.

I want to first give thanks to my Lord and Savior Jesus Christ. None of this would be possible without Him giving me the strength. I dedicate this book to my loving wife April and our kids. They stood by my side through it all. Your prayers and sacrificial love made the difference. I also want to thank the following people for helping to bring this work to fruition: Vinson Synan–Thanks for the opportunity to work with you. Estrelda Alexander–Thanks for empowering me to write my dissertation. Jon Ruthven–Thanks for believing in me from day one.

VINSON SYNAN

I dedicate this book to the fine professors and Ph.D. graduate students at the Regent University School of Divinity who have advanced the cause of African and African-American religious studies. They are: Professors Estrelda Alexander, Clifton Clarke, and Antipas Harris and Ph.D. Graduates: Charles Fox, Lewis Brogdan, Jean Batiste Roamba, and Fitzroy Willis.

Table of Contents

Preface

For several years I have been in conversation with Lloyd Hildebrand about doing a book with Bridge-Logos publishers. During this time I became Dean of the School of Divinity at Regent University. In 2003 I helped inaugurate a Ph.D. program in Renewal Studies that was the first of its kind anywhere in the world. Among the faculty we recruited to work in this program and the Doctor of Ministry program were two fine African-American scholars: Dr. Estrelda Alexander, and Dr. Antipas Harris. We also hired a missions professor from England who has great missions experience in England and Africa, Dr. Clifton Clarke.

As we developed the Ph.D. program, many fine students enrolled from America and around the world. Among these were African-American students Charles Fox, Lewis Brognan, and Fitzroy Willis from the United States, and Jean Batiste Roamba from Burkino Faso in East Africa. Each of these produced fine dissertations dealing with Pentecostal and Charismatic movements in America and Africa. Charles Fox's excellent biography of William J. Seymour earned him a Ph.D. degree at Regent in 2009. Dr. Estrelda Alexander was the Chairperson on his dissertation.

About this time, Lloyd Hildebrand called me about doing a book with Bridge-Logos. I immediately suggested that Charles and I produce a unique book on Seymour that would include two parts. The first half would be the biographical dissertation by Charles and the second half would be all the known signed articles and sermons that Seymour published in the *Apostolic Faith* in Los Angeles from 1906 to 1909, plus his only book, *Doctrines and Discipline*, which was published in 1915 to serve as the governing document of his new denomination. In the past this book has been difficult to find in its original and unabridged form, although Larry Martin published it in an abridged and corrected form in the year 2000.

It was my purpose to take the original book and present it in the most exact form possible—to keep the fonts, pagination, and even the typos that were in the original version. Now scholars can have the complete unchanged version of the original (with the same page numbers) for research and writing projects. It will also be quite interesting for the average reader who wants to know more about Seymour and his remarkable ministry.

I have many people to thank for bringing this book to life. First of all I thank Lloyd Hildebrand for his encouragement and support during all phases of the project. And, of course, I thank Charles Fox for his enthusiastic cooperation as we moved forward towards publication. As usual, my wife Carol Lee worked diligently to help bring the *Doctrines and Discipline* back to life in its original form. This took many weeks of exacting labor trying to match fonts and spacing from the original. It was not easy, but we did it. Also I want to thank Harold J. Chadwick for helping edit and correct the Seymour book so it would be as accurate as possible. He did a great job. Thanks also to Jackie Van Hauen for her hard work and tenacity in the layout of this book, and to Susan Parr for her expertise and brainstorming with Jackie to get the job done.

It is our hope that the reader will learn much more about the mind and spirit of William Joseph Seymour from this biography and collection of his published works.

Vinson Synan
Regent University
Virginia Beach, VA
January, 2012

Introduction

Although *Life Magazine* and *USA Today* list the Azusa Street Revival as one of the top one hundred nation-impacting events of the Twentieth Century, there still remains a degree of vagueness about its black leader, William Joseph Seymour. After one hundred years, the Pentecostal/Charismatic movement has grown to over 600 million adherents globally. Particularly within the North American context, where many of these believers trace their roots either directly or indirectly to Azusa Street, it is becoming more important to investigate the significance of Seymour. Though, in recent decades, some Pentecostal historians have tried to make people more aware of his significance, few have specifically concentrated on the contribution that Seymour's theology has made to the movement.

One of the reasons for this oversight is that because of his lack of formal education, most historians have viewed Seymour as simply a catalyst for the world-wide Pentecostal movement rather than an astute Pentecostal theologian. Because of such attitudes, the theological depth of his writings and sermons is often missed.

Thus, this book is not just another history of Seymour and the Azusa Street Revival, it is a book that digs deeper into the mind of William J. Seymour and gives him a voice that actually speaks to us today. Accordingly, section one of this work will examine his theology, with particular emphasis on his views on sin and salvation (soteriology), the Holy Spirit (pneumatology), and his view of the Church (ecclesiology) in an attempt to understand him in his own context, and discover the implications of his theology for Pentecostals and Charismatics of today.

Section One of this book broadens the overall knowledge of Seymour in several areas. First, it examines the historical context and sources that shaped Seymour's theology by tracing his associations with, Martin Wells Knapp, the "Evening Light Saints" (also known as the Church of God Reformation Movement), Charles Harrison Mason, Charles Price Jones, and Charles Fox Parham. Second, it seeks to recover Seymour's central message and the ensuing pivotal early controversies that surrounded him. Third, it considers the implications for the ongoing process of shaping contemporary Pentecostal/ Charismatic theology.

Section Two of the book lets Seymour speak for himself by providing two important primary sources from him. Part A of Section Two will help those interested in Pentecostalism to grasp Seymour's sermons at the Azusa Street Mission. This section furnishes the signed articles of William J. Seymour from 1906-1908 in the Apostolic Faith, which was a periodical that was sent out to nearly 50,000 people to keep them informed about Azusa's happenings. Also included are some of the topics that were preached by Seymour: marriage, sanctification, gifts of the Holy Spirit, and baptism of the Holy Spirit.

Part B of Section Two provides readers with the entire *Doctrines and Discipline of the Apostolic Faith Mission of Los Angeles, California*, which Seymour published in 1915. Though major parts of the Doctrines and Discipline were adopted from a Discipline of the African Methodist Episcopal Church, several parts were written by Seymour to establish the doctrines, identity, and constitution of his own church. The Doctrines and Discipline also help us to see a more mature

Seymour who has evolved in his theology of tongues as initial evidence.

The conclusion of Section One of this thorough examination of Seymour's thought yields a picture of his contribution to Pentecostal theology that is much richer than that for which he has previously been credited. Furthermore, this exploration moves the conversation of Pentecostal experience to a more robust understanding of Holy Spirit baptism and the Spirit-empowered life.

SECTION ONE

WILLIAM J. SEYMOUR:
Pioneer of the Azusa Street Revival

by

Charles R. Fox, Jr.

CHAPTER ONE

From Louisiana to Azusa Street

Catholic Roots in Louisiana

On May 2, 1870 in Centerville, Louisiana beside Bayou Teche, William J. Seymour, son of former slaves Simon Seymour and Phillis Salaba Seymour, came into this world. Simon Seymour had recently moved from New Iberia, twenty miles up the bayou, and at the center of Acadian, or Cajun, country. During the Civil War, he was among the fifteen thousand African American volunteers to join the Union army.[1] Because Lincoln's Emancipation Proclamation was directed only at areas under Confederate control, it did not free those slaves who lived in St. Mary and surrounding parishes, where Simon lived. Therefore, he took advantage of an exception clause by volunteering to take up arms against the South, thereby earning immediate freedom in exchange for his military service.[2]

Although Lincoln was committed to ending slavery and had declared that all slaves would be free as of January 1, 1863, he did not want to put the Union army at a tactical disadvantage by having to care for homeless freed slaves while the North was still fighting a war. Therefore, Simon

1 Cecil M. Robeck Jr., *The Azusa Street Mission and Revival: The Birth of the Global Pentecostal Movement* (Nashville: Nelson Reference and Electronic, 2006), 20.

2 John Hope Franklin, *From Slavery to Freedom: A History of Negro Americans*, 4th ed. (New York: Knopf, 1974), 223-224; and Howard A. White, *The Freedmen's Bureau in Louisiana* (Baton Rouge: Louisiana State University Press, 1970), 101.

took the only option that a slave living in St. Mary Parish, and desperately desiring freedom could take; on October 10, 1863, he became an infantryman in the *Corps d'Afrique*, later called the U.S. Colored Infantry.[3] Simon served his country for three years in Louisiana and in Florida and was honorably discharged September 7, 1866.[4]

Seymour's mother, Phillis Salaba, was born November 23, 1844, and, according to Cecil M. Robeck, had been owned by Mr. Adelard Carlin, one of the wealthiest plantation owners in St. Mary Parish.[5] It was reported that Carlin owned 2,110 acres of land along with 112 slaves, 80 horses, 40 mules, 30 milk cows, 16 oxen, 150 pigs, and 150 "other" cattle.[6] The 112 slaves included Phillis Salaba, her parents and her siblings.

Simon and Phillis were married July 27, 1867, and since neither could read or write, they each signed their wedding license by placing an "X" on the license and having it witnessed.[7] Not long afterward, the Seymours had a daughter named Rosalie, and in 1870 they had a son named William. These two would be joined by Simon, Amos, Julia, Jacob, Isaac, and Emma over the next fifteen years.[8]

Religious life in southern Louisiana was dominated by the Roman Catholic Church due to the influence of the French settlers who gained control of the region by the eighteenth century. Loyalty to the Roman Catholic Church was imposed on anyone under its territorial jurisdiction. A generation earlier, in 1724 the mayor of New Orleans, Jean Baptiste Le Moyne Bienville issued *Le code noir*, "The Black Code," requiring all slave-owning settlers to instruct and baptize their slaves in the Roman Catholic faith. The Seymour family was one of the many African American families to be instructed in the ways

3 Robeck, *Azusa Street Mission and Revival*, 21.
4 Ibid.
5 Ibid., 19.
6 Ibid.
7 Ibid., 23.
8 Ibid.

of the Catholic Church. Accordingly, each child was escorted to the Catholic Church in nearby Franklin, Louisiana, where they were baptized.[9] William J. Seymour was baptized when he was just a four-month-old infant, on September 4, 1870. He was to be raised a Roman Catholic.[10]

Nevertheless, William was probably influenced by various local religions, often of African origin and interwoven into Catholicism. One of the most dominant religions in Louisiana during Seymour's time was one of several forms of Voodoo.[11] A majority of the slaves that arrived in southern Louisiana from Africa, had not totally embraced classic Voodoo, but did bring with them many of its tenets, superstitions, and fears, which were then bequeathed to the next generation of slaves.[12]

However, in spite of their differences with Christians, the African slave religion held many beliefs in common with the Christian worldview. These included the belief in a divine spirit, signs and wonders, miracles and healings, invisible spirits, trances, spirit possession, and visions and dreams.[13] Against this backdrop it is easy to understand why some scholars assert that the African religion, along with the conditions of slavery under which a black understanding of Christianity was formed, may have been influential in the formation of Seymour's brand of Pentecostalism, or black Pentecostalism.[14] Therefore, Seymour's formative years, with its emphasis on dreams, visions, and the supernatural, should be kept in mind while observing his spiritual pilgrimage leading up to Azusa Street.

9 Ibid., 23-24.
10 Ibid., 24.
11 Ibid., 22.
12 Ibid., 23.
13 Ibid.
14 Iain MacRobert, *The Black Roots and White Racism of Early Pentecostalism in the USA* (New York: St. Martin's Press, 1988), 9; and Leonard Lovett, "Black Origins of the Pentecostal Movement," in *Aspects of Pentecostal-Charismatic Origins*, ed. Vinson Synan (Plainfield, NJ: Logos International, 1975), 123-141.

Slavery and Emancipation

In 1877, when Seymour was seven years old, Reconstruction[15] ended, leaving blacks feeling betrayed by their liberators, as Republicans agreed to withdraw federal troops from the South.[16] The promise of freedom that was guaranteed in President Lincoln's Emancipation Proclamation of January 1, 1863 was mere rhetoric for most southern blacks, as they were denied basic liberties such as the right to vote, the right to obtain an education, and the right to benefit from employment opportunities.

Additionally, blacks suffered unspeakable atrocities at the hands of white supremacists. For example, on April 13, 1873, four years before federal troops departed, 100 black men were killed when the White League, a paramilitary group intent on fortifying white rule in Louisiana, clashed with Louisiana's almost all-black state militia in Colfax, Louisiana.[17] From 1876 to the end of the century, white leaders brutally enforced supremacy and segregation throughout the South.

Like much of the South, the city of Centerville had deep racial conflicts that had evolved through a clear chain of events, spanning many decades. Settlers arrived in the area shortly after President Thomas Jefferson purchased the Louisiana Territory from Napoleon Bonaparte in 1803, in effect doubling the size of the United States.[18] By 1808 the boat-landing at Franklin (six miles up the bayou from Centerville) had become large enough to make Franklin the first town in the parish. In 1820, Franklin became the seat of the parish. Enthusiastic fortune hunters came to seek small fortunes through the sale of refined

---

15 Reconstruction was the period after the Civil War when the southern states were reorganized and reintegrated into the union; 1865-1877.

16 John Hope Franklin, *From Slavery to Freedom: A History Negro Americans,* 3rd ed. (New York: Knopf, 1967), 332; and Nelson, "For Such a Time as This," 155.

17 http://www.pbs.org/wgbh/americanexperience/features/general-article/grant-colfax/.

18 Ibid., 151.

sugar, and to build larger fortunes from the sale of the rum that was made from sugar. These recently arrived entrepreneurs used the Mississippi River to commute from New Orleans northward and westward through the Bayou Plaquemines and other bayous, traveling as far as Bayou Teche, which was midway between New Orleans and the land beyond the Sabine River, later to be known as Texas.[19]

Whites knew that strong backs were needed to toil in the sugar cane fields. During harvest time, they made sure to keep an adequate supply of African slaves, who would sometimes work eighteen to twenty hours a day in an area known to be one of the most hot and humid regions on earth.[20] The backs of these black slaves were bloodied by whips and painfully bent as their white oppressors forced them to a life of slashing and severing the two-inch fibrous stalks just above the soil. Even beasts of burden were not fit for such demanding labor in the dreadful Louisiana heat. Mrs. Amy Jackson, a former Louisiana slave, gave a clear description of a day in the life of slave.

> As slaves we were forced to be up in the mornings and in the fields at 4:00 a.m., and our work day lasted until 11:00 p.m.—sometimes later...How well I remember those beatings! The scars are still on my back. ...Two men held my hands and two held my feet, while with my back bare, I lay on my stomach. The master plied the lash until my skin lay open in great gashes, large enough to put your hands in, and a pool of warm blood formed underneath.[21]

19 Beverly Bernard Broussard, "A History of St. Mary Parish" (unpublished MS, Franklin, LA: 1968), 6-8, as cited in Nelson, "For Such a Time as This," 151.
20 Nelson, "For Such a Time as This," 151; and Franklin, *From Slavery to Freedom*, 144.
21 Jewel Lynn de Grummond Delaune, "A Social History of St. Mary Parish, 1845-1864" (master's thesis, Louisiana State University, 1984), 108, as cited in Nelson, "For Such a Time as This," 170.

By the 1830s, real estate in St. Mary Parish skyrocketed due to over-zealous speculation of the fertile land that was able to produce vast amounts of new wealth by means of slave labor.[22] Also in 1830, after a decade of mounting fears of slave rebellion, Louisiana passed laws forbidding anyone to instruct slaves in reading and writing, under penalty of one year in jail. These apprehensions were justified. In 1831, Nat Turner led a slave insurgency that killed 60 whites in Southampton County, Virginia.[23] The fear of more rebellions precipitated widespread anti-education laws being enacted against the Africans. For the slaves, any form of schooling faded into an unattainable dream.

Apprehension by slave masters about the explosive consequences of slavery had been present since the Haitian slave revolt of 1791 when five-hundred-thousand blacks destroyed not only sugar plantations, but also their overseers. By 1798, and perhaps with an eye toward the Haitian revolt while also surveying the ominously increasing number of American slaves, all U. S. states declared the slave trade, but not slavery itself, to be illegal. A further step in this direction came on January 1, 1808, when the importation of slaves was banned by the federal government. This ban, however, did not eliminate the influx of slaves, but merely allowed for the creation of a profitable black market, which was controlled by men such as the pirate Jean Lafitte, who plied his trade

22 Broussard, "History of St. Mary Parish," 8, as cited in Nelson, "For Such a Time as This,"151.

23 Nat Turner believed that he had been divinely chosen by God to deliver his people from slavery. Turner selected August 21 as the day for his revolt, which resulted in the death of sixty whites within a twenty-four hour period, until the main group of insurgents were overcome by state and federal troops. More than one hundred slaves were killed because of the uprising. Turner was eventually captured on October 30 and hanged on November 11, 1831. Franklin, *From Slavery to Freedom*, 161-163; and for a more thorough treatment also see Nat Turner and Thomas R. Gray, *The Confessions of Nat Turner: Leader of the Late Insurrection in Southampton, Va., as Fully and Voluntarily Made to Thomas R. Gray... and Acknowledged by Him ... When Read Before the Court of Southampton, Convened at Jerusalem, November 5, 1831, for His Trial* (1830-1839?).

from Barataria Bay (forty miles south of New Orleans) to within a short distance of Bayou Teche.[24]

While brother fought against brother in the Civil War of 1861-1865, it was sometimes difficult to differentiate the attitudes of either side toward African Americans, or even toward the local economy. Union forces commanded by General Benjamin Butler had choked off Louisiana's commercial existence with an extended blockade of New Orleans, concluding with the capture of the city on May 1, 1862. The withdrawing Confederate army aided in the destruction by burning all boats, docks, and warehouses, including cotton and sugar stocks. The outcome of General Butler's war effort was an 1862 harvest gross of a mere eight million dollars; less than one-third of the previous year's crop. In fact, the estimated losses to sugar planters throughout the war totaled in excess of one hundred seventy million dollars and virtually ruined the entire sugar industry.[25]

Lincoln's 1863 Emancipation Proclamation deeply impacted most Louisiana slaves, but not all. Since the Proclamation was directed to those areas under Confederate control, it did not free the slaves in Teche country (which included St. Mary and its neighboring parishes), because this area was under federal jurisdiction.[26] As for General Butler, despite his position in the Union Army, he returned runaway slaves to their masters until his successor, General Nathanael P. Banks, stopped the practice in January 1864.[27]

In December 1865 all slaves were freed with the ratification of the 13th Amendment. The Emancipation Proclamation was recited publicly on every Louisiana plantation, with written copies in English and French given to newly freed slaves. In addition to the public reading of the Proclamation, a special

24 Franklin, *From Slavery to Freedom*, 106-110.
25 White, *Freedmen's Bureau in Louisiana*, 5.
26 Franklin, *From Slavery to Freedom*, 223-224.
27 White, *Freedmen's Bureau in Louisiana*, 101.

admonition went out to the town of Franklin, where blacks were illegally prohibited from owning property, carrying firearms, and assembling for worship without a permit.[28]

While the federal government's Freedmen's Bureau was trying to educate and enfranchise black people, violence erupted when secret white terrorist groups, such as the Ku Klux Klan and White League, arose to keep blacks oppressed through fear and brutality. St. Mary Parish, as well as other neighboring areas suffered vicious attacks against its black residents. On July 30, 1866 in New Orleans, an attempted constitutional convention of African Americans was met with an attack that left thirty-four dead and 146 injured at the hands of whites.

Twenty-five freed blacks were attacked and murdered between September 1865 and November 1866; however, as of March 9, 1867, the Freedmen's Bureau acknowledged that no white person had been prosecuted for killing a freedman. The trend accelerated. By September 30, 1867 the Bureau counted fifty-one such murders, sixty-nine assaults with the intent to kill, and fifty-six reports of assault and battery. The next year brought 166 more murders and 225 other provocations against former slaves. Attempts to bring offending whites to justice by the civil authorities were feckless; the guilty seemed immune from the law.[29]

28 Ibid., 135-136.
29 White, *Freedmen's Bureau in Louisiana*, 144-146.

RECONSTRUCTION, RACISM, AND MIGRATION

Reconstruction

In November 1876, dubious election results in Louisiana and South Carolina led to a compromise in Washington. In exchange for the presidency, Republicans agreed to remove federal troops from the South. When the newly elected Rutherford B. Hayes became president, he kept his covenant with southern (white) voters by withdrawing federal troops from the South in 1877. In effect, this ended the enforcement of Reconstruction laws that aided African Americans toward their civil rights and freedom.[30]

Despite many achievements, the Freedmen's Bureau was regrettably not able to supply needed economic resources for the advancement of black freedom, due to lack of federal funding from Congress, which merely reflected the prevailing attitudes of the American people. The constitutional right guaranteeing political equality was worthless at this time, because freedmen were denied not only voting rights, but education and employment as well. The dream of "forty acres and a mule" was nothing more than a fantasy, as blacks were abandoned by their liberators.[31]

It was during this period that Seymour grew into manhood in Louisiana. It was also against this backdrop of heightening racism that made him seek to relocate to an area more accommodating for blacks who wanted freedom from oppression, and an opportunity to live the American dream.

During Seymour's lifetime, African Americans endured indescribable hostility and incalculable atrocities. Suppressed by terrorism and random acts of violence in the ashes of a failed Reconstruction policy, the sobering fact was that after the Civil War, former slaves lived on the most fruitful plantation areas

30 Franklin, *From Slavery to Freedom*, 267.
31 White, *Freedmen's Bureau in Louisiana*, 63.

of the South, often outnumbering whites. Having superior numbers, however, was not enough because the ex-slaves were not able to realize their new Constitutional right to vote. Therefore, they could not control the richest agricultural lands of the nation. Whites justified their actions with such phrases as "necessity knows no law"; "self-preservation is the first law of life"; and "this is war, not politics."[32] White domination of African Americans in the South had few boundaries; certainly very few boundaries imposed by the federal government, which tacitly conceded the end of Reconstruction in 1876. The nation's attention seemed diverted by the saga of "Custer's last stand" at the Little Big Horn, which led to further atrocities against Native Americans. The rights of ex-slaves in the South had become old news.

Racism

In the years from 1876 to the end of the century white racial leaders imposed their brand of supremacy and segregation throughout the South, returning slavery in all but name. Jim Crow laws and the "Black Codes" became the norm, which communicated a separate world of totalitarian regulation for African Americans. Such regulations against blacks ranged from separate drinking fountains and toilets, to controlled wages and constant unrestrained violence. In the last sixteen years of the nineteenth century, twenty-five hundred people were lynched or burned at the stake; virtually all of these were black residents of Mississippi, Alabama, Georgia, and Louisiana.[33]

In 1896 the United States Supreme Court formally sanctioned white governance in its harsh "separate but equal"

32 Richard Wright, introduction to *Native Son* (New York: Harper, 1940), xi-xii.
33 Franklin, *From Slavery to Freedom*, 322-323.

decision.[34] Two years later Seymour's home state of Louisiana conceived the "grandfather clause," which stated that no citizen be allowed to vote unless their father and grandfather were eligible on January 1, 1867. This practically eliminated all blacks from participating in the voting process. The few African American voters who met this stringent condition were forced to satisfy strict educational and property rules, which further eliminated otherwise qualified voters. Although there were 130,344 African Americans registered to vote in 1896, a majority in twenty-six parishes, the final number of those who were actually qualified to vote fell to 5,320 by 1900, with no majority in any parish.[35]

Migration

Though many historians allege that the primary reason young African American men left the South was related to economic opportunity, another more practical explanation was related to the inability of African Americans to defend against indiscriminate violence.[36] For southern African Americans, it really did not matter how submissive they were, or even if they were able to enjoy some measure of financial success; the potential for violence from white oppressors was always present. Such was the case with the tragic story of Anthony Crawford, who owned 427 acres of prime cotton land, and was the wealthiest black farmer in Abbeville County, South Carolina.[37]

34 Smithsonian Institution, "Separate but Equal," *Smithsonian National Museum of American History*, http://americanhistory.si.edu/brown/history/1-segregated/separate-but-equal.html. The context of this ruling by the Supreme Court of the United States occurred when Homer Plessy, an African American, decided to get arrested for refusing to move from a seat reserved for whites on a train car. Judge John H. Ferguson upheld the law, and the case of *Plessy v. Ferguson* gradually moved up to the Supreme Court. On May 18, 1896, the U.S. Supreme Court, with only one dissenting vote, ruled that segregation in America was constitutional.

35 Franklin, *From Slavery to Freedom*, 274-275.

36 Milton C. Sernett, *Bound for the Promised Land: African American Religion and The Great Migration* (Durham: Duke University Press, 1997), 12.

37 Ibid., 9.

Crawford was a successful man that had raised a family of twelve sons and four daughters through hard work and tenacity. On October 21, 1916, Crawford got into an argument with W. D. Barksdale over the price of cotton. Barksdale was the owner of a mercantile store in Abbeville. It was reported that Barksdale called Crawford a liar, and being offended, Crawford cursed Barksdale. In no time at all a white mob had gathered at the store. Crawford tried to escape and sought refuge in a moderately covered pit in the ground at a nearby cotton gin. In his attempts to defend himself from the violent mob, Crawford armed himself with a sledgehammer and managed to smash the skull of one of his attackers before he finally succumbed to the mob's violent frenzy, when he was struck with a rock and knifed from behind.

When the Abbeville sheriff arrived on the scene, he was able to keep the bloodthirsty mob at bay temporarily with the promise that Crawford would be confined to the jail until it was determined whether Crawford's first attacker would survive the effects of the sledgehammer. What happened next was an all too familiar scenario that plagued black communities. Outraged by speculation that the sheriff might help Crawford get away on the four o'clock train, a second white mob broke into the jail, violently seized Crawford, tied a rope around his neck, and dragged him through the black section of town to his death.[38]

In Louisiana, Seymour had apparently seen enough such inhumane treatment of African Americans, along with their lack of economic enfranchisement, and he sought a new life in the North.[39] He left the South before the actual start of the Great Migration, when thousands of African Americans moved from the rural South to the urban North. Many of these folks hoped to escape the enduring problem

38 Ibid., 10.

39 *Indianapolis City Directories*, 1896-1899.

of racism in the South, and truly believed they would find greater economic opportunity and an overall improved life in the North. It is estimated that over one million African Americans participated in this mass movement between 1910 and 1930.[40] The Great Migration aided in facilitating the development of the first large, urban, black communities in the North, thus causing the North's African American population to grow about twenty percent during this time.[41] Cities such as Chicago, Detroit, New York, and Cleveland saw some of the greatest proportional increases.

When Seymour migrated north to Indianapolis around 1896, he found that black people were given equal protection as citizens, the right to vote, and the right to hold public office. Seymour was able to find employment as a waiter in a large downtown restaurant.[42] Each edition of the *Indianapolis City Directory* from 1896-1899 listed Seymour's occupation as a waiter. He was employed in three upscale Indianapolis hotels: the Bates House, the Denison House, and the Grand Hotel.[43] It is noteworthy that Seymour, the son of former slaves, and a southerner fresh off Louisiana's sugar cane fields, could adjust so quickly to such comparatively luxurious venues.

Most important during his years in Indianapolis, was Seymour's claim to have had a conversion experience. Charles Shumway, a Methodist minister who was writing a baccalaureate thesis for the University of Southern California

40 Sernett, *Bound for the Promised Land*, 57-86; and Digital History: Online American History Textbook. "The Jazz Age: The American 1920's," *Digital History*, http://www.digitalhistory.uh.edu/database/article_display.cfm?HHID=443. The Great Migration was a massive movement of 1.5 million southern blacks that decided to move to northern cities to escape racism, poor wages and sharecropping.
41 Sernett, *Bound for the Promised Land*, 57-86; and Public Broadcasting Service, "Great Migration," *Public Broadcasting Service*, http://www.pbs.org/wnet/aaworld/reference/articles/great_migration.html.
42 *Indianapolis City Directories*, 1896-1899; and Charles W. Shumway, "A Study of 'the Gift of Tongues'" (master's thesis, University of Southern California at Los Angeles, 1914), 173.
43 Robeck, *Azusa Street Mission and Revival*, 27; and *Indianapolis City Directories*, 1896-1899.

in 1914 interviewed Seymour and reported that while Seymour was in Indianapolis he had been converted in a "colored Methodist Episcopal Church."[44] According to Douglas Nelson, Seymour joined the Simpson Chapel Methodist Episcopal Church, located beside the White River Canal at Missouri and Eleventh Streets. This was a black congregation affiliated with the interracial Methodist Episcopal Church. The MEC refused to separate racially even when provision was made for black clergy in 1876 to form conferences within the denomination.

Robeck asserts that we cannot be certain in which congregation Seymour actually came to faith in Christ, because there were two other possible churches that he may have attended during this time.[45] One was Bethel African Methodist Episcopal Church, which was the strongest African American congregation in Indianapolis, and close to Seymour's apartment. The second was the Meridian Street Methodist Episcopal Church, which was across the street from Seymour's second address.[46]

Some argue that Seymour's affiliation with the Methodist Episcopal Church in Indianapolis was significant because it was the first indication of Seymour's desire for interracial fellowship.[47] If this was Seymour's initial sign of interracial inclusion, it is not surprising that he would join the Methodists, considering the fact that they were one of the first denominations to actively reach out to African Americans.[48]

At this juncture of Seymour's life, he undoubtedly gained a certain amount of admiration for the teachings of John Wesley,

44 Shumway, "A Study of the 'Gift of Tongues'," 173.
45 Robeck, *Azusa Street Mission and Revival*, 28.
46 Ibid.
47 Nelson, "For Such a Time as This," 155. Nelson believed Seymour's decision to join the more interracial Methodist Episcopal Church was the first clear indication he gave of seeking interracial reconciliation.
48 John Wesley, "Thoughts upon Slavery," *Global Ministries of the United Methodist Church*, http://new.gbgm-umc.org/umhistory/wesley/slavery/?search=thoughts%20upon%20slavery.

the founder of Methodism. However, Shumway reports that Seymour soon left the Methodist church over two important issues: the doctrine of premillennialism, and the role of "special revelations."[49] Like most Protestant churches of this period, the Methodist church did not adhere to premillennialism, which essentially asserts the physical return of Jesus prior to a literal one thousand years when the Lord will rule over the earth. The Methodists held to an "amillenial stance," viewing the millennium as a spiritual reality, instead of a literal return of the Lord. Further, Seymour gave high place to "special revelations," while the Methodist church did not.[50] This was apparent from Seymour's own experience and resulting stance on visions and dreams.

While Shumway believed that Seymour left the Methodist Church for theological reasons, Douglas Nelson believed Seymour left due to race.[51] Racial prejudice was not restricted to the South. By 1900, racial feelings in Indiana had shifted to the point that there was little communication between blacks and whites. Despite constitutional guarantees, the earlier optimism that blacks had embraced quickly dissipated as they encountered discrimination (augmented by mob violence), and increased episodes of black lynching. This trend continued for two decades, culminating in the vastly underreported "red summer of 1919," in which countless blacks were massacred in major northern cities.[52] Unfortunately, the racial harmony in

49 Shumway, "A Study of the 'Gift of Tongues'," 173.

50 Shumway, "A Study of the 'Gift of Tongues'," 173; and Robeck, *Azusa Street Mission and Revival*, 28. In Shumway's interview with Seymour, he mentions that the Azusa leader stated that the [Methodist] "Church [did] not endorse premillennialism or 'special revelation'."

51 Nelson, "For Such a Time as This,"162.

52 Alana J. Erickson, "Red Summer," in *Encyclopedia of African-American Culture and History*, ed. Jack Salzman, David Lionel Smith, and Cornel West (New York: Simon and Schuster Macmillan, 1996): 4:2293-2294; and Public Broadcasting Service, "Red Summer," *Public Broadcasting Service*, http://www.pbs.org/wnet/jimcrow/stories_events_red.html. The Red Summer refers to the summer and fall of 1919, in which race riots ignited in a number of cities in both the North and South. The three most violent incidents occurred in Chicago IL, Washington DC, and Elaine AR.

the Methodist Episcopal Church also succumbed to the racism of the times, as interracial togetherness became nothing more than an administrative formality.[53] Whether due to his opposing theological stances, or the change in interracial cooperation in the Methodist Episcopal Church, Seymour decided that his tenure in Indianapolis was over. In 1900, he moved about one hundred miles southeast to Cincinnati, Ohio.

In Cincinnati, Seymour may have briefly attended God's Bible School under the ministry of Holiness evangelist Martin Wells Knapp, who favored racial inclusion.[54] Though precise details have yet to be documented about Knapp's direct impact on Seymour's theology, there appears to be general consensus among scholars that Knapp did have an effect on him.[55]

Knapp's ministry, however, was not the only one that Seymour visited during his tenure in Cincinnati. He apparently joined the Reformation Church of God, which was also known as the "Evening light Saints." This was a group of singing, happy, and jubilant Christians who believed that the last spiritual outpouring (or evening light) was being given to the saints just before the close of history. Seymour became attracted to the movement because it vigorously reached out to include African Americans. Cincinnati was extremely important to Seymour's theological growth, because there he became involved in radical Holiness theology, which taught second blessing entire sanctification. The Saints emphasized Christian holiness in preparation for the consummation of history, along with divine healing, and the need to forsake denominationalism in favor of the true "Church of God."[56]

In 1903, Seymour left Cincinnati and returned south to find his family in Houston, Texas. The move to Houston

53 Nelson, "For Such a Time as This," 162.
54 Nelson, "For Such a Time as This," 163; and Robeck, *Azusa Street Mission and Revival*, 31. Oral tradition asserts that Seymour may have been influenced by evangelist and Holiness teacher, Martin Wells Knapp.
55 Ibid.
56 Nelson, "For Such a Time as This,"164.

would be of inestimable importance to his life and ministry. Seymour did not know that he would have a "divine connection" by joining a small Holiness church pastored by a black woman named Lucy Farrow. In 1905, just before Farrow relocated to Kansas to take employment as a governess in the home of Charles Fox Parham (the Holiness preacher who had been leading a Midwest Pentecostal movement since 1901), she asked Seymour to assume the office of pastor in her church.[57] Farrow returned to Houston in October 1905 with a new experience of speaking in tongues, which she accepted under Parham's influence,[58] and she immediately put Seymour in contact with Charles Fox Parham. Seymour probably never imagined that his connection with a white Holiness preacher from the Midwest would impact so many people in the years to come.

In December of 1905, Parham moved his Bible School to Houston, where he taught that the evidence of receiving the baptism of the Holy Spirit was speaking in tongues.[59] Although Seymour was hungry for more biblical training, the Jim Crowism of the South prevailed; he was not allowed to participate in Parham's school as a regular student due to the color of his skin. Because of racial segregation, Parham had Seymour sit in the hallway outside the classroom's open door; from there he could listen to Parham's Pentecostal teachings. After a short time under Parham's teaching, Seymour wholeheartedly accepted Parham's doctrine concerning tongues, even though he had not experienced this phenomenon himself.

The year 1906 would prove to be of great significance for Seymour. It was in this year that he was invited to help Julia Hutchins pastor a Holiness church in Los Angeles,

57 Ibid., 167.
58 Ibid.
59 Ibid.

California. This invitation came through Miss Neely Terry, who had heard Seymour preach at Farrow's church while she was visiting relatives in Houston. Terry described Seymour as a man well qualified.[60] When Seymour reached Los Angeles, an enthusiastic congregation greeted him and nightly meetings began immediately at 9th and Santa Fe Streets. Seymour preached on a variety of Christian topics, including holy living, divine healing, and the impending return of Jesus. Of all the topics Seymour preached on, none sent more shockwaves through the community than his advocating of glossolalia as a sign attending baptism with the Holy Spirit. Seymour preached the new Pentecostal doctrine using Acts 2:4 as his text. However, Julia Hutchins, the co-pastor of the church, rejected Seymour's teaching on tongues as evidence of the baptism of the Holy Spirit and padlocked the door to censor Seymour's teaching.[61]

Although Hutchins did not respond favorably to Seymour's Pentecostal message, there were others who were more receptive. Seymour was invited to stay at the home of Richard and Ruth Asberry at the now historic 214 Bonnie Brae Street; it was here that, on April 9, 1906, several people began to speak in tongues.[62] It did not take long for the good news about the new Pentecost to spread. The strange events at Bonnie Brae Street drew so much attention that Seymour was forced to preach on the front porch to crowds gathered in the street. At one point, the crowd grew so large that the porch floor collapsed.[63] It was at this point that Seymour

60 Ibid., 187.
61 Shumway, "A Study of the 'Gift of Tongues'," 173.
62 Charles W. Shumway, "A Critical History of Glossolalia" (PhD diss., Boston University, 1919), 116; also see Nelson, "For Such a Time as This," 189. Reportedly, Edward Lee (a janitor) was the first to receive the baptism of the Holy Spirit and spoke in tongues on April 9, 1906, after Seymour laid hands on him. After Lee received his personal Pentecost, seven others, including Jennie Evans Moore, received Spirit baptism and spoke in tongues. Ironically, Seymour did not receive the experience until April 12, three days later.
63 Nelson, "For Such a Times as This," 191.

began his search for a bigger building, anticipating a mighty outpouring of the Holy Spirit. The search ended as Seymour found an old structure that was once an African Methodist Episcopal church, but more recently had been used as a stable and warehouse; the location was 312 Azusa Street.[64] What happened at Azusa Street for the next three years would fascinate church historians for decades; Seymour conducted three services a day, seven days a week, where thousands of seekers received the baptism of the Holy Spirit.

The revival at Azusa Street, under Seymour's leadership, also stood in opposition to the racism and segregation of the times, as blacks and whites worshipped together under a black pastor. Frank Bartleman, a white Azusa participant, captured the spirit of the historic meeting by these words: "The 'color line' was washed away in the blood."[65] There was a great outpouring of the Holy Spirit, and Seymour was God's chosen leader at this crucial time in history. Seymour's leadership qualities blossomed in a time when African Americans were not considered to have the capacity for leadership. Nevertheless, Seymour would dispel these racist myths by leading one of the greatest revivals in American Church history.

64 Ibid., 192.
65 Frank Bartleman, *Azusa Street* (South Plainfield, NJ: Bridge Publishing, 1980), 54.

CHAPTER TWO

Seymour's Pilgrimage: Who Influenced His Pentecostal Faith?

It is often maintained that to truly understand a person, it is important to know the relative foundation which helped them arrive at their personal methodology. In other words, one's personal history, in a particular sociopolitical setting, serves as an essential factor in forming the attitude and content of their theological perspective.[66] This chapter examines the people who helped form Seymour's theology by tracing his associations with "Martin Wells Knapp, the Evening Light Saints" (also known as the Church of God Reformation Movement), Charles Harrison Mason, Charles Price Jones, and Charles Fox Parham.

Martin Wells Knapp

According to oral tradition, Seymour moved to Cincinnati, Ohio in 1900 where his interest in the Methodist Church and holiness doctrines were revitalized due to the influence of evangelist Martin Wells Knapp. Knapp was a Holiness preacher and teacher who included blacks in his meetings in the downtown Revivalist Chapel, and conducted classes at God's Bible School and Missionary Training Home.[67] The motto of

66 James H. Cone, preface to *God of the Oppressed* (New York: Seabury Press, 1975), vi.
67 Nelson, "For Such a Time as This," 163.

the school was "Back to the Bible." The advertisements for God's Bible School that circulated in various publications described it as "Pentecostal" and "non-sectarian."[68] Though the school used terms like "Pentecostal" to describe itself, it did not imply speaking in tongues, but rather identified with those who believed in two works of grace: salvation and sanctification.[69] Knapp was also a stalwart supporter of holiness, divine healing, and the second coming of Christ. Though precise details have yet to be documented about Knapp's direct influence on Seymour and Azusa Street, there appears to be a cross-pollination of ideologies, as the two men are examined. After using a familiar passage dealing with race and gender equality in Galatians 3:28 as a backdrop, Knapp described the condition of the Church in his social context:

> Barriers of race and color, and social position have no true place in Christ's Church...High toned social clubs, claiming to be churches, but throwing stones of criticism and ostracism at saints of God because of caste or color, are among the most stupendous of Satan's frauds which curse the earth today. Respecters and selectors of persons...What a contrast to the Body of Christ.[70]

Seymour expressed sentiments at Azusa that were analogous to Knapp's in speaking on the issue of equality. Seymour's newspaper, the *Apostolic Faith*, captures the equality of the fellowship:

68 Cecil M. Robeck Jr., *The Azusa Street Mission and Revival: The Birth of the Global Pentecostal Movement* (Nashville: Nelson Reference and Electronic, 2006), 31.
69 Ibid., 32.
70 Martin Wells Knapp, *Lightning Bolts from Pentecostal Skies, or Devices of the Devil Unmasked* (Cincinnati: Office of the Revivalist1898), 173.

> This meeting has been a melting time. The people are all melted together.... made one lump, one bread, all one body in Christ Jesus. There is no Jew or Gentile, bond or free, in the Azusa Street Mission... He is no respecter of persons or places.[71]

Equality in the Spirit became a central theme at Azusa, and was evidenced by Seymour's empowerment of visiting ministers from different denominations, the diversity in Azusa's leadership, and the role of women at the mission.

Robeck argues that there were three important factors that must have attracted Seymour to Knapp's Bible school: the school was racially inclusive, Knapp was an avowed premillennialist, and he believed in "special revelation."[72] In fact, a decade before Knapp started God's Bible School, he authored the book, *Impressions*, which taught how to distinguish whether a person had received "impressions" from God or "impressions" from Satan.[73] Of the factors that might have attracted Seymour, Knapp's belief in "special revelation" possibly impressed Seymour the most, because of his African background and growing up in southern Louisiana, where dreams, visions, and hearing voices were the norm. Knapp took the idea of "special revelation" serious as he wrote about dreams, visions and internal voices, while admonishing his readers to discern the spirits in order to recognize which manifestations were from God.[74] If Seymour was indeed influenced by Knapp in the area of "special revelation," it definitely would have benefited him in Los Angeles years later, as attendees claimed visionary experiences, and local spiritualists came looking for acceptance at the Azusa Mission.

71 William J. Seymour, ed., Untitled article, *Apostolic Faith* 1, no. 4 (December 1906): 1.

72 Robeck, *Azusa Street Mission and Revival*, 33.

73 Ibid.

74 Martin Wells Knapp, *Impressions* (1892; repr., Cincinnati: Tyndale House, 1984), 7-73.

Though Seymour may not have been in direct contact with Knapp, because of Knapp's untimely death in 1901,[75] it is likely that he embraced the Cincinnati evangelist's teaching in the areas of "special revelation," premillennialism, and racial inclusion. These same themes would become evident at the Azusa Street Mission.

The Evening Light Saints

While Seymour was in Cincinnati, he also became interested in the local ministry of the "Evening Light Saints" (also known as the Church of God Reformation Movement); a movement founded by Reverend Daniel S. Warner in 1880 in Ohio, Indiana, and Michigan.[76] The passion of the movement in vigorously reaching out to black people, along with their central message of Christian fellowship, probably initially attracted Seymour. In 1901, for instance, the movement's publishing house printed Saints leader William G. Shell's book, *Is the Negro a Beast?*, as a reply to Charles Carroll's racially motivated book, *The Negro a Beast*. Schell portrayed blacks in a positive light by depicting their lineage as coming from great black civilizations, and showed them as being fully human, equivalent to whites, and equal before the law.[77] He became America's voice of conscience by proclaiming that all men are created equal, and insisting that racial prejudice be eradicated.

In *An Introduction to the Negro Churches in the Church of God Reformation Movement*, James Earl Massey observes that African Americans like Seymour were characteristically

75 *Cincinnati City Directories* (Cincinnati, 1901, 1902, 1904). In 1901, Seymour is listed as a waiter living in rooms at 23 Longworth. In 1902, he is also listed as a waiter living in the rooms at 437 Carlisle Ave. And in 1904, he is noted as a laborer dwelling in the rooms at 337 W. Front. As previously mentioned, oral history has Seymour's arrival in Cincinnati in 1900; however, this arrival does not correspond with the Cincinnati directory.
76 Nelson, "For Such a Time as This," 164.
77 Ibid.

displeased "over the sectarianism in which they as members of various religious bodies were involved...and were quick to see and claim the spiritual and social implications inherent in the Movement's [Evening Light Saints] central message of Christian fellowship."[78] In fact, African Americans "embraced the Movement's essential theological forms, sentiments, opinions, faith, and practices."[79] While racial discrimination abounded during the late nineteenth century, the Evening Light Saints detested such thinking, and upheld interracial worship as a litmus test of the true church, which would function in holiness and unity. Merle D. Strege helped to articulate the unifying spirit of the Saints, and explained how someone like Seymour might have been attracted to the movement:

> It was not uncommon for members of both ethnic groups to attend the same tent meetings and revivals, on occasion drawing the ire of local residents for transgressing such racial taboos as mixed seating. In some instances Whites served as ministers to biracial gatherings; in other cases Black ministers took the lead. The pattern of racial unity in the movement's early decades was driven by a literal reading of Galatians 3:28 as normative status of the true New Testament church: "In Christ there is neither Jew nor Greek; there is neither bond nor free, there is neither male nor female: for ye are all one in Christ Jesus."[80]

According to historian Charles E. Brown, Warner and his early followers "were more rigid and stern in their stand... for justice to the Negro," than most Holiness churches.[81]

78 James Earl Massey, *An Introduction to the Negro Churches in the Church of God Reformation Movement* (New York: Shining Light Press, 1957), 17.
79 Ibid., 18.
80 Merle D. Strege, *I Saw the Church: The Life of the Church of God Told Theologically* (Anderson, IN: Warner Press, 2002), 145-147.
81 Charles E. Brown, *When the Trumpet Sounded* (Anderson, IN: Warner Press, 1951): 156.

In his December 1906 article in the *Gospel Trumpet,* W. J. Henry declared:

> There is no room for prejudice of any kind in the hearts of sanctified people. If you, as a white man find any of this in your heart toward the black man as an individual or toward his people, you need to go to the Lord for cleansing; to the black brother, I will say the same. All prejudice of every kind is outside the church of God.[82]

The Azusa leader's initial contact with the Saints was in Indianapolis, while Seymour was attending a Methodist Episcopal church. When Seymour joined the "Evening Light Saints," he reportedly made a "second" trip to the altar after hearing the testimonies of the Saints, and prayed until he testified to being wholly sanctified.[83] The Azusa leader's experience was claimed by most Holiness people, as they deemed sanctification to be an instantaneous work that God wrought in the soul, and which cleansed the heart of all sin. Though the Church of God (Evening Light Saints) never adopted a statement of faith on the issue, they have been continuously recognized as strong proponents of sanctification as a second work of grace. The Saints followed the teachings of John Wesley, who taught that sanctification was a more complete reception of the Holy Spirit than mere "salvation"; it was similar to the day of Pentecost. Furthermore, Daniel S. Warner's first book was entitled, *Bible Proofs of a Second Work of Grace.*[84]

82 W. J. Henry, "The Color Line," *Gospel Trumpet*, December 20, 1906, 3.

83 James S. Tinney, "William J. Seymour: Father of Modern Day Pentecostalism," in *Black Apostles: Afro-American Clergy Confront the Twentieth Century,* ed. Randall K. Burkett and Richard Newman (Boston: GK Hall, 1978), 216.

84 Daniel S. Warner, *Bible Proofs of the Second Work of Grace, or Entire Sanctification as a Distinct Experience, Subsequent to Justification: Established by the United Testimony of Several Hundred: Including a Description of Great Holiness Crisis of the Present Age, by the Prophets* (Goshen, IN: EU Mennonite Publication Society, 1880).

William J. Seymour was also influenced by the Saints' stringent standard of holy living. For example, early Saints would not drink tea or coffee. Women were not permitted to wear lace and ruffles. Men would refrain from wearing neckties, and neither gender was allowed to wear gold. These strict principles would not only affect Seymour, but would also influence the Pentecostal movement in general.

Though the Saints' doctrines on sanctification and racial harmony were significant to Seymour's theological formation and his future ministry, the church's views on Christian unity proved to be paramount to Seymour. This teaching included the destruction of racial barriers and sectarian obstacles, and the obliteration of impediments that stymied the empowerment of class and gender. According to the Evening Light Saints, unity was much more than just a teaching; it was a reality.[85] Seymour demonstrated his position on the issue of Christian unity primarily through his actions, as he promoted interracial fellowship, denominational camaraderie, and gender equality at the Azusa meetings.

The Cleansing of the Sanctuary

Although several inferences have been presented regarding the Evening Light Saints' influence on Seymour, a more direct connection was made by Scott Lewis. In his *Wesleyan Theological Journal* article entitled, "William J. Seymour: Follower of the 'Evening Light' (Zech. 14:7)," Lewis noted Seymour's utilization of a "central metaphor of the Saints' theology to propagate...his doctrine of the baptism of the Holy Spirit and his entire theological system."[86] Seymour apparently utilized the "cleansing of the Sanctuary" metaphors employed

85 John W. V. Smith, *A Brief History of the Church of God Reformation Movement* (Anderson, IN: Warner Press, 1976), 107, 121-124.

86 Scott B. Lewis, "William J. Seymour: Follower of the Evening Light (Zech. 14:7)," *Wesleyan Theological Journal* 39, no. 2 (Fall 2004): 179-180.

by Warner and Riggle in their book entitled, *The Cleansing of the Sanctuary*.[87] Seymour used Warner and Riggle's diagram of "The Tabernacle" in his own book, *The Doctrines and Discipline of the Azusa Street Apostolic Faith Mission of Los Angeles California*.[88] For Seymour, the diagram foreshadowed "full salvation." The tabernacle typified the progression of that "full salvation" from justification (represented by the "brazen altar"), to sanctification (symbolized by the "golden altar"), and finally, baptism of the Holy Spirit (signified by the "Holy of Holies"). Warner and Riggle's diagram supported a Holiness paradigm of salvation that was represented by two works of grace: justification (signified by the "Golden Altar"), and sanctification (typified by the "Holy of Holies"). For Warner and Riggle, the illustration represented Daniel 8:14, which states, "And he said unto me, unto 2,300 days: then shall the sanctuary be cleansed." According to Warner and Riggle, the cleansing of the sanctuary was something that was to be fulfilled in their day.[89] This passage in Daniel, along with Zechariah 14:7 (which states that there will be light in the evening time), served as a "prophetic self-understanding for the early Saints' movement which believed they were living in the last of the 2,300 days mentioned in Daniel."[90] Moreover, the "light" shining in this "evening time" was thought to be the "cleansing" of the Church, which God was accomplishing through the Saints. Warner and Riggle affirmed this belief in the following excerpt:

> The Work of cleansing the literal sanctuary, which Antiochus had defiled, which was accomplished by Judas Maccabeus at the completion of the 2,300 days

87 Daniel S. Warner and H. M. Riggle, *The Cleansing of the Sanctuary* (1903; repr., Guthrie, OK: Faith Publishing House, 1967), 99.
88 Seymour, *Doctrines and Discipline*, 99.
89 Lewis, "William J. Seymour: Follower of the Evening Light," 180; and Warner and Riggle, *Cleansing of the Sanctuary*, 99.
90 Lewis, "William J. Seymour,"180.

> of Daniel 8:14, was a perfect figure of the great work of cleansing the spiritual sanctuary, or church, which is now going on. Judas Maccabeus burned the heathen altars, set up the altars of the Lord, and reinstated the true worship of Jehovah according to the ancient custom. See 1 Macc. 4:36:55. So today, with the fire of holiness and truth, we burn the false religions of the earth, and restore the true worship of God as in days of old—as it existed in apostolic times.[91]

The Saints believed that God was using them to cleanse the Church of "sectism," and to restore true worship, as in apostolic times. According to the Saints, the restoration of "full salvation" included justification and the succeeding work of sanctification. "Sin," according to the Saints, was the root problem of denominations and sects, and "the only cure for this plague was a thorough-going experience of sanctification that would melt believers into spiritual and physical union."[92] At the core of the Saints' vision of unity was sanctification by Spirit baptism.[93] This sanctification experience was essential to the Saints' overall message of vision and unity; this understanding of sanctification was believed to be the cleansing that God was accomplishing to unify the Church. The Evening Light Saints envisioned a Church that was liberated from racial discrimination, gender, age, and sectarianism, with its members completely unified in the Spirit.

The theology of Seymour would follow this same model. The concept of tabernacle typology governed Seymour's views on justification, sanctification, and Spirit baptism throughout the *Apostolic Faith* periodicals.[94] But Seymour's progression

91 Warner and Riggle, *Cleansing of the Sanctuary*, 435.
92 Strege, *I Saw the Church*, 21; and Lewis, "William J. Seymour," 181.
93 Lewis, "William J. Seymour," 181.
94 William J. Seymour, "The Way into the Holiest," *Apostolic Faith* 1, no. 2 (October 1906): 4; Geo. E. Berg, "Baptized with the Holy Ghost," *Apostolic Faith* 1,

of salvation was different from the Saints in his added third experience—the baptism of the Holy Spirit, which was due to the influence of his mentor, Parham.

Seymour's relationship with the Evening Light Saints during his tenures in Indianapolis and Cincinnati assisted in shaping his theological-ecclesial convictions, which stayed embedded in his life and ministry.[95] An article in the *Apostolic Faith* underscored Seymour's commitment to unity in the church. In it, Seymour affirmed that "Azusa Mission stands for the unity of God's people everywhere. God is uniting his people, baptizing them by one Spirit into one body."[96] Similar to the Saints, Seymour had earlier declared that Pentecostalism was too large to be restricted to a denomination or sect.[97] In his own article, Lewis rightly asserts that Seymour's "heritage of following the 'evening light' produced a self-conscious identity that was rooted in temple imagery and biblical prophecy for the advocacy of Christian holiness and unity."[98]

CHARLES HARRISON MASON AND CHARLES PRICE JONES

Reportedly, Seymour was directed by "special revelation" to Jackson, Mississippi in the winter of 1904-1905, to seek counsel from a prominent black clergyman.[99] But who was this black clergyman? According to Robeck, two options quickly emerge; the clergyman was either Charles Price Jones

no. 4 (December 1906): 3; and William J. Seymour, ed., "Salvation According to the True Tabernacle," *Apostolic Faith* 1, no. 10 (September 1907): 3.

95 Lewis, "William J. Seymour," 183.

96 William J. Seymour, ed., "Beginning of World Wide Revival," Apostolic Faith 1, no. 5 (January 1907): 1.

97 William J. Seymour, ed., Untitled article, *Apostolic Faith* 1, no. 1 (September 1906): 1.

98 Lewis, "William J. Seymour," 183.

99 Nelson, "For Such a Time as This," 166.

or Charles Harrison Mason.[100] Both men had been ministers in the Missionary Baptist Church Association, but had been asked to leave because each had accepted the Holiness stance of sanctification as a second work of grace. After being excommunicated, they together formed the Church of God in Christ.

Charles Harrison Mason

C. H. Mason, according to the late Bishop Ithiel Clemmons, is one of "the most significant figures in the rise and spread of the modern Pentecostal movement."[101] In 1895, Mason met Charles Price Jones, the newly elected pastor of Mt. Helms Baptist Church in Jackson, Mississippi, and the two men became fast friends. Like Mason, Jones was heavily influenced by the Holiness movement, and before long the pair caused a commotion with their teachings, leading to their expulsion from the Baptist Association, as mentioned previously. Afterwards, Mason and Jones sought for the future direction of what had become, under their influence, independent "sanctified" congregations.[102] Through much prayer and Scripture study, Mason received a revelation of the name, Church of God in Christ (COGIC). Thus in 1897, a major African American denomination was born. Through the dynamic preaching ministry of Mason, and the prolific writings and hymnology of C. P. Jones, Holiness churches sprang up throughout the South and Southwest bearing the name Church of God in Christ.

100 Robeck, *Azusa Street Mission and Revival*, 36.
101 Ithiel Clemmons, "Charles Harrison Mason," in Burgess, McGee, and Alexander, *Dictionary of Pentecostal and Charismatic Movements*, 585.
102 Ibid., 586.

Mason's Connection to Seymour

As the work moved forward, Mason continued to seek a more complete consecration of his life.[103] Reports about a Pentecostal revival in Los Angeles sparked Mason's interest. Upon hearing the good news of the spiritual outpouring out West, he traveled to California and received the baptism of the Holy Spirit under the ministry of William J. Seymour on March 19, 1907. Mason wrote about the experience:

> ...led by the Spirit to go to Los Angeles where the great fire of the latter rain of Holy Ghost had fallen on many. It was March 1907 when I received Him, Jesus my Lord in the Holy Ghost.[104]

After five weeks with Seymour and the Azusa faithful, Mason returned to Memphis and Jackson, eager to share his new experience with the brethren. However, his Pentecostal message was met with great resistance by the church. Consequently, after several days and nights of intensive debate, Mason and Jones separated; the church split. Those who sided with Mason convened in September 1907 to reorganize the COGIC, and C. H. Mason was elected as general overseer.[105] Mason would continue to lead the COGIC until his death in 1961. Under his direction, the church experienced phenomenal growth as thousands of his followers, migrating from South to North and Southwest to far West, carried his "Pentecostal" teachings and evangelistic spirit to virtually every major city in the United States.[106]

---

103 Ibid., 587.

104 James Oglethorpe Patterson, German R. Ross, and Julia Mason Atkins, eds., *History of the Formative Years of the Church of God in Christ: Excerpts and Commentary from the Life and Works Bishop C. H. Mason* (Memphis: Church of God in Christ, 1969), 17, as cited in Ithiel Clemmons, *Bishop C. H. Mason and the Roots of the Church of God in Christ* (Bakersfield, CA: Pneuma Life Publishing, 1996), 26.

105 Clemmons, "Charles Harrison Mason," in Burgess, McGee, and Alexander, *Dictionary of Pentecostal and Charismatic Movements*, 587.

106 Ibid.

At this point, it is important to pose some questions about the timing of the Mason and Seymour relationship. One can clearly ascertain the historical connection between the two men in Los Angeles; their time together in California has already been well documented. However, did Mason know Seymour prior to his visit to Azusa Street in 1907? Was C. H. Mason the mysterious black clergyman in Jackson, Mississippi that Douglas Nelson wrote about in his dissertation, "For Such A Time As This: The Story of Bishop William J. Seymour and the Azusa Street Revival"?[107] It is important to remember Seymour's attraction to the topic of special revelation. With this fact in mind, it is conceivable that C. H. Mason might emerge as a most worthy candidate to have influenced Seymour during his brief stay in Jackson.

Charles Mason focused on the issue of "special revelation" throughout his long tenure as Chief Apostle and Bishop of the Church of God in Christ. In fact, there are several photographs that show Mason encircled by what are sometimes described as, "oddities of nature."[108] Though some people see in these photographs an example of slave religion, and others imagine Mason as a conjurer who divined strange objects in order to attain revelation, Mason himself consistently appealed to Psalms 19:1-4b to explain his unorthodox methods for deciphering what he believed were God's messages:

> The heavens declare the glory of God; and the firmament sheweth His handiwork. Day unto day uttereth speech, and night unto sheweth knowledge. There is no speech nor language, where their voice is

107 Nelson, "For Such a Time as This," 166.

108 Patterson, Ross, and Atkins, *History of the Formative Years*, vii, x, xii, as cited in Robeck, *Azusa Street Mission and Revival*, 36. Mason believed with the help of the Holy Spirit he could discern the message that God placed in rare artifacts when they were created.

> not heard. Their line is gone out through all the earth, and their words to the end of the world.[109]

Though Mason was a firm believer that he could hear the voice of God in strange objects, there were others who would bear witness to Mason's dexterity in discerning messages. Such was the case in the late 1960s with Elder C. G. Brown, the first Secretary of the Department of Home and Foreign Missions for the Church of God in Christ. Brown vividly recalled Mason's "exploits" in the following manner:

> ...Elder Mason will calmly pick up a stick, shaped in exact likeness of a snake in its growth, or a potato shaped in the exact likeness of the head and ears of a pig in its growth, and demonstrate with such power that thousands of hearers are put on a wonder. It appears that he is reading his message from a scroll which is concealed within some one of the recesses of the object from which he is preaching.[110]

Brown's language reveals a side of Mason that would have definitely attracted Seymour, the son of former slaves and familiar with the supernatural. According to Robeck, "there is a sense in which Mason baptized into Pentecostal practice something he had seen in the surrounding African American conjure culture."[111] Standing in the place of a shaman or root worker, and using the same signs they would use, Mason gave these signs new meaning and filled them with Christian understanding, thereby preserving the historic African cultural basis.[112]

Though Seymour might have been interested in Mason's

109 Robeck, *Azusa Street Mission and Revival*, 37.
110 Mary Mason, ed., *The History and Life Work of Elder C. H. Mason, Chief Apostle and His Co-Laborers* (1924; repr., Memphis: Church of God in Christ, 1987), 92-93.
111 Robeck, *Azusa Street Mission and Revival*, 38.
112 Ibid.

focus on "special revelation," there is no evidence that Seymour ever participated in similar activities at the Azusa Street Mission.[113] The two would become lifelong friends, and although it appears that their relationship may have begun in Jackson, it seems quite likely that it crystallized as a result of Mason's visit to Azusa in 1907, when he received the baptism of the Holy Spirit under Seymour's ministry.

Charles Price Jones

Charles P. Jones, the distinguished black Holiness preacher who became founder and bishop of the Church of Christ (Holiness), was an extremely successful pastor of Christ's Tabernacle Church in Jackson, Mississippi at the time of Seymour's visit. Originally from northern Georgia, Jones benefited from the instruction of several gifted teachers, and developed a notable love for books.[114] Before settling in Mississippi, the gifted clergyman accepted his first pastorate while enrolled as a student in Arkansas Baptist College. He was ordained by the dean of the college, C. L. Fischer, a graduate of Morgan Park Divinity School in Chicago (now part of the University of Chicago). Jones graduated in 1891, and that same year met Joanna P. Moore, a white northern Baptist missionary, who had worked expansively among African Americans in the South for several decades. Interestingly, it was reported that Moore prophesied in 1891 to Jones these words: "God is going to fill you with the Holy Ghost."[115] This prophecy seemed to resonate with Jones, for

113 Ibid., 39.

114 Dale T. Irvin, "Charles Price Jones: Image of Holiness," in *Portraits of a Generation: Early Pentecostal Leaders,* ed. James G. Goff Jr. and Grant Wacker (Fayetteville: University of Arkansas Press, 2002), 38.

115 J. H. Green, introduction to *An Appeal to the Sons of Africa: A Number of Poems, Readings, Orations and Lectures, Designed Especially to Inspire Youth of African Blood with Sentiments of Hope and True Nobility as well as to Entertain and Instruct All Classes of Readers and Lovers of Redeemed Humanity,* by Charles Price Jones (n.p.: Truth Publishing, 1902), xi.

beyond his intellectual prowess and pastoral gifts, he "yearned for apostolic life and power."[116]

In 1894, while serving as pastor of Tabernacle Baptist Church in Selma, Alabama, Jones claimed to have a spiritual experience that he classified as the experience of holiness, of being sanctified, and of being filled or baptized with the Holy Ghost. Jones believed that sanctification was an act of divine grace that made a person holy. According to the Holiness preacher, his inclination to sin was removed due to sanctification. However, holiness for Jones not only enabled the believer to overcome sin, but to experience healing from disease. Jones saw in this experience an effective means of spiritual empowerment for his own life and ministry, as well as for the churches in the South.[117]

Jones' Possible Connection to Seymour

According to Douglas Nelson, Seymour developed a warm friendship with Jones, and left Mississippi, being more firmly grounded in his beliefs, and especially premillennialism.[118] However, in *Portraits of a Generation: Early Pentecostal Leaders,* Dale Irvin raised some important questions concerning Jones's possible influence on Seymour.[119] Irvin encourages the reader to investigate the relationship between Jones and Seymour more closely, as he contends, "Indeed, I know of no direct reference by Jones to having met Seymour, even though such a claim would certainly have fit his pattern of relating firsthand experiences with those involved in events about which he was writing."[120]

116 Ibid.

117 Irvin, "Charles Price Jones," in Goff and Wacker, *Portraits of a Generation,* 38.

118 Nelson, "For Such a Time as This," 166.

119 Irvin, "Charles Price Jones," in Goff and Wacker, *Portraits of a Generation,* 43-45.

120 Ibid., 43.

By 1906, Jones claimed to be familiar with the writings of Charles Parham, whom he credited with being the originator of the doctrine of speaking in tongues as initial evidence of Spirit baptism.[121] He also recalled an encounter in Denver where he met Agnes Ozman, the first person to speak in tongues under Parham's ministry; however, he was not convinced of the authenticity of her experience.[122] Surprisingly, the Holiness clergyman did not have much more to say about his friend Seymour. Jones only mentioned that he had read Seymour's *Apostolic Faith* papers, and after a preliminary affirming response, decided to not distribute them any longer.[123] Jones casts more doubt on his relationship to Seymour through his response to an inquiry that compared his work to other Holiness groups around the nation in the first decade:

> The Tongues cult started in Kansas a few years ago under a man named Parham. Afterward, in 1906 I believe, it broke out afresh in a colored mission in Los Angeles, California. It became immediately almost a world-wide sensation and many good and earnest people were deceived by it.[124]

Considering this statement, it is not surprising that Jones contended against the Pentecostal doctrine of baptism of the Holy Spirit with the evidence of tongues (as advocated by Seymour at Azusa) to such a degree, that it caused a split between him and his ministry partner, Charles Harrison Mason, who was a recipient of this "Pentecostal experience." It is also worth mentioning that Jones made no mention of his friend

121 Charles Price Jones, *Characters I Have Met* (Los Angeles: National Publishing Board of the Church of Christ Holiness, 1996), 38-39, as cited in Irvin, "Charles Price Jones," in Goff and Wacker, *Portraits of a Generation,* 43.
122 Jones, *Characters I Have Met*, 41, as cited in Irvin, "Charles Price Jones," in Goff and Wacker, *Portraits of a Generation,* 43.
123 Jones, *Characters I Have Met*, 39-40.
124 Charles Price Jones, *The Gift of the Holy Ghost in the Book of Acts* (Los Angeles: National Publishing Board of the Church of Christ Holiness, 1996), 42.

Seymour in the article, even though Nelson had previously stated that the two men developed a warm friendship.

However, despite Jones's silence, recent Pentecostal historiography has often directly linked Seymour to Jones, primarily because of Nelson's 1981 dissertation, "For Such a Time as This."[125] The source for Nelson's confidence in Jones's influence on Seymour stems from a footnote found in Charles W. Shumway's 1914 A.B. thesis, completed at the University of Southern California. While researching for this thesis, Shumway conducted several interviews with some early Pentecostals, including Seymour. Shumway recorded the following, based on the interview with the Azusa leader:

> In the winter of 1904-05 [Seymour] went "by special revelation" to Jackson, Miss., to receive spiritual advice from a well know colored clergyman there. There he was grounded more firmly in his millenarianism and he came away a more firm believer than ever in the value of "special revelations."[126]

Further support of Nelson's assertion of Jones's influence on Seymour was evidenced in an interview he conducted in 1979 with Elder C. C. Carhee in Los Angeles, who confirmed to Nelson that the mysterious clergyman was C. P. Jones.[127]

It is also noteworthy that at the time of Seymour's visit to Jackson, Jones was the most widely read black Holiness teacher in the country, and his convocations were attracting people from considerable distances.[128] Therefore, it is difficult to conceive of Seymour traveling to Jackson that winter

125 Nelson, "For Such a Time as This," 166.

126 Charles W. Shumway, "A Study of 'the Gift of Tongues'" (master's thesis, University of Southern California at Los Angeles, 1914), 173.

127 Irvin, "Charles Price Jones," in Goff and Wacker, *Portraits of a Generation*, 381 n. 29. "Carhee is listed in Cobbins, *History of the Church of Christ*, 58-59, as an evangelist from Louisiana who initially met Jones in Jackson, Mississippi, in 1906 and joined the Church of Christ in 1907, being ordained finally in 1910. Nelson does not say how Carhee knew of Seymour's visit to Jackson in 1905" (ibid.).

128 Irvin, *Portraits* ,44.

to meet with someone other than Jones. The fact remains, however, that Jones did not indicate that he had met the Azusa leader, when writing of Seymour several years later.[129]

Nevertheless, one must question what spiritual advice Jones might have given to Seymour.[130] Jones was a proponent of special revelation, which many Pentecostals and Charismatics today would label as the gift of prophecy. This lines up with Seymour's promotion of the doctrine of special revelation, and seems to give credence to the proposal that he met with Jones. However, since Jones did not place much emphasis on millenarianism, some scholars find it difficult to reconcile Seymour's explanation, as found in Shumway's thesis, with Jones's teachings.[131] Furthermore, Jones's Christocentric or Christ-centered doctrine appears more closely related to that of William H. Durham, whose stance on the timing of sanctification (or the "finished work" doctrine) Seymour opposed.[132] Reportedly, Jones even used the phrase, "finished work" at times to describe the sufficiency of Christ for the fullness of salvation.[133]

One explanation that could help resolve the issue of Jones' influence on Seymour is offered by Dale Irvin. According to Irvin, the answer may be found in the December 29, 1904 edition of *Truth*, with an invitation requesting "the ministers" (possibly those who had identified themselves with the ministry and whose names were printed in the same edition) to come "to the class in January."[134] It was most likely this

129 Ibid.
130 Ibid.
131 "The President's Message," *Proceedings of the Fortieth Annual Session of the Church of Christ (Holiness) U.S.A* (Chicago National Publishing Board, 1936), 35-37, as cited in Irvin, "Charles Price Jones," in Goff and Wacker, *Portraits of a Generation*, 44. Here, Irvin points out that Jones held a moderate millennial stance, holding that the end of the age was near.
132 Irvin, "Charles Price Jones," in Goff and Wacker, *Portraits of a Generation*, 44.
133 Ibid.
134 Charles Price Jones, *Truth* (Jackson, MS) 9, no. 25 (December 29, 1904): 7, as cited in Irvin, "Charles Price Jones," in Goff and Wacker, *Portraits of a Generation*, 44.

minister's seminar, conducted January 1905 in Jackson that a decade later Seymour recollected as having attended. The announcement made no mention as to the identity of the person teaching the class, but Jones was probably involved. It is also quite plausible that a discussion on millennial teaching occurred, which may have resonated with Seymour, and left a lasting impression in his thinking about the subject.[135] Most important, if this hypothesis is further carried out, it would suggest that Jones's emphasis on special revelations (the gift of prophecy) in this minister's class would likely have had a significant influence on Seymour's understanding of the Holy Spirit's ministry in the Church.

A final link between Jones and Seymour should be noted at this point. In 1917, Jones structured a new congregation in Los Angeles, and eventually became a permanent fixture in that city. Interestingly, Seymour was still serving in ministry at Azusa Street, which had incorporated into a local church. Since the two men spent five years concurrently ministering in the same city (Seymour died in 1922), it is possible that they crossed paths at some point.[136] Interestingly, the two men were buried in the same cemetery in Los Angeles, less than one hundred feet apart.[137]

Charles Fox Parham

Though Seymour gained spiritual insight and clarity from his brief tenure in Jackson, Mississippi, his life would be forever changed by the teachings he embraced during his time in Houston, Texas. Shortly after Seymour's arrival in Houston, the Houston press announced that Reverend Charles Fox Parham would soon hold public meetings. Parham, evangelist

135 Seymour, "Behold the Bridegroom Cometh!" *Apostolic Faith* 1, no. 5 (January 1907): 2. This article brings illumination to Seymour's positions on the Second Coming and catching away of the saints.
136 Irvin, "Charles Price Jones," in Goff and Wacker, *Portraits of a Generation*, 45.
137 Ibid.

and founder of the historic Bible school in Topeka where the Pentecostal movement initially began, had first gained notoriety when one of his students (Agnes Ozman) began speaking in tongues on January 1, 1901.[138] After several days had passed, Parham and about half of the student body had similar experiences.

The summer of 1900 would prove to be a significant time as Parham embarked on a Holiness tour of religious centers.[139] Central to this twelve-week expedition was Frank W. Sandford's Holiness commune at Shiloh, Maine. Parham's attraction to Sanford's commune at Shiloh was due in large part to the leader's infatuation with the Holy Spirit's "latter rain" outpouring that was emphasized throughout the Holiness movement.[140] Parham wanted a greater manifestation of this power in his own life, and through Sandford had heard isolated reports of xenolalia among missionaries.[141] For Parham, the discovery of xenolalia was of particular importance, because he viewed these foreign tongues as proof of Spirit baptism, since it made all beneficiaries instant missionaries.[142] Convinced that Christ's premillennial return would take place on the heels of a worldwide revival, Parham viewed the emergence of a large number of divinely trained missionaries and the restoration of apostolic power in the last days as two important antecedents that would prompt the global renewal.[143]

138 James. R. Goff Jr., "Charles Fox Parham," in Burgess, McGee, and Alexander, *Dictionary of Pentecostal and Charismatic Movements*, 660; See also James R. Goff Jr., *Fields White unto Harvest: Charles F. Parham and the Missionary Origins of Pentecostalism* (Fayetteville: University of Arkansas Press, 1988), 67.

139 Ibid.

140 Ibid.

141 Xenolalia, a synonym of xenoglossia, describes glossolalia when the language that is spoken is identifiable among over six thousand languages across the globe. For more information, see R. P. Spittler, "Glossolalia," in Burgess, McGee, and Alexander, *Dictionary of Pentecostal and Charismatic Movements*, 336.

142 Goff, "Charles Fox Parham," in Burgess, McGee, and Alexander, *Dictionary of Pentecostal and Charismatic Movements*, 660.

143 Ibid.

Excited about what he learned during his time at Sandford's Shiloh community, Parham returned to Topeka in September 1900, and secured an elaborate old mansion ("Stone's Folly") to use for a Bible School that would prepare prospective missionaries for the outpouring of the Holy Spirit. In this old building Parham taught his students the essentials of Holiness doctrine, and encouraged them to search for the true evidence of Holy Spirit reception. The Holiness leader then strategically directed his students to the account of Acts 2 where xenolalia had sparked the initial phase of Christian growth on the day of Pentecost in Jerusalem. As he departed town for three days on a speaking engagement, Parham left his students with a homework assignment; he asked them to find the scriptural evidence for the reception of the baptism with the Holy Spirit.[144] Upon his return, Parham asked the students to state their conclusion, and they all responded that the evidence was speaking in tongues (which they deduced from the four recorded instances in Acts when glossolalia accompanied the baptism with the Holy Spirit).[145]

Firmly convinced that this was the correct interpretation, Parham and his students conducted a watch night service on December 31, 1900, with this in mind. On this night Agnes Ozman asked Charles F. Parham to lay hands on her to receive the baptism of the Holy Spirit with evidential tongues, and (as previously mentioned) began speaking in tongues shortly after midnight, on the first day of the twentieth century. As the other students began to speak in tongues, along with Parham himself, the happenings in "Stone's Folly" reached the

144 Synan, *Holiness Pentecostal Tradition*, 90-91.

145 Robert Mapes Anderson, *Vision of the Disinherited: The Making of American Pentecostalism* (Peabody: Hendrickson, 1992), 52-57; and Goff, *Fields White unto Harvest*, 66-72. It is interesting that Pentecostal scholars Robert Mapes Anderson and James R. Goff, Jr. believe that Parham was already convinced that tongues was the evidence that a person was baptized in the Holy Spirit resulting in "missionary tongues" prior to the Topeka outpouring. Hence, they view the "student consensus theory" as Parham's manipulations to establish a doctrine that he had already formulated.

presses at Topeka and Kansas City. Parham tried to follow the Topeka outpouring with a determined effort to spread what he believed was the true "apostolic faith," but his plans were dashed by that April, because of negative publicity and poor attendance.[146]

Parham's Apostolic Faith movement gained some momentum, however, through a late 1903 revival outbreak in Galena, Kansas, where the message of Pentecostalism merged with the message of divine healing. Consequently, on the strength of the revival in Galena, Parham set his sights on Houston, Texas, and in 1905 promptly established a string of *Apostolic Faith* churches in the suburbs of Houston.[147] He sought to reestablish the "apostolic faith" of the early Christian Church, believing that history was rapidly approaching its final phase, and glossolalia was an important sign of the end times. In keeping with his mode of operation in Kansas, Parham launched a short-term Bible school in Houston in December of 1905. Under Parham's direction, classes were offered in a variety of theological subjects, including: conviction, repentance, conversion, consecration, sanctification, healing, the Holy Spirit in His different operations, prophecies, the book of Revelation, and other practical topics.[148] Of particular interest for this ten-week training session was the attendance of William J. Seymour.

Seymour learned of the school through his friendship with Lucy Farrow. Farrow entered the picture of emerging Pentecostalism through her contact with Parham, while she was still serving as pastor of her church. In 1905, Parham offered her a position as his family governess for the summer in Kansas. In order to take advantage of the opportunity

146 Goff, "Charles Fox Parham," in Burgess, McGee, and Alexander, *Dictionary of Pentecostal and Charismatic Movements*, 660-661.
147 Ibid., 661.
148 Sarah E. Parham, *The Life of Charles F. Parham: Founder of the Apostolic Faith Movement* (Joplin, MO: Garland Publishing, 1985), 140.

with Parham, Farrow asked Seymour to fill the pulpit in her absence, and Seymour accepted. Having experienced tongues in Kansas under Parham, Farrow returned to Houston in late October with the Parham family, and began working as a cook in Parham's Bible School.[149] Farrow's role was significant, because she sparked Seymour's interest by mention of her Kansas experiences, including a lustrous account of having spoken in tongues in the Parham residence. She informed Seymour that glossolalia was not merely a part of the early Christian church but was intended for the present age. Though Seymour had some reservations about the strange new teaching because of his background with the Evening Light Saints, his desire to experience God overpowered his theological bias. With Farrow's persuasion, and by his own determination, he gained admission into Parham's short-term Bible study course.

According to James Goff, Parham was "neither a racial reformer nor a champion of white supremacy; but occupied a paternalistic middle ground typical of many white ministers from the Midwest."[150] Despite his compliance with the specifics of the Jim Crow laws, Parham felt compelled to evangelize the black community, and consequently preached alongside Seymour to African Americans in the Houston area. This outreach to Houston's blacks showed evidence of his belief that the Pentecostal message was for all races. Though scholars still debate Parham's dormant racism, he clearly had an indelible influence on Seymour's life.

Seymour left abruptly after only completing about five weeks of training in Parham's school, because of an unexpected offer to pastor a small church in Los Angeles. The time he spent in Parham's school, however, was long enough for Seymour to

149 Nelson, "For Such a Time as This," 167. Apparently Parham had relocated to Houston from Kansas.
150 Goff, *Fields White unto Harvest*, 111.

assent to his teacher's central thesis that a third work of grace, substantiated by speaking in tongues, would transform the world through spiritual power and missionary zeal.[151]

Clearly, Parham greatly affected Seymour's personal life and theology. Though Seymour had yet to receive the Pentecostal experience, he preached the new doctrine with confidence upon his arrival in Los Angeles. Interestingly, though Seymour initially accepted Parham's main thesis of tongues as the Bible evidence of Holy Spirit baptism, he would later question this position because of unfortunate circumstances with Parham and other whites who placed too much emphasis on tongues, at the expense of love.

It was Parham who coined the name "Apostolic Faith movement"; a term that Seymour would use for his own monthly newspaper, and eventually, for his mission. Parham also issued ministerial credentials to Seymour, and raised an offering to help offset the Azusa leader's travel expenses to Los Angeles. Parham's effect on Seymour was evidenced in his letter sent to Parham in August 1906 from Los Angeles:

> Dear Bro. Parham:
>
> Sister Hall has arrived, and is planning out a great revival in this city, that shall take place when you come. The revival is still going on here that has been going on since we came to this city. But we are expecting a general one to start again when you come, that these little revivals will all come together and make one great union revival. Now please let us know about the date that you will be here, so we can advertise your coming and the date. I shall look for a large place, by God's help, that will accommodate the people. Hallelujah to God! Victory through the all cleansing blood of Jesus Christ! I expect an earthquake to happen in Los

151 Ibid.

> Angeles when you come with the workers filled with the Holy Ghost; that God will shake this city once more...[152]

Seymour's jubilation over the long-awaited visit of his spiritual father would soon turn into hurt and disappointment, because of Parham's repudiation of the revival shortly after his late October arrival. However, the seeds of Pentecost that were planted in Seymour through the teaching of Charles Fox Parham would soon change the landscape of Christianity in North America, and the rest of the world.

Conclusion

William J. Seymour's associations with Martin Wells Knapp, the "Evening Light Saints," Charles Harrison Mason, Charles Price Jones, and Charles Fox Parham were foundational to the Azusa leader's theological worldview. These influences provided the theological underpinning that would remain a part of Seymour's life, and help him articulate his message of Pentecost in the *Apostolic Faith* newspaper, as well as his own *Doctrines and Discipline* publication. It is important to now investigate the extent that some of these antecedents had permanently affected a more mature Seymour in three doctrinal areas: sin and salvation (soteriology), the Holy Spirit (pneumatology) and his view of the church (ecclesiology).

152 Sarah E. Parham, *Life of Charles F. Parham*, 154-155.

CHAPTER THREE

SEYMOUR'S THEOLOGY

Having interacted with the sources that helped shape Seymour in his more formative years, we will now focus on how Seymour lived out his Pentecostal faith at the Azusa Street Mission. In order to accomplish this goal, the chapter will explain the theology of Seymour by examining three specific areas: his soteriology (view of sin and salvation), his pneumatology (view of the nature and work of the Holy Spirit), and his ecclesiology (view of the church).

Soteriology

As shown in chapter three, Seymour was heavily influenced by Holiness teaching, and he enthusiastically embraced the movement's two central assertions about the mature Christian life. For him, the first phase of the salvation experience was conversion, with sanctification being understood as a subsequent second work of grace that brought about the "double cure" that was required because of mankind's sin.

Justification

According to Seymour, the first work of grace that occurred in conversion was expressed as justification. In justification, God offered the individual forgiveness from sins, as well as acquittal from the retribution of those sins. Justification occurred at a definite moment in time and was experienced by the individual at conversion. In the occurrence of conversion, repentant sinners recognized their moral failures against God and pleaded for forgiveness of their sins on the basis of Christ's redemptive work on the Cross. God's reply to the repentant sinner was that He removed the guilt of their sin, and received them into the kingdom of God. Due to their exoneration from the culpability of sin, they became prime candidates to make it into heaven, saved from eternal damnation in hell. A short article by Seymour found in the *Apostolic Faith* entitled, "The Way into the Holiest," helps to illustrate this point:

> A sinner comes to the Lord all wrapped up in sin and darkness. He cannot make any consecration because he is dead. The life has to be put into us before we can present any life to the Lord. He must get justified by faith. There is a Lamb without spot and blemish slain before God for him, and when he repents toward God for his sins, the Lord has mercy on him for Christ's sake, and put [sic] eternal life in his soul, pardoning him of his sins, washing away his guilty pollution, and he stands before God justified as if he had never sinned.[153]

According to Seymour, justification meant that a person was pardoned and had been received into God's favor. An individual who received Christ was considered to be in a justified state, but must continue in the faith to be finally saved.[154] Seymour's Arminianism is even more noticeable in regard to believers and willful sin. Christians participating in wayward acts, in Seymour's mind, forfeited their faith and could not have reacquired justifying faith without repenting

153 William. J. Seymour, "The Way into the Holiest," *Apostolic Faith* 1, no. 2 (October 1906): 4.
154 William J. Seymour, *Doctrines and Discipline of the Azusa Street Apostolic Faith Mission of Los Angeles, Cal.* (Los Angeles: 1915), 27.

yet again. It is easy to surmise how Seymour could arrive at this point of view, due to his Methodist background and the influence of John Wesley. However, Seymour was able to demonstrate a degree of sophistication on the cardinal doctrine of justification, because of his firm grasp of Scripture. For instance, when asked about an apparent contradiction over the nature of justification and works, as found when Paul's summary of Abraham in Romans is compared to James' teaching on justification by works, Seymour gave this response:

> St. Paul speaks of that justification which was when Abraham was seventy-five years old, about twenty-five years before Isaac was born. St. James [speaks] of that justification, which was when he offered up Isaac on the altar; 2nd. [sic] Because they do not speak of the same works: St. Paul [is] speaking of works that precede faith; St. James, of works that spring from it.[155]

The quote above demonstrates that Seymour understood Paul's message in the fourth chapter of Romans to mean that Abraham was not justified by any previous works, but by faith alone, while James' use of the term in the second chapter of his book necessitates that our faith produce acts of righteousness. Noteworthy is the fact that a self-educated black man with humble beginnings preserved the biblical tension between justification and works better than the reformer Martin Luther, who struggled to reconcile the two terms in the book of James, finally referring to it as the "epistle of straw."

Sanctification

The second work of grace that Seymour championed was sanctification. To him, this was an act of cleansing

155 Ibid., 28.

rather than forgiveness. Seymour, like many Christians who had been influenced by the Holiness movement, believed that sanctification dealt with sin in the singular, or the "sin nature," or "original sin." The focus in this instance was on the general inclination to sin, rather than on distinct acts of sin or specific actions that transgressed the law of God. In the act of sanctification, God supernaturally removes the basic desire to sin from the human heart. According to most Holiness theologians, this purification does not insinuate that the urge to sin, which humankind inherited from Adam, is rendered inoperative in an individual's life. Rather, sanctification makes it possible for Christians to live a life that is free from sin. However, some radical Holiness teachings in Seymour's time suggested that sanctification totally eradicated the sin nature from human beings; however, this was never the position of the majority. Similar to justification, many in the Holiness movement taught that sanctification occurred at a specific point in time. In a sermon to the Azusa faithful entitled, "Sanctified on the Cross," Seymour said:

> Sanctification makes us holy and destroys the breed of sin, the love of sin and carnality. It makes us pure and whiter than snow. ...Any man that is saved and sanctified can feel the fire burning in his heart, when he calls on the name of Jesus.[156]

Not only did sanctification free the individual from sin, but Seymour and those who surrounded him at the Azusa Mission, believed that a justified person had the ability to feel a heightened sense of God's presence after having their petition for sanctification answered.

In effect, Seymour's two-stage view of grace was essential for the Azusa leader's theology of the mature Christian life.

156 William J. Seymour, "Sanctified on the Cross," *Apostolic Faith* 2, no. 13 (May 1908): 2.

Justification and sanctification were absolutely necessary if a person would ever partake of the third experience, the baptism of the Holy Spirit. This experience was not a third work of grace, but was a "gift of power" to assist the saved (justified) and sanctified believer in the ministry of the gospel to others.[157] Moreover, the *Apostolic Faith* paper routinely reported incidents of recipients who experienced this three-fold experience, having been saved, sanctified, and filled with the Holy Spirit. For Seymour, these three experiences were significant and they could only take place in this particular order. An anonymous excerpt in the April 1907 issue of the *Apostolic Faith* underscores the significance that the Azusa leader placed on justification and sanctification as prerequisites for those who would receive the gift of the Holy Spirit:

> Before you can receive the baptism of the Holy Ghost, you must have a thorough, definite experience of justification and sanctification, which are through the Blood of Jesus, and they are two distinct acts of grace. First, what God has done for you, second what God has wrought within you. Then and only then are you prepared to receive your baptism from the Father, by Jesus Christ His Son.[158]

Seymour himself, in a latter issue of the paper, would expound further on this three-fold progression:

> The first thing in order to receive this precious and wonderful baptism with the Holy Spirit [is] to have a clear knowledge of justification by faith according to the Bible...the second step is to have a real knowledge of sanctification, which frees us from original sin...

157 William J. Seymour, ed., "The Apostolic Faith Movement," *Apostolic Faith* 1, no. 1 (September 1906): 2.
158 William J. Seymour, ed., Untitled article, *Apostolic Faith* 1, no. 7 (April 1907): 3.

> then after we [are] clearly sanctified, we pray…for the baptism with the Holy Spirit.[159]

Though Douglas Jacobsen has charged that Seymour never fully developed the logic for his three-stage position of Christian maturation,[160] he possibly overlooked how Seymour utilized temple imagery to articulate his stance. Again, the tabernacle typology governed Seymour's views on justification, sanctification, and Spirit baptism throughout the *Apostolic Faith* periodicals. Although Seymour imbibed the "cleansing of the sanctuary" metaphors, as used by the Evening Light Saints in Warner and Riggle's book, *The Cleansing of the Sanctuary*,[161] his incorporation of the baptism of the Holy Spirit in the tabernacle model makes a sharp distinction from the Holiness paradigm of the Evening Light Saints. An unsigned article in the *Apostolic Faith* entitled, "Salvation According to the True Tabernacle" communicated the difference between the Azusa leader's stance on "full salvation" from that of Warner and Riggle.

> First we come to the court of the tabernacle. This is where the sinner does his first works. Here we find the brazen altar which stands for justification. We receive pardon and regeneration right at the brazen altar…Here is pardon and regeneration combined. As soon as a soul is pardoned, he is washed and the work of regeneration is wrought in his soul…Now the believer comes to the golden altar…Now he can consecrate himself to be sanctified. Here he finds on the altar the Blood of Jesus, which represents Christ

159 William J. Seymour, "Letter to One Seeking the Holy Ghost," *Apostolic Faith* 1, no. 9 (June to September 1907): 3.

160 Douglas Jacobsen, *Thinking in the Spirit: Theologies of the Early Pentecostal Movement* (Bloomington: Indiana University Press, 2003), 71.

161 For a plenary explanation of Seymour's utilization of Warner and Riggle's progression of "Full Salvation," see the chapter entitled Chapter 2 "Seymour's Pilgrimage: Who Influenced his Pentecostal Faith?"

> the sanctifier of His people...We can see that the baptism with the Holy Ghost is not a work of grace for there is no altar in the Holy of Holies. This is another step, the gift of the Holy Ghost. Instead of an altar, there is an ark of gold, which represents the Lord Jesus Christ perfected in you, for in Christ you have the experience of justification, sanctification and the baptism with the Holy Ghost.[162]

In essence, Seymour and the Azusa faithful believed that justification, sanctification, and the baptism of the Holy Spirit constituted the "full blessing" of Christ, as symbolized by the Azusa leader's utilization of tabernacle imagery. All three experiences were purchased on the Cross, and Spirit baptism was readily available for every believer.[163]

Pneumatology

With the many testimonies regarding supernatural elements at Azusa, it is evident that Seymour emphasized the work of the Holy Spirit. Speaking in tongues, prophesying, and dramatic healings were common place at Azusa Street. However, Seymour based these occurrences on the Word of God. He accepted as true the words of Scripture in Acts 2:1-4 and Acts 4:29-31, which indicated that accompanying signs would follow the church.[164] However, to understand Seymour's doctrine of the Holy Spirit, it is necessary to examine his position on tongues and the baptism of the Holy Spirit.

Initially, Seymour advocated the understanding of his mentor, Charles Fox Parham, that tongues was the evidence of a new baptismal event. From the inception of the Azusa Street

162 William J. Seymour, ed., "Salvation According to the True Tabernacle," *Apostolic Faith* 1, no. 10 (September 1907): 3.
163 Ibid.
164 Seymour, *Doctrines and Discipline*, 10.

Mission's paper, the *Apostolic Faith*, the connection between tongues and the baptism of the Holy Spirit took "center stage." The baptism of the Holy Spirit was considered to be a "gift of power upon the sanctified life," and evidence of this blessed event was the individual would speak in "new tongues."[165] In the first issue of the *Apostolic Faith*, dated September 1906, Seymour clearly distinguished his theology of the Holy Spirit from the historic Wesleyan-Holiness movement by approving the following statement:

> Too many have confused the grace of Sanctification with the endowment of Power, or the Baptism with the Holy Ghost; others have taken "the anointing that abideth" for the Baptism, and failed to reach the glory and power of a true Pentecost.[166]

Albeit Seymour's teaching was dissimilar to, and even confrontational towards, the Wesleyan-Holiness position, it was his belief that speaking in tongues "provided an important distinction that held profound implications for world evangelization."[167]

According to Seymour, the baptism of the Holy Spirit brought the power of God upon believers, which enabled them "to speak in all the languages of the world."[168] Seymour exhorted his followers to preach "all of it"; and *all* included "justification, sanctification, healing, the baptism with the Holy Ghost, and signs following."[169] The Azusa leader alleged that Spirit baptism was one of power, which came with a commission. An unsigned article in the *Apostolic*

165 William J. Seymour, ed., "The Apostolic Faith Movement," *Apostolic Faith* 1, no. 1 (September 1906): 2.

166 Ibid.

167 Cecil M. Robeck Jr., "William J. Seymour and 'the Bible Evidence'," in *Initial Evidence: Historical and Biblical Perspectives on the Pentecostal Doctrine of Spirit Baptism*, ed. Gary B. McGee (Peabody: Hendrickson, 1991), 77.

168 William. J. Seymour, "The Precious Atonement," *Apostolic Faith* 1, no. 1 (Sept. 1906): 2.

169 Ibid.

Faith underscores Seymour's early stance regarding the evangelization of the world through the gift of tongues: "The gift of languages is given with the commission, 'Go ye into all the world and preach the Gospel to every creature.'"[170] Seymour seemed to take a significant amount of pride in the fact that the "Lord ha[d] given [such] languages" as German, Latin, French, Italian, Chinese and several others to people who were uneducated.[171]

Seymour believed that glossolalia enabled believers to be more efficacious in global evangelization. In this he initially affirmed the theory of his mentor, Charles Fox Parham, that speaking in tongues served as the "Bible evidence" that one had been baptized in the Holy Spirit. In an unsigned article in the *Apostolic Faith* entitled, "Tongues as a Sign," in referring to a passage in the sixteenth chapter of Mark's Gospel, verses 16-17, the author (who was likely Seymour himself) made the following statement:

> Here a belief and baptism are spoken of, and the sign or evidence given to prove that you posses [sic] that belief and baptism. This scripture plainly declares that these signs shall follow them that believe.[172]

The writer of the article later reprimanded people for "running off with blessings and anointings with God's power, instead of tarrying until [the] Bible evidence of Pentecost came."[173] Thus, the author associated the ideas of *signs following them that believe* with the "Bible evidence" of baptism with the Holy Spirit.

170 William J. Seymour, ed., Untitled article, *Apostolic Faith* 1, no. 1 (September 1906): 1.
171 Ibid.
172 William J. Seymour, ed., "Tongues as a Sign," *Apostolic Faith* 1, no. 1 (September 1906): 2.
173 Ibid.

While speaking in tongues was linked with proof of Spirit baptism by Seymour and the Azusa faithful, the Azusa leader was always vigilant to maintain a sense of balance in regard to the goal of having this experience. Seymour admonished his followers, even in the earlier stages of the revival, that speaking in tongues was not something to be sought as an end in itself. If a person came to Azusa seeking tongues, it was clear to Seymour that the individual did not really understand the baptism of the Holy Spirit. At one point, Seymour wrote:

> Beloved...we are not seeking for tongues, but we are seeking the baptism with the Holy Ghost and fire. And when we receive it, we shall be so filled with the Holy Ghost, that He Himself will speak in the power of the Spirit.[174]

Not only did Seymour urge his followers not to focus on glossolalia, but he specifically implored those who sought the experience to "pray for the baptism of the Holy Ghost and God would throw in the tongues"[175] as an extra blessing. Thus, even though speaking in tongues was an important experience confirming Spirit baptism, the main goal for Seymour, from the very beginning of the revival, was the baptism of the Holy Spirit.

By the middle of 1907, Seymour's stance that tongues were the "Bible evidence" of Holy Spirit baptism had begun to change. Though the *Apostolic Faith* supported speaking in tongues as the "evidence" of Spirit baptism through May of that year, the Azusa leader began to argue that the ability to speak in tongues was only one of the signs of Spirit baptism. This shift in Seymour's thinking was evidenced in a September 1907 article addressed to the "baptized saints":

174 William J. Seymour, "The Baptism with the Holy Ghost," *Apostolic Faith* 1, no. 6 (February to March 1907): 7.
175 Ibid.

> Tongues are one of the signs that go with every baptized person, but it is not the real evidence of the baptism in the every day life. Your life must measure with the fruits of the Spirit. If you get angry, or speak evil, or backbite, I care not how many tongues you may have, you have not the baptism of the Holy Spirit.[176]

It is apparent that Seymour's stance on tongues as the prerequisite of Spirit baptism had changed. Not only did he revise his previous position on the issue, but he drew on his Wesleyan-Holiness background by insisting that one's life must "measure with fruits of the Spirit," to prove that the recipient had a genuine experience of Spirit baptism. It is important to ask what precipitated this change in Seymour's ideology. Furthermore, did Seymour have a specific individual in mind when he described, "getting angry, speaking evil or backbiting"? And what caused Seymour to insist that individuals who partook of such fleshly activities did not truly possess the baptism of the Holy Spirit? The answers to these questions indicate that Charles Fox Parham played a key role in Seymour's pneumatological evolution.

Ironically, the same person who introduced Seymour to what has become the defining Pentecostal doctrine (tongues as evidence of Spirit baptism) was also the individual who prompted Seymour to adjust his theology by broadening his definition of Holy Spirit baptism. The major reason for this theological shift was his former teacher's questionable actions at Azusa. In October 1906, Parham arrived in Los Angeles, after receiving critical reports from his Los Angeles friends concerning Negro influences at Azusa. As mentioned in the previous chapter, Seymour knew Parham only through

176 William J. Seymour, ed., "To the Baptized Saints," *Apostolic Faith* 1, no. 9 (J to September 1907): 2.

several weeks of study at his school in Houston. However, Seymour still honored Parham as the movement's leader,[177] because it was under Parham that Seymour discovered the "lost gift" of Christian glossolalia.

Parham came to Azusa at the apex of his career, following successful campaigns in Houston, and Zion City, Illinois. He was determined to assume what he considered to be his rightful place as leader of the revival, and of the new movement. Further, Parham wanted to put an end to offensive behavior such as, "white people imitating unintelligent, crude negroisms of the Southland, and laying it on the Holy Ghost."[178] Though Parham believed in interracial cooperation, which was evident in his relationship with Seymour in Houston, he favored race-mixing only under controlled conditions.[179] In Los Angeles, Parham attempted to reprimand the Azusa leadership for allowing things to get out of control. However, the Azusa leadership rejected his admonition, and asked him to leave. Parham's retelling of the incident indicates his disgust:

> I hurried to Los Angeles, and to my utter surprise and astonishment I found conditions even worse than I had anticipated. Brother Seymour came to me helpless, he said he could not stem the tide that had arisen. I sat on the platform in the Azusa Street Mission, and saw manifestations of the flesh, spiritualistic controls, saw people practicing hypnotism at the altar over candidates seeking the baptism; though many were

177 William J. Seymour, ed., "Letter from Bro. Parham," *Apostolic Faith* 1, no. 1 (September 1906): 1. Seymour honored Parham as the leader of the movement before he came to Azusa Street.

178 Charles F. Parham, "Sermon by Chas. F. Parham," *Apostolic Faith* (Baxter Springs, AR) 3 (April 1925): 10; and Douglas J. Nelson, "For Such a Time as This: The Story of Bishop William J. Seymour and the Azusa Street Revival," (PhD diss., University of Birmingham, UK, 1981), 208.

179 James R. Goff Jr., *Fields White unto Harvest: Charles F. Parham and the Missionary Origins of Pentecostalism* (Fayetteville: University of Arkansas Press, 1988), 131. Seymour and Parham preached together to the blacks while Seymour attended Parham's Bible training school in Houston, Texas.

> receiving the real baptism of the Holy Ghost. After preaching two or three times, I was informed by two of the elders, one who was a hypnotist...that I was not wanted in that place.[180]

Though Parham did not agree with the emotional display at Azusa, there were two deeper issues that disturbed him significantly. One was the degree of racial equality that was exhibited by its participants; the other was the lack of evidence for xenoglossia, or foreign tongues, in the Azusa Street services.[181] Again, Parham had demonstrated some sensitivity to the spiritual needs of blacks in his interaction with Seymour, and his outreach to African Americans in the Houston area. However, according to James R. Goff Jr., Parham's stance on race was similar to many whites in the early twentieth century, in that he assumed white superiority and feared miscegenation.[182] Consequently, Parham's paternalistic attitude toward blacks gave way to a more calloused and palpable racism. When the Azusa elders rejected his attempts to correct them or take over, Parham became blatantly critical of black religious expression and wantonly imprudent in his remarks regarding Seymour and the Azusa faithful. This change in attitude was apparent in 1912, as Parham reflected on what he had seen at Azusa Street:

> Men and women, whites and blacks, knelt together or fell across one another; frequently, a white woman, perhaps of wealth and culture, could be seen thrown back in the arms of a big "buck nigger," and held tightly

180 Charles F. Parham, "The Latter Rain: the Story of the Origin of the Original Apostolic or Pentecostal Movements," *Apostolic Faith* (Baxter Springs, AR) 2, no. 7 (July 1926): 5-6; and Sarah E. Parham, *The Life of Charles F. Parham: Founder of the Apostolic Faith Movement* (Joplin, MO: Garland Publishing, 1985), 163.

181 Goff, *Fields White unto Harvest*, 131.

182 Ibid. According to Goff, the Anglo-Israel theory convinced Parham that white Anglo-Saxons held a unique place in history and miscegenation would weaken the bloodlines of the chosen race.

> thus as she shivered and shook in freak imitation of Pentecost. Horrible, awful shame![183]

Seymour had not only invited Parham because of their friendship, but had wanted him to lead an area-wide Los Angeles revival to strengthen the movement. The Louisiana native understood some of the limitations that his race presented at this critical juncture in American history. He was depending on the help of Parham, and other whites, for the global leadership of the movement.[184] But Seymour's vision of an area-wide revival was shattered upon Parham's repudiation.

In addition to Parham's racial intolerance at Azusa, he was concerned that verifiable xenolalia should mark the reception of Spirit baptism in the life of every Pentecostal believer. Essential to Parham's theology was a strong emphasis on tongues as foreign languages. He believed that the presence of xenolalia gave credence to the movement's justification as an end-time revival. Parham shared the same belief as several Azusa participants (including Seymour initially) that xenoglossia would enable the recipients to be effective in missionary work. Although Parham was satisfied with this aspect of the Azusa Revival, he held strong reservations about the authenticity of some other tongue speech that he observed there. He criticized Azusa worshipers for their "babbling," and accused some of the altar workers of using trickery, such as suggesting certain words and sounds for the seeker to repeat, along with "the working of the chin, or the massaging of the throat."[185] Parham's critique of the "spurious" tongues is evidenced as follows:

> There are many in Los Angeles who sing, pray and talk wonderfully in other tongues, as the Spirit

183 Charles F. Parham, "Free Love," *Apostolic Faith* (Baxter Springs, AR) 1, no. 10 (December 1912): 4-5; and Goff, *Fields White unto Harvest*, 132.

184 Nelson, "For Such a Time as This," 210.

185 Sarah E. Parham, *Life of Charles F. Parham*, 169.

> gives utterance, and there is *jabbering* here that is *not tongues at all.*[186]

Notably, Parham did affirm that people at Azusa were having genuine experiences of the Spirit. But his theology of xenolalia as proof of Spirit baptism, would not allow him to accept the authenticity of those who did not appear to be speaking a known language.

Due to his rejection by the Azusa Street elders, Parham opened revival meetings at the Los Angeles' Women's Christian Temperance Union Building, which lasted until December.[187] In his worship services, he vehemently attacked Seymour and the Azusa Street Revival, and continued to condemn the revival at every given opportunity during following years. Parham's decision to separate from Azusa and compete with it undermined Seymour's leadership and seriously weakened the movement. Seymour became the scapegoat for alleged extremes at Azusa, while the true reasons behind these criticisms were probably racist.

Considering the hurt Seymour endured at the hands of his "spiritual mentor," (Parham) it is apparent how his view of Spirit baptism could have been altered.

However, there may have been another reason for Seymour's departure from Parham's "Bible evidence" doctrine.

In July of the summer of 1907, while he was in San Antonio, Parham was arrested and charged with committing an "unnatural offense."[188] Parham was accused of sodomy with a young man named J. J. Jourdan. Although he was released, and denied any wrong doing, the incident severely damaged his reputation, and diminished his status in the Pentecostal

186 Ibid.
187 Ibid.
188 "Evangelist is Arrested," *San Antonio Light,* July 19, 1907, 1; and "Preacher is Out of Jail," *San Antonio Light,* July 23, 1907: 7. After his release on bond, Parham immediately announced that he was innocent and that the charges were "trumped up."

movement. It is possible that Seymour had Parham in mind when, just six months after Parham's arrest, he published the following article in the *Apostolic Faith,* pertaining to the "real evidence" of Spirit baptism:

> Divine love, which is charity. Charity is the Spirit of Jesus. They will have the fruits of the Spirit. Gal. 5:22. "The fruit of the Spirit is love, joy, peace, longsuffering, gentleness, goodness, meekness, faith, temperance; against such there is no law. And they that are Christ's have crucified the flesh with the affections and lusts." This is the real Bible evidence in their daily walk and conversation; and the outward manifestations; speaking in tongues and the signs following; casting out devils, laying hands on the sick and the sick being healed, and the love of God for souls increasing in their hearts.[189]

Seymour again appealed to the fruit of the Spirit in the article, and singled out a variety of charisms, but his comments about fleshy "affections and lusts" seem most applicable to Parham. While Parham, in his training school in Houston had taught Seymour to expect tongues as the "Bible evidence of the baptism of the Holy Spirit," Seymour had clearly expanded his comprehension of Spirit baptism to include an ethical dimension.[190]

Elmer Fisher was pastor of "the Upper Room," which was Azusa Street Mission's chief rival congregation during the historic meetings, in addition to the place where Charles F. Parham had been allowed to hold temporary gatherings after his expulsion from Azusa. The words Fisher offered regarding Parham's fall seem to give credence to the possibility that Seymour's response was indeed provoked by this fall. "Don't allow any of the counterfeits of the devil or *the failures of*

189 William J. Seymour, ed., "Questions Answered," *Apostolic Faith* 1, no. 11 (October to January 1908): 2.

190 Robeck, "Seymour and 'the Bible Evidence'," in McGee, *Initial Evidence,* 81.

men to cause you to lower the standard of the Word of God," Fisher continued, "...those who receive the full baptism of the Holy Ghost *will speak in tongues* as the Spirit gives utterance *always*" [191] (emphasis added). With these comments, Fisher implied that Seymour had lowered the "standard of the Word of God" by choosing to focus on the weakness of man (Parham's alleged fall) rather than focusing on the "Bible evidence."

From 1915, until his untimely death in 1922, the Azusa leader's stance on tongues as evidence of Spirit baptism went through a significant transformation. Due to the wounds Seymour suffered under the harshness of Parham, the African American leader from Louisiana began more directly to challenge his mentor's thesis that speaking in tongues was the prerequisite of Spirit baptism. An unsigned article entitled, "Character and Work of the Holy Ghost," in the May 1908 issue of the *Apostolic Faith* gives more insight into Seymour's thought:

> If you find people that get a harsh spirit, and even talk in tongues in a harsh spirit, it is not the Holy Ghost talking. His utterances are in power and glory and with blessing and sweetness...He is a meak [sic] and humble Spirit—not a harsh Spirit.[192]

It is significant that the word "harsh" appears three times in this short article. Parham had been extremely harsh in his assessment of Azusa, even referring to the revival as "sewerage."[193] A more direct response from Seymour to

191 E. K. Fisher, "Stand for the Bible Evidence," *The Upper Room* 1, no. 1 (June 1909): 3.

192 William J. Seymour, ed., "Character and Work of the Holy Ghost," *Apostolic Faith* 2, no. 13 (May 1908): 2.

193 Charles F. Parham, ed., "Lest We Forget," *Apostolic Faith* (Baxter Springs, AR) 1, no. 6 (August 1912): 6; Charles F. Parham, ed., Untitled article, *Apostolic Faith* (Baxter Springs, AR) 1, no. 7 (September 1912): 10; Charles F. Parham, ed., "Baptism of the Holy Ghost," *Apostolic Faith* (Baxter Springs, AR) 1, no. 8 (October 1912): 8-10; and Charles F. Parham, ed., "Free Love," *Apostolic Faith* (Baxter Springs, AR)

Parham's repudiation of Azusa Street came in the form of his ninety-five page book published in 1915, *The Doctrines and Discipline of the Azusa Street Apostolic Faith Mission of Los Angeles, Cal.* This work demonstrated that Parham's evidential theory, once championed by Seymour, had been clearly rejected. In the preface to this work, Seymour wrote:

> Wherever the doctrine of the Baptism in the Holy Spirit will only be known as the evidence of speaking in tongues, that work will be an open door for witches and spiritualists, and free loveism [sic]. That work will suffer, because all kinds of spirits can come in. The word of God is given to Holy men and women, not to devils. God's word will stand forever. 1 Peter 1:22-23.[194]

In other words, Seymour was not only challenging Parham's thesis, but he was now suggesting that focusing narrowly on tongues as evidence of Spirit baptism could make one susceptible to the demonic.

In short, Seymour concluded that tongues might demonstrate that a person had truly received the baptism of the Holy Spirit, but to say that tongues was the "evidence" was to go beyond what Scripture had to say about the subject. Robeck makes a compelling argument in his analysis of Seymour's stance on tongues, affirming that for Seymour, the doctrine of tongues as the "Bible evidence" could not be the definite evidence, because it was a "human construct, a theological formulation which bound God."[195] Seymour's words in his *Doctrines and Discipline* give credence to Robeck's observation:

1, no. 10 (December 1912): 4-5.

194 Seymour, *Doctrines and Discipline*, 5.

195 Robeck, "Seymour and 'the Bible Evidence'," in McGee, *Initial Evidence*, 87.

> So many people have made shipwreck of their faith by setting up a standard for God to respect or come to. When we set up tongues to be, the Bible evidence of Baptism in the Holy Ghost and fire only [sic]. We have left the divine word of God and have instituted our own teaching.[196]

Seymour challenged Parham's thesis because it restricted the ways in which the Holy Spirit might choose to operate in a person's life. According to Seymour, God was at liberty to choose His desired manifestation(s), which included tongues. Seymour became convinced that God was not limited to speaking in tongues being the evidence of Spirit baptism. The Azusa leader again addressed the topic in the May 1908 issue of the *Apostolic Faith*.[197] In this particular article, Seymour presented the Azusa Street Mission's official stance, clearly avoiding the term "evidence:"

> The Azusa standard of the baptism with the Holy Ghost is according to the Bible in Acts 1:5, 8; Acts 2:4 and Luke, 24:49. Bless His Holy name. Hallelujah to the Lamb for the baptism of the Holy Ghost and fire and speaking in tongues as the Spirit gives utterance. ...So, beloved, when you get your personal Pentecost, the signs will follow in speaking with tongues as the Spirit gives utterance. This is true. Wait on God and you will find it a truth in your own life. God's promises are true and sure.[198]

196 Seymour, *Doctrines and Discipline*, 91.

197 Although this may have been the last time that Seymour addressed the topic in the *Apostolic Faith*, it was not the last time he addressed the issue of tongues as one can observe from his writings in his *Doctrines and Discipline*, which was written in 1915. However, the May 1908 issue entitled, "The Baptism of the Holy Ghost" is significant because it seemed to be (at least for the time being) the official standard for the baptism of the Holy Spirit at the Azusa Street Mission.

198 William J. Seymour, "The Baptism of the Holy Ghost," *Apostolic Faith* 2, no. 13 (May 1908): 3.

Importantly, although Seymour did not promote a doctrine of the "Bible evidence" in this statement, he still believed that when people were truly baptized with the Spirit, they would speak in tongues. However, now he described the ability as a sign which should follow the experience, as the Spirit made it possible.[199]

Though Seymour believed in a "Spirit-filled" church, he also believed that people who were truly baptized in the Spirit would demonstrate the fruits of the Spirit (Galatians 5:22). The Azusa leader clearly broadened his understanding of Spirit baptism to include an ethical dimension that was lacking under the earlier teaching of Charles Parham, who trained him to focus on speaking in tongues as "the Bible evidence."[200] For Seymour, the ability to speak in tongues was satisfactory, but it was not the standard for Christian spirituality. Seymour wanted to make sure that his followers were balanced in their Christianity. Even though he supported spiritual manifestations, he did not promote them. Seymour warned his readers of the potential dangers of excesses in an unsigned article in the *Apostolic Faith*:

> Keep your eyes on Jesus and not on the manifestations, not seeking to get some great thing more than somebody else. The Lord God wants you just as humble as a baby, looking for Him to fill you with more of God and power. If you get your eyes on manifestations and signs you are liable to get a counterfeit, but what you want to seek is more holiness, more of God.[201]

In short, Seymour believed that signs and charismatic gifts had a legitimate place in the church; but preoccupation

199 Robeck, "Seymour and 'the Bible Evidence'," in McGee, *Initial Evidence*, 82.
200 Ibid., 81.
201 William J. Seymour, ed., Untitled article, *Apostolic Faith* 1, no. 11 (October to January 1908): 4.

with them was unbiblical, particularly in the doctrine of initial evidence, or "*Bible evidence.*"

Interestingly enough, there are many classical Pentecostals who would disagree with Seymour's conclusions about tongues and its role in Spirit baptism. However, Seymour could appropriately be considered the forerunner of the modern Charismatic renewal, because he envisioned Pentecostalism in a much broader sense than the narrow approach of Parham and many later North American Pentecostals.[202] Seymour was inclusive in that he believed all who received Christ, could, through faith, receive from God an outpouring of the Holy Spirit upon a holy sanctified life. Though Seymour did not believe that one's faith should rest upon whether they spoke in tongues, he accepted as true the concept that one who was filled with the Spirit could speak in tongues as the Spirit gave utterance.[203] As one reflects upon the pneumatology of Seymour, it appears that he had a more balanced view of the work of the Spirit, as it pertained to the makeup of what it meant to be a "Spirit-filled believer," than his contemporaries (particularly Parham) and most classical Pentecostals living today.

Seymour urged his followers to seek the baptism of the Holy Spirit by focusing their attention on the giver of the gift, rather than on one particular manifestation of the Spirit. According to Seymour, gifts were to be used for the glory of God. The nature of tongues as evidence for the baptism of the Holy Spirit on "all flesh" was an implicit service meant to demonstrate the equality of all peoples under God. Just as the Church in Acts received various ethnic communities into the fold via the evidence of speaking in tongues, so it was at Azusa; the white Church was forced to confront its exclusiveness in

202 Robeck, "Seymour and 'the Bible Evidence'," in McGee, *Initial Evidence*, 88.
203 Seymour, *Doctrines and Discipline*, 51-52.

light of blacks, Hispanics, and all other races which received this Pentecostal experience.

Ecclesiology

Arguably, the best primary source for Seymour's ecclesiology is the Azusa leader's 1915 work, *Doctrines and Discipline*. Though Seymour adopted most of its content, including his twenty-four articles of religion from the *Doctrines and Discipline of the African Methodist Episcopal Church*,[204] some sections in Seymour's discipline contain his original thoughts. This is particularly true regarding his views on the Church. Seymour, for example, believed that the authority of the Church was derived directly from God.[205] The Lordship of Christ was foundational to Seymour's doctrine, and particularly to his understanding that the Church on earth was clearly to be subject to Jesus. Moreover, Seymour held the authority of the believer in high esteem, because of his strong belief in the supremacy of Christ in all things. Still, he believed the authority of the Church was designed to ensure a conduct and conversation of godliness in all its members.[206]

A Unified Church

The words of an article in the *Apostolic Faith* embody Seymour's zeal for unity in the church, and stand as a stinging rebuke to those who would try to perpetuate a spirit of division. In it the author stated, "We recognize every man that honors the blood of Jesus Christ to be our brother, regardless

204 Frank Madison Reid, A. J. Allen, H. Y. Tookes, W. A. Fountain, J. H. Clayborn, and George W. Baber, ed., *The Doctrine and Discipline of the African Methodist Episcopal Church*, 34th rev. ed. (Philadelphia: A.M.E. Book Concern, 1948), 48-56. As mentioned in the previous chapter, the Articles of Religion in Seymour's *Doctrines and Discipline of the Azusa Street Apostolic Faith Mission* and the Articles of Religion in the *Doctrine and Discipline of the African Methodist Episcopal Church* has almost identical wording.

205 Seymour, *Doctrines and Discipline*, 9.

206 Ibid.

of denomination, creed, or doctrine."[207] Seymour argued for the practice of divine love that set believers free to be in unity rather than in the adaptation of creeds and confessions that divided Christians. The Azusa leader wanted those members of the body of Christ outside of the Pentecostal movement to know that this young movement was inclusive and that they were not considered the opposition. The *Apostolic Faith* in September 1906 captures the mood of the Seymour's thinking on the issue:

> We are not fighting men or churches, but seeking to displace dead forms and creeds and wild fanaticisms with living, practical Christianity. "Love, Faith, Unity" are our watchwords, and "Victory through the Atoning Blood" our battle cry.[208]

Another article from the September 1906 *Apostolic Faith* stated the ecumenical nature of the Azusa Revival:

> Jesus was too large for the synagogues. He preached outside because there was not room for him inside. This Pentecostal movement is too large to be confined in any denomination or sect. It works outside, drawing all together in one bond of love, one church, one body of Christ.[209]

Even in the earliest moments of the revival, Seymour realized that the Azusa happenings were of great significance to the history of Christianity. It was "too large" in the overall scope of things to be restricted to any one church, sect or location. According to Seymour, those who were truly baptized

207 William J. Seymour, ed., "Pentecost with Signs Following: Seven Months of Pentecostal Showers. Jesus, Our Projector and Great Shepherd," *Apostolic Faith* 1, no. 4 (December 1906): 1.
208 William J. Seymour, ed., "The Apostolic Faith Movement," *Apostolic Faith* 1, no. 1 (September 1906): 2.
209 William J. Seymour, ed., Untitled article, *Apostolic Faith* 1, no. 1 (September 1906): 1.

in the Holy Spirit were united in love; and this passionate love would enable recipients of this "new baptism" to spread the good news, thereby infecting the entire body of Christ.

Not only did Seymour promote a spirit of unity, but he also wanted to ensure that his followers respected other denominations and churches who did not embrace this particular version of Christianity. An article possibly written by Seymour in the *Apostolic Faith*, entitled, "The Church Question," warned supporters not to judge other churches based on doctrinal differences:

> All these denominations are our brethren. The Spirit is not going to drive them out and send them to hell. We are to recognize every man that honors the Blood. So let us seek peace and not confusion.[210]

Though Seymour believed that the baptism of the Holy Spirit was for everyone, he was also Christocentric, contending that the Holy Spirit did not have the "time to magnify anything else but...our Lord Jesus Christ."[211] He was adamantly opposed to the idea of criticizing other churches because of their refusal to accept the tenets of the revival. The main thing for the Azusa leader was that an individual put their trust in Christ. This is what is meant by the phrase, "we are to recognize every man that honors the Blood." Seymour tried to eliminate doctrinally-superior attitudes by admonishing his followers about their danger of falling the moment they felt that they had "all of the truth or more than anyone else."[212]

As the revival progressed, Seymour's ecumenism became even more pronounced. In a question and answer segment in the October to January 1908 issue of the *Apostolic Faith* entitled, "Questions Answered," Seymour provided this

210 William J. Seymour, ed., "The Church Question," *Apostolic Faith* 1, no. 5 (January 1907): 2.
211 Ibid.
212 Ibid.

answer to a question about speaking in tongues as the standard for fellowship with other Pentecostals:

> ...Our fellowship does not come through gifts and outward manifestations but through the Blood by the Spirit of Christ. There is nothing more loving than the Blood of Jesus Christ in our hearts...If a man is saved and living according to the word of God, he is our brother, if he has not got [sic] the baptism with the Holy Spirit with tongues.[213]

Here, again, Seymour linked true fellowship to the sacrificial death of Jesus, and not through glossolalia, spiritual gifts, or any other manifestations. However, in this article he was more firm in his stance concerning Christian unity, and demonstrated his desire for believers outside of the movement (who did not have the experience of the baptism of the Holy Spirit with tongues) to understand that they were brothers and sisters in Christ.

In essence, Seymour believed that the recipe for revival in the body of Christ was to follow the standard of Jesus, which happened to be the "baptism of the Holy Ghost and fire."[214] He was fully convinced that the secret to the success of the Azusa Revival was that believers were united in purpose, similar to the day of Pentecost in the book of Acts. Seymour supposed that unity was guaranteed as people came together with one heart, believing for the "great power." In other words, as believers waited together in anticipation for the baptism of the Holy Spirit, "Pentecostal results" would follow, and the people would become even more united. An article written by Seymour, late in the revival in 1908 entitled, "The Baptism of the Holy Ghost," accentuates this last point:

213 William J. Seymour, ed., "Questions Answered," *Apostolic Faith* 1, no. 11 (October to January 1908): 2.
214 William J. Seymour, "The Baptism of the Holy Ghost," *Apostolic Faith* 2, no. 13 (May 1908): 3.

> Apostolic Faith doctrine means one accord, one soul, one heart...O how my heart cries out to God in these days that He would make every child of His see the necessity of living in the 17th chapter of John, that we may be one in the body of Christ, as Jesus has prayed.[215]

It is clear that Seymour not only believed that unity was a good idea, but he viewed it as instrumental to define the movement. He yearned to see every believer comprehend the importance of unity in the body of Christ. This passion for unity was not only evident in the life of Seymour; it figured prominently in lives of many Azusa Street faithful, because of his vision. Anna Hall, an associate of Charles Fox Parham, gave the following testimony in the *Apostolic Faith* in October 1906:

> If this movement stands for anything, it stands for unity of mind. It was raised up to answer the prayer of Jesus: "That they might be one, as thou Father art in me and I in thee." What is the matter with the world today? Here is a little selfish sect and there a denomination by itself. They do not love one another as God would have them. Let us honor every bit of God there is in one another. Let us honor the Holy Ghost to teach men to get them out of their error.[216]

Though Seymour was ecumenical and desired fellowship with people of different theological backgrounds and denominations, he preferred only to associate with people who held Scripture in high regard. Again, he promoted inclusiveness in the church by embracing those who honored the blood of Christ as brothers and sisters, "regardless of

215 Ibid.

216 Anna Hall, "Honor the Holy Ghost," *Apostolic Faith* 1, no. 2 (October 1906): 4.

denomination, creed, or doctrine."[217] However, this was a *conditional inclusiveness* contingent on a person's view of the Word of God. A comment in the *Apostolic Faith* immediately followed a sentence on unity: "But we are not willing to accept any errors, it matters not how charming and sweet they may seem to be. If they do not tally with the Word of God, we reject them."[218]

Even though these words seem harsh and lacking in tolerance to our modern ears, for Seymour and the Azusa faithful, the Bible was the infallible word of God. As children of their time, they held that true unity could only be realized upon the sure foundation of the authority of Scripture. In *Doctrines and Discipline*, Seymour maintained that Scripture was the divine revelation given by God to men, and maintained that it was a complete, infallible guide.[219] He held Scripture to be the standard of authority in all matters of religion and morals.

A Mission-oriented Church

Seymour saw the duty of the church as fulfilling the great commission by following the teachings of Jesus in Matthew 28:19-20, which declares:

> "Go ye therefore and teach all nations, baptizing them in the name of the Father, and of the Son, and the Holy Ghost. Teaching them to observe all things whatsoever I have commanded you."

The Church was not to deviate from the teachings of Christ; it was to continue to walk in obedience until His coming. For Seymour, the sending of missionaries was a clear

217 William J. Seymour, ed., "Pentecost with Signs Following: Seven Months of Pentecostal Showers. Jesus, our Projector and Great Shepherd," *Apostolic Faith* 1, no. 4 (December 1906): 1.
218 Ibid.
219 Seymour, *Doctrines and Discipline*, 7.

mandate of Scripture and an indication of that obedience. The missionaries sent out from Azusa Street were also vital to the spread of the worldwide Pentecostal movement. It is important to remember that Seymour initially agreed with Charles Fox Parham's thesis that tongues were actually human languages, given for the purpose of missionary use. For a short period, Seymour was in full agreement with his mentor and believed that those who were baptized in the Holy Spirit, with the evidence of tongues, were prepared to accomplish God's end-time missionary mandate. Seymour believed that the tongues that were spoken when one was baptized in the Holy Spirit would be an indication of the country that they would eventually go to.

While defending the position alleging that the Azusa Street Mission was the birthplace of global Pentecostalism, Mel Robeck argued that Seymour and the Azusa faithful followed a simple four-step process when a person spoke in a tongue to determine if they were called to go to the mission field.[220] First and foremost in this four-stage program, they attempted to identify the language. Second, they tried to determine whether or not the orator believed that they had received a "missionary call." Third, if the person who spoke in tongues claimed such a call, mission personnel sought to establish whether the call was legitimate, and whether the individual was actually prepared to go. Finally, if all these requisites were satisfied, they would give the candidate the finances to reach their mission field. In general, upon receiving the money, the individual left town within days or in some cases, even hours.

A. G. and Lillian Garr provided an example of how this four-fold process worked. The Garrs had only been at the Azusa Street Mission for a couple weeks before they were

220 Cecil M. Robeck Jr., *The Azusa Street Mission and Revival: The Birth of the Global Pentecostal Movement* (Nashville: Nelson Reference and Electronic, 2006), 239.

baptized in the Holy Spirit. The pair were former leaders of a local ministry in Los Angeles, and associated with the Burning Bush organization.[221] As pastors of this nearby ministry, they had the trust of the local people. This confidence led the Azusa faithful to fully embrace the Garrs when A. G. announced that he had received the Hindustani language of India, and Lillian claimed that she had the ability to speak Chinese. After making their public declarations, the couple offered themselves without delay as Azusa Street's first missionaries to the foreign field. Within fifteen minutes the enthusiastic couple received an offering of twelve hundred dollars in cash to send them on their way.[222]

However, the Garrs were not the only Azusa pilgrims who experienced this kind of missionary support. Seymour repeatedly provided similar support to others who sensed a call to go to the mission field. According to Robeck, once a missionary received the finances for their trip, an energized congregation, often accompanied him or her to a nearby railroad station, singing and shouting.[223] The group would often hold public meetings in the station until the train departed.[224]

Though Seymour and his congregation were extremely supportive of those who sensed a missionary call, they practiced a degree of perspicacity by subjecting missionary candidates to a process of discernment. Such was the case with George and Daisy Batman who believed that they were called to Monrovia, Liberia in Africa. George Batman testified that he was able to speak in six different languages, which were bestowed upon him "at God's command."[225] Though they

221 William J. Seymour, ed., "Good News from Danville, VA," *Apostolic Faith* 1, no. 1 (September 1906): 4.
222 Robeck, *Azusa Street Mission and Revival*, 240.
223 Ibid.
224 Ibid.
225 G. W. and Daisy Batman, "En Route to Africa," *Apostolic Faith* 1, no. 4 (December 1906): 4.

were excited about the opportunity to go to a place named the "white man's graveyard,"[226] along with their three little children, their faith was tested when they did not immediately receive provision for the trip. Instead, they were forced to wait until the individual who would finance the majority of the expedition could receive 'revelation' from God. This came one night before the Batmans left.[227]

Vinson Synan labeled those who participated in Azusa's missionary program as, "missionaries of the one way ticket," since most of them were sent out with only enough money to get them to their destinations, and little or no guarantee of provision for a return ticket.[228] Seymour's rationale for his unorthodox missions program appeared to have eschatological dimensions since he and the mission faithful believed that Christ would return before their missionaries needed to return home.[229] However, if it became necessary for the missionary to return home prematurely, the congregation was fully convinced that the tickets home would be, somehow, supplied by God.

Though it would be difficult to criticize the zeal, willingness, and compassion of Seymour and these early Pentecostal pioneers for their faith to trust God, or the sacrifices they were more than willing to make, their method of running the missionary program led to some unsurprising problems. Their belief in the ability to preach in unknown tongues to the natives led many to go out from Azusa without any training or theological instruction. They knew nothing about the languages or the customs of the countries that they felt themselves called to. For example, using these unconventional methods, the Garrs were originally unsuccessful in India in

226 Ibid.
227 Ibid.
228 Vinson Synan, *The Holiness-Pentecostal Tradition: Charismatic Movements in the Twentieth Century* (Grand Rapids: William B. Eerdmans, 1997), 133.
229 Robeck, *Azusa Street Mission and Revival*, 240.

1907; but their work proved more productive in Hong Kong, after they employed more traditional linguistic methods.[230]

Even with their lack of training, Seymour and his staff did everything in their power to spread the "full gospel" as they issued credentials and supplied the necessary funds to would-be missionaries. The number of missionaries who went out from the Mission during the first three years of its existence is simply astonishing. A headline in the January 1907 edition of the *Apostolic Faith* provides evidence of how Seymour and his staff perceived the global nature of the movement: "Beginning of the Worldwide Revival." Missionaries from Azusa were responsible for Pentecostal outbreaks in places such as Jerusalem, India, China, Europe, South America, Africa, and the islands of the sea.[231] Important for Seymour and the Azusa faithful was the insistence that all races of humankind were suitable to receive the gospel. Universal missionary activity logically required a universal equality of all humanity, and Seymour appeared to be just the man to lead such an endeavor.

A Loving Church

Central to Seymour's ecclesiology was his understanding of divine love. Again, the theological metamorphosis that Seymour underwent moved him from the assertion that tongues were the evidence of Spirit baptism, to the conviction that divine love was the sign of baptism in the Holy Spirit. However, Seymour did not discontinue his teaching on the significance of tongues. Instead, he earnestly wanted his

230 Vinson Synan, "William Joseph Seymour," in *Dictionary of Pentecostal and Charismatic Movements*, ed. Stanley M. Burgess, Garry B. McGee, and Patrick H. Alexander (Grand Rapids: Zondervan, 1988), 781.

231 William J. Seymour, ed., "Good News from Danville, VA," *Apostolic Faith* 1, no.1 (September 1906): 4; William J. Seymour, ed., "Missionaries to Jerusalem," *Apostolic Faith* 1, no. 1 (September 1906): 4; G. W. and Daisy Batman, "En Route to Africa," *Apostolic Faith* 1, no. 4 (December 1906): 4; and William J. Seymour, ed., "Revival in India," *Apostolic Faith* 1, no. 4 (December 1906): 4. For more examples of missionary activity among Azusa participants, see *Apostolic Faith* (September 1906 through May 1908).

listeners to understand that, though the ability to speak in other tongues was *one* of the evidences, divine love was the key result for all those who were inaugurated into the new baptism. His admonition in the *Apostolic Faith* helps one to grasp Seymour's heart on the issue:

> Many may start in this salvation, and yet if they do not watch and keep under the Blood, they will lose the Spirit of Jesus, which is *divine love*, and have only gifts which will be as sounding brass and a tinkling cymbal, and sooner or later these will be taken away. If you want to live in the Spirit, live in the fruits of the Spirit every day.[232]

From the early days of the revival, Seymour believed that love was the real evidence of the baptism of the Holy Spirit, though he remained convinced that it was usually accompanied by the sign of speaking in other tongues. An article signed by the name Apostolic Light, possibly written by Seymour in the *Apostolic Faith* clarifies his position:

> Those who receive the baptism with the Holy Ghost and speak in tongues and backslide from this state may retain the speaking in tongues for a while after divine love is gone, but gradually this gift also will melt away.[233]

From this statement, one ascertains the significance that Seymour placed on divine love, juxtaposed to speaking in tongues. In Pastor Seymour's estimation, a person who was genuinely baptized in the Spirit would demonstrate divine love. Once the person turned away from walking in love, and developed harshness in their speech toward a fellow believer,

232 William J. Seymour, ed., "To the Baptized Saints," *Apostolic Faith* 1, no. 9 (June to September 1907): 2 (emphasis added).
233 Apostolic Light, Untitled article, *Apostolic Faith* 1, no. 4 (December 1906): 4.

it was only a matter of time before speaking in tongues would also fade away. Seymour's perception of love was summed up in the early months of the Azusa Revival in October of 1906: "Divine love to all, especially to the church, the body of Christ, of which every justified soul is a member."[234] Azusa pilgrim and historian Frank Bartleman helped to describe the early mood at Azusa (and affirmed Seymour's position) through his declaration that divine love was wonderfully manifested in the meetings and that the Azusa faithful "lived in a sea of pure divine love."[235]

The fruit of Seymour's teaching on love was evidenced in the testimonies of those who received the baptism of the Holy Spirit, as the statement of a man with a Nazarene background attests:

> It was a baptism of love. Such abounding love! Such compassion seemed to almost kill me with its sweetness! People do not know what they are doing when they stand out against it. The devil never gave me a swet [sic] thing, he was always trying to get me to censuring people. This baptism fills us with divine love.[236]

In one instance, a preacher was filled with the Holy Spirit during a service at Azusa Street, and immediately stood up and shouted, "Hallelujah!" When the man spoke in tongues, his wife and children became frightened, and believed their loved one had lost his mind. However, when his family sensed "the sympathy and *divine love* which the Holy Ghost [placed] in people's hearts, they said, 'Papa was never so sane in his life.'"[237]

---

234 William J. Seymour, ed., "Marks of Fanaticism," *Apostolic Faith* 1, no. 2 (October 1906): 2

235 Frank Bartleman, *Azusa Street* (South Plainfield, NJ: Bridge Publishing, 1980), 54.

236 William J. Seymour, ed., Untitled article, *Apostolic Faith* 1, no. 1 (September 1906): 1.

237 William J. Seymour, ed., Untitled article, *Apostolic Faith* 1, no. 1 (September 1906): 2 (emphasis added).

Interestingly, in the *Apostolic Faith* in the October 1906 article entitled, "Praying for the Holy Ghost," an anonymous writer (possibly Seymour) wrote the following about Charles Fox Parham, complimenting the controversial leader in regard to his "love walk":

> Before another issue of this paper, we look for Bro. Parham in Los Angeles, a brother who is full of *divine love* and whom the Lord raised up five years ago to spread this truth.[238]

Noteworthy is the fact that Parham's demonstration of love is what impressed Seymour most about the man. One might imagine that Seymour would have been most attracted to Parham's revolutionary teaching on the Bible evidence of Spirit baptism, which would have thereby been highlighted in the article detailing Parham's imminent visit to Los Angeles. However, Seymour's emphasis on the significance of divine love, which he believed to observe in Parham's life in Houston, was most important to the Azusa leader. This demonstrates the high value Seymour placed on the concept of love among believers in the Body of Christ.

Ironically, this perception of the element of divine love in Parham would be short-lived when the former Methodist preacher visited Azusa Street in October 1906, and repudiated the revival by disrespecting Seymour and the Azusa leadership. Though it has already been noted that Seymour believed strongly that divine love was an essential factor of the authenticity of an individual's Holy Spirit baptism, Parham's volatile comments on race, and rejection of the revival helped Seymour to further elucidate his theology of love.

Such behavior would have raised several questions for Seymour, as to how Parham could be truly baptized in the Holy

238 William J. Seymour, ed., "Praying for the Holy Ghost," *Apostolic Faith* 1, no. 2 (October 1906): 3 (emphasis added).

Spirit when he had a problem with the color of Seymour's skin. This would naturally lead him to question whether tongues were sufficient evidence of Holy Spirit baptism, and whether love had anything to do with the event. Although these questions may seem a bit exaggerated, Seymour's writings reflect comparable reactions. Seymour summarized what he believed was the central doctrine in the *Apostolic Faith*:

> The Pentecostal power, when you sum it all up, is just more of God's love. If it does not bring more love, it is simply a counterfeit. Pentecost means to live right in the 13th chapter of First Corinthians, which is the standard. When you live there, you have no trouble to keep salvation. This is Bible religion. It is not a manufactured religion. Pentecost makes us love Jesus more and love our brothers more. It brings us all into one common family.[239]

The racism Seymour endured at the hand of whites, particularly Charles Parham, may have caused him to come to the conclusion that some people who claimed genuine "Pentecostal experiences," in fact, had none. In Seymour's estimation, the "Pentecostal power" enabled an individual to love a person of a different race or another denomination. This is why Seymour could not understand those who claimed Holy Spirit baptismal experiences, and yet tightly held racial or denominational prejudices. In the following quote from an *Apostolic Faith* article entitled, "The Church Question," Seymour gives further clarification regarding those who perpetuated a spirit of division:

> When people run out of the love of God, they get to preaching something else, preaching dress, and

239 William J. Seymour, ed., Untitled article, *Apostolic Faith* 2, no. 13 (May 1908): 3.

meats, and doctrines of men, and preaching against churches.[240]

For Seymour, love was the often-missing ingredient required to create a proverbial culinary masterpiece in the Spirit. Without it, saints in the body of Christ became preoccupied with other things, and would eventually become hostile towards one another.

A Holy (Sanctified) Church

Although the topic of divine love was important to Seymour, his holiness convictions secured his belief that the proper fabric for the character of the Church was men and women saved from sin, dedicated to live free from sin and all uncleanness.[241] In short, Seymour tightly held to a life of holiness, and fervently believed that God could only use clean vessels to achieve His mighty works, one of which was the obliteration of the "color line" within the Christian community.

It is important to revisit Seymour's stance on sanctification, because of its prominence in the ontological framework of his ecclesiology. Seymour repeatedly stressed the sanctified church motif throughout the *Apostolic Faith*. In one sermon, entitled, "Rebecca; Type of the Bride of Christ-Gen. 24," he used Ephesians 5:25-27 to implore his followers to prepare themselves for Christ, who was coming back for a church without "spot or wrinkle."[242] According to Seymour, the only people who were eligible to meet Jesus at His coming were the sanctified ones. These people made up the "glorious church" that Seymour alluded to in this interpretation of Ephesians,

240 William J. Seymour, ed., "The Church Question," *Apostolic Faith* 1, no. 5 (January 1907): 2.
241 Seymour, *Doctrines and Discipline*, 10.
242 William J. Seymour, "Rebecca; Type of the Bride of Christ-Gen. 24," *Apostolic Faith* 1, no. 6 (February to March 1907): 2.

who were also prime candidates to receive the baptism of the Holy Spirit with fire (which was considered a gift only for the sanctified). An anonymous article, possibly written by Seymour, in the June-September 1907 edition of the *Apostolic Faith*, shared comparable sentiments about the importance of maintaining purity in the Church:

> Jesus wants a clean people, a sanctified people, a holy people, washed through His own precious Blood... O it is so sweet to live this sanctified experience, living in the presence of Christ and His Blood flowing, washing and putting away our sins every moment of our lives.[243]

Seymour's Wesleyan-Holiness background convinced him that believers should be ideal men and women, because they had Jesus, who happened to be a perfect model to emulate.

According to Seymour, Christ was not merely concerned with the Holy Spirit baptizing individuals, and bodily healing; but instead, He was walking in the midst of His people, putting "His finger on every wrong and mean thing in the church."[244] One such "wrong thing," in Seymour's eyes, was the issue of impure doctrine. The Azusa leader was a proponent of unity, but not at any cost. He commented in the sermon, "Christ's Messages to the Church" in the *Apostolic Faith*, that "Jesus hates impure doctrine just as much as when He rebuked the Pharisees for their impure doctrine."[245] Doctrinal purity had to be preserved, if the Church of Jesus Christ was to be truly effective in the last days. Seymour's posture concerning the significance of maintaining right doctrine in the church is evident:

243 William J. Seymour, ed., Untitled article, *Apostolic Faith* 1, no. 9 (June to September 1907): 4.
244 William J. Seymour, "Christ's Messages to the Church," *Apostolic Faith* 1, no. 11 (October to January 1908): 3.
245 Ibid.

> We find many of Christ's people tangled up in these days, committing spiritual fornication as well as physical fornication and adultery. They say "Let us all come together; if we are not one in doctrine, we can be one in spirit." But, dear ones, we cannot all be one, except through the word of God.[246]

Seymour reaffirmed his stance on conditional inclusiveness by drawing a proverbial line in the sand for those who did not hold his convictions about the authority of Scripture. For Seymour, the only true rationale for fellowship in the Spirit was doctrinal purity. In essence, he envisioned a victorious Church that was filled with God's Spirit, and abounded in love. However, for Seymour, it must be a "sanctified" Church, free from sin and all impurity, as he never abandoned his high ideals for the Church, but continued to emphasize holiness until he died.

A Racially-Inclusive Church

Although many testimonies have been recorded about the miracles that occurred at Azusa under Seymour's leadership, the greatest miracle may have been the interracial harmony. Most are familiar with the Frank Bartleman's assertion that at Azusa, "the color line was washed away in the blood."[247] Many historians are fascinated by the reality that people of various nationalities and races attended services and became united under a black pastor from Louisiana. The fact that blacks and whites were able to work together in leadership during a time when the unjust Jim Crow laws were the precedent is even more fascinating.

The kind of racial diversity that this revival enjoyed for a season was remarkable in itself. Black hands were laid on white heads, as many received the baptism of the Holy Spirit.

246 Ibid.
247 Bartleman, *Azusa Street,* 54.

An example of this interracial cooperation was evidenced in the experience of G. B. Cashwell, a white Holiness leader in North Carolina. Cashwell had read about the Azusa Street Mission in September of 1906 and decided to come to Los Angeles to get a closer look at the "New Pentecost." Upon his arrival at Azusa, Cashwell cringed when a young black man touched him while praying for him. Yet after several services, and days of internal wrestling with his own racist attitudes, Cashwell had a change of heart and asked Seymour to pray for him. After his Pentecostal experience, which only came about because of his willingness to submit himself, he returned to North Carolina to become the "Apostle of Pentecost" to the South. His ministry was pivotal in bringing the Pentecostal message to that entire region.[248] For a brief time, white people at Azusa forgot that they were *white*. They were not concerned about their reputations, or how they would be perceived by those of their own race. The only thing that mattered to them was that they had to receive what this humble black preacher had. White Azusa leader, Florence Crawford testified about her first encounter with Seymour:

> They sang a little, but that did not seem to touch my heart. They went down in prayer but that didn't move me at all...Finally a big colored man got up on his feet. He said, 'Hallelujah!' It just went through my soul. He waited a minute, and again he said,

248 Vinson Synan, "Gaston Barnabas Cashwell," in Burgess, McGee, and Alexander, *Dictionary of Pentecostal and Charismatic Movements*, 109-110; Gaston Barnabas Cashwell, "Came 3,000 Miles for His Pentecost," *Apostolic Faith* 1, no. 4 (December 1906): 3; and Nelson, "For Such a Time as This," 198. After leaving Azusa Street, Cashwell returned to Dunn, North Carolina where he brought the Pentecostal message to a local Holiness church on December 31, 1906. Cashwell then invited to ministers of Holiness churches around the region to attend Pentecostal services in January in Dunn. The Dunn meetings garnered so much attention that they lasted through the month of January 1907 and became an East Coast counterpart to the Azusa Street meetings. For more information on Cashwell, see Doug Beacham, *Azusa East: The Life and Times of G. B. Cashwell* (Franklin Springs, GA: LSR Publications, 2006), 42-55.

> 'Hallelujah!' I thought, "God, I have heard the voice from heaven. I have heard it at last. ...He has the thing my heart is reaching out after. I forgot everything else, for I heard the voice of the great Shepherd of the sheep. ...The one thing I wondered was, [h]ow could I get it? How could I receive that wonderful blessing on my soul that I had hungered for so long, and that this man had? ...Oh, the hunger that God planted in my soul! It didn't matter what my people would say—my friends and all—but only, could I get it.[249]

Like Florence Crawford, several other white people came to Azusa because of a deep hunger for God. White southern ministers made the long journey to California in order to receive the blessings of the Spirit through the prayers and intercessions of their African American brothers and sisters. Even more significantly, pastors returned to their congregations in the South (and other areas of the country) less racially prejudiced because of their association with the black people of Azusa.[250]

It might be taken for granted that nothing but a miracle of racial harmony allowed the races to come together for a brief period of time in the midst of Jim Crowism. But were there other dynamics that aided in fostering Azusa's environment to make it ripe for this miracle to take place? Was glossolalia the amalgamating factor that broke down the color barrier? Or did Seymour's ecclesiological stance on racial inclusiveness play a significant role in obliterating the color line in his Mission for a short period of time?

Seymour's theology of race was already formed before he assumed leadership at the Azusa meetings, and provided the

249 Raymond Robert Crawford, *The Light of Life Brought Triumph: A Brief Sketch of the Life and Labors of Florence L. (Mother) Crawford 1872-1936* (1936; repr., Portland: Apostolic Faith Publishing House, 1955), 9-10.

250 Gaston Barnabas Cashwell, "Came 3,000 Miles for His Pentecost," *Apostolic Faith* 1, no. 4 (December 1906): 3.

impetus for the racial solidarity. The Azusa leader's personal experiences were important in shaping his theological perspective concerning racial equality. Seymour was forced to endure the harshness of racial discrimination while growing up in Centerville, Louisiana. As the son of former slaves, he left his home in the South in search of racial congruity. He was attracted to racially sensitive organizations such as the Evening Light Saints, the Methodist Episcopal Church, and the ministry of Martin Wells Knapp. It is not surprising, that, when given the chance to lead his own congregation, Seymour was able to cast a vision of interracial cohesiveness, which provided a template for his followers to also employ. In his first issue of the *Apostolic Faith,* Seymour made his conviction known: "multitudes have come. God makes no difference in nationality, Ethiopians, Chinese, Indians, Mexicans, and other nationalities worship together."[251]

However, the remarkable occurrence of racial harmony at this juncture in American Church history ought not to be overlooked. Given the racial climate in America during the Azusa Street meetings, the level of racial togetherness should certainly be considered miraculous. Yet, it must be acknowledged that the monumental achievement of racial harmony that was realized at Azusa occurred because of one individual who was truly dedicated to equality. A final excerpt from the *Apostolic Faith* helps us to understand the kind of atmosphere that Seymour created at the Mission:

> No instrument that God can use is rejected on account of color or dress or lack of education. This is why God has so built up the work. ...The sweetest thing of all is the loving harmony."[252]

251 William J. Seymour, ed., "The Same Old Way," *Apostolic Faith* 1, no. 1 (September 1906): 3.

252 William J. Seymour, ed., "Gracious Pentecostal Showers Continue to Fall," *Apostolic Faith* 1, no. 3 (November 1906): 1.

Clearly, Seymour was attributing the success of Azusa Street to certain intentionality, as it pertained to race and class. Further, this statement stood in contrast to the more providential view held by Azusa participants like Frank Bartleman, who explained the secret of Azusa as simply a move of God.[253]

Azusa's interracial fellowship was no accident. Rather, it was a defining mark, related to the vision of a man that spent his entire life searching for true Christian fellowship without limitations. For Seymour, racial inclusiveness was the sign of the true Church that was birthed on the day of Pentecost, as people from all nations gathered to hear the gospel in their own native language.

Seymour's ecclesiology, then, both shaped, and reflected his views on racial harmony. His emphases on the themes of Church unity, missions, sanctification, and the expression of divine love as evidence of the Spirit's sanction in Azusa's interracial community, all implicitly or explicitly demonstrated the legitimacy of racial integration against a hostile world.

As one considers Seymour's theology, particularly his views on soteriology, pneumatology, and ecclesiology, he becomes more than a humble man with his face in a shoe box.[254] Seymour was a person of substance with deep theological convictions regarding the doctrines of sin, the Holy Spirit and the Church.

His soteriology held that justification, sanctification, and baptism of the Holy Spirit constituted the "full blessing" of Christ, as symbolized by the Azusa leader's utilization of tabernacle imagery. In Seymour's mind, all three experiences

253 Bartleman, *Azusa Street*, 48.

254 Ibid., 58. Frank Bartleman commented that Seymour was so humble that he usually prayed with his face inside one of the two empty crates which held shoeboxes that were probably being used as a makeshift pulpit during the meetings. Although Bartleman's depiction of Seymour is somewhat accurate in regard to the Azusa leader's meekness, Bartleman had a tendency to not give proper credit to Seymour's other qualities, such as his leadership and theological prowess.

were purchased on the Cross, and Spirit baptism was accessible for every believer, because the gift of the Spirit came upon those who had been sanctified.

Pneumatologically, Seymour had a more balanced view of the work of the Spirit (as pertaining to that which constituted a "Spirit-filled believer") than most of his contemporaries. Pastor Seymour encouraged his congregants to seek the baptism of the Holy Spirit by focusing their attention on God alone, rather than on one particular gift of the Spirit. The gifts of the Holy Spirit were to be used for the glory of God. Glossolalia (as evidence for the baptism of the Holy Spirit on "all flesh") served implicitly to prove the egalitarianism of all ethnicities, as people from all races were receiving this experience at Azusa.

Finally, Seymour's ecclesiology pleaded for the Church to break free from the fetters of divisiveness and racial disharmony, to allow the Holy Spirit to bring it into true Christian fellowship. According to Seymour, the chief task of the Holy Spirit was not to produce glossolalia as the distinctive mark of Pentecostal solidarity, as many white Pentecostals believed. Instead, Seymour was convinced that the work of the Holy Spirit was to bring together all races and nations into one universal family through divine love.

CHAPTER FOUR

Seymour in Dialogue and Conflict

This chapter shows how Seymour was perceived by his peers within the early Pentecostal movement by placing him in dialogue with three of his contemporaries: Florence Crawford, Charles Fox Parham, and William H. Durham. As Seymour's theological understanding is compared and contrasted with others, a more complete picture of Seymour's teachings emerge, as well as some of the subsequent controversies within early Pentecostal movement.

Florence Crawford

Arguably, Florence Crawford may have been the woman who most influenced the Pentecostal movement beyond the initial Azusa Street Revival, because of her pioneering work with the Apostolic Faith Mission in Portland, Oregon.[255] Moreover, Crawford claimed to be the first white woman to receive the baptism of the Holy Spirit in 1906 at Azusa Street.[256]

However, before Mrs. Crawford became known as a Pentecostal pioneer, she was a person who suffered many

255 Estrelda Alexander, *The Women of Azusa Street* (Cleveland: Pilgrim Press, 2005), 59. Affectionately called "mother" by her followers, Crawford was considered to be heavy-handed in her leadership style. Her Apostolic Faith Mission is responsible for 122 churches around the world.

256 William J. Seymour, ed., "The Same Old Way," *Apostolic Faith* 1, no. 1 (September 1906): 3. Though Crawford claimed she was the first white woman to receive the baptism, the *Apostolic Faith* paper argued that another white woman named May Evans (Mrs. Evans) was the first to receive the Pentecostal experience with speaking in tongues.

childhood illnesses. As a teenager, Crawford was thrown from a carriage, and landed on a stump, injuring her back. The injury caused Crawford to be bedridden for weeks. Further, she suffered debilitating bouts of spinal meningitis, as well as tuberculosis.

Crawford, like many others had made the trip south to California from her native Oregon in 1890 in search of physical healing. Crawford later recalled that she had migrated to the "sunny south," Los Angeles out of sheer desperation.[257] Unfortunately for Crawford, healing from her physical ailments failed to materialize during her early years in Los Angeles.

Just eighteen years old when she arrived at the downtown Los Angeles rail station in 1890, Florence (formerly Florence L. Reed) was married at the end of the year to Frank M. Crawford, and entered motherhood by the close of the following year.[258] By 1900, the Crawfords were permanent fixtures within the Los Angeles economic and social life. Florence attended teas, dances, and other social events, as well as caring for her growing family. All the while, she continued her search for relief from her unrelenting physical ailments. The turning point in the life of Florence Crawford occurred around 1900 when she claimed that she heard the voice of God while dancing in one of the city's ballrooms. This incident caused the Oregon native to search out an unnamed friend who led her in a prayer for salvation.[259]

After Crawford's conversion, she threw herself wholeheartedly into church and rescue work. She became

257 Florence Louise Crawford, Untitled Sermon, *Apostolic Faith* (Portland), April 4, 1923: 4.

258 *Los Angeles City Directory*, 1900, 1906, 1908. The Crawford family lived in the nearby farming region of Riverside County where their son, Raymond was born in Menefee Valley. Her daughter Mildred was born in 1897.

259 Raymond Robert Crawford, *The Light of Life Brought Triumph: A Brief Sketch of the Life and Labors of Florence L. [Mother] Crawford, 1872-1936* (1936; repr., Portland: Apostolic Faith Publishing House, 1955), 3-4.

involved in a number of community groups, such as the Women's Christian Temperance Union (WCTU), and became a church hopper as she worshipped with the Methodists, the Presbyterians, the Christian and Missionary Alliance at the Gospel Tabernacle Church, and with Joseph Smale's First New Testament Church.[260] Though Crawford experienced a degree of fulfillment through her social causes, she grew dissatisfied with her justification experience. She wanted more, and claimed that she was searching for sanctification despite ministers' attempts to convince her that she already had been sanctified. Crawford's search ended when an acquaintance informed her that she would find what she sought at the Azusa Street Mission.[261] After several days of praying at the mission, Crawford testified that the "Holy Ghost came down from Heaven and fell upon my life and baptized me with the Holy Ghost and fire, [and] spoke through me in another language."[262] Shortly after her Pentecostal experience, Crawford claimed that she was healed and removed a brace that she had worn for eleven years.[263]

Crawford quickly ascended within the Azusa leadership ranks, and became one of six women who served on the Azusa Street administrative board. The Oregon native became known at Azusa for praying for those who wanted to receive the baptism of the Spirit, physical healing, salvation, and sanctification.[264] She also served as co-editor (along with Seymour and Clara Lum) of *The Apostolic Faith* newspaper, and was second only to Seymour in the number of signed

260 Ibid., 6.

261 Ibid., 8-10. Florence Louise Crawford testified in *Light of Life Brought Triumph* that "fire fell" on her one Friday afternoon at the Azusa Street mission when the preacher (most likely Seymour) stopped preaching and said, "Somebody in this place wants something from God." Crawford then pushed the chairs away from the altar and claimed that God had sanctified her.

262 Ibid., 13-14.

263 Ibid., 14-16.

264 Alexander, *Women of Azusa Street*, 62.

articles in the paper.[265] Due to Crawford's work ethic and zeal for ministry, Seymour named her State Director in California, and entrusted her to plant new works throughout the state in the name of the Apostolic Faith.

Seemingly then, Seymour and Crawford had an exceptional beginning. Again, Crawford was initially enamored with Seymour, and on hearing him speak, remarked that he had "the thing my heart is reaching out after. I forgot everything else, for I heard the voice of the great Shepherd of the sheep."[266] Both she and Seymour were strong proponents of sanctification as a definite second work of grace, with the baptism of the Holy Spirit coming upon the sanctified life.[267]

However, by the middle of 1907 things began to change between Crawford and Seymour. As California State Director of the Pacific Coast Apostolic Faith movement, she established herself as a credible leader, leading a group of workers in September 1906 to Northern California, Oregon, and Washington. She was accustomed to taking extended ministry trips away from the mission. But by the end of the summer of 1907, Crawford parted ways with Seymour, and permanently moved to Portland with her daughter Mildred, and associate and longtime friend, Will Trotter (with his family).[268] The reason for the breach between Seymour and Crawford has been debated among scholars. The majority opinion is that Crawford justified her break from Seymour because of his alleged compromise on the teaching of

265 Ibid.

266 Raymond Robert Crawford, *Light of Life Brought Triumph*, 9-10.

267 Florence Louise Crawford, "Entire Sanctification," in *Sermons and Scriptural Studies*, comp. Raymond Robert Crawford (Portland: Apostolic Faith Mission, 1931), 39; and William J. Seymour, ed., "The Apostolic Faith Movement," *Apostolic Faith* 1, no. 1 (September 1906): 2. Like Seymour, Crawford believed that the baptism of the Holy Spirit was a gift of power on the "clean life."

268 Cecil M. Robeck Jr., *The Azusa Street Mission and Revival: The Birth of the Global Pentecostal Movement* (Nashville: Nelson Reference and Electronic, 2006), 300. Though Florence Crawford would later maintain that her formal separation from Seymour did not occur until nearly 1908, the break was essentially complete by September of 1907.

sanctification.[269] Evidently, Crawford had heard rumors that Seymour no longer held the Wesleyan position, which championed entire sanctification as a second work of grace, after conversion. Crawford maintained that she had returned to Los Angeles to resolve the conflict, but that intervention had been ineffective.[270] However, there is no evidence to suggest that Seymour ever wavered from traditional Wesleyan Holiness teaching on sanctification. So one must question what really caused Crawford to accuse him of such compromise, and whether her critique of Seymour was valid. In order to understand the possible reasons for the breach between the two, it is important to examine Crawford's theology more closely, as well as the accompanying circumstances.

Again, Crawford was a strict proponent of entire sanctification as a second work of grace. Crawford's stance on this doctrine was evidenced in her sermon entitled, "Entire Sanctification":

> Sanctification is a second definite work of grace in the heart. It is impossible to teach on sanctification without teaching on justification. The one subject does not go into the other, but it leads up to the other. ...After the soul is born again and sins are blotted out, there still remains in the heart the root of sin, the inbred nature, the depravity of the fallen nature, that must be cleansed away—not blotted out, not forgiven. You yourself did not transgress in order to bring into your life the inbred nature. You did not commit the inbred sin in your heart. You committed the transgressions that were the result of the inbred sin. But the inbred sin itself, the bruise of the fall, you inherited from your

269 Ibid.; and Alexander, *Woman of Azusa Street*, 66.
270 Robeck, *Azusa Street Mission and Revival*, 300.

> forefathers, and for that reason you cannot repent of your inbred nature, but you can repent of your actual transgressions.[271]

In addition to her stance on holiness, Crawford, like many early Pentecostals, held radical eschatological views about the imminent return of Jesus Christ. Her position was outlined in a message entitled, "The Second Coming of Christ":

> There can be no question concerning the manner of the second coming of Christ. Many Doctors of Divinity say that He comes in the spirit at death to take us home...If we die we shall be carried by the angels to Paradise. And when Jesus comes He shall call forth the bodies of the sleeping saints...The coming of Jesus is the Christian's hope. How could we live if we did not have that hope of meeting the Lord in the air?[272]

Because of her view of the Second Coming of Christ, she believed that normal activities, such as marriage and the raising of families, were counterproductive, because of the pressing need to spread the Pentecostal message before the soon return of Christ. Apparently, in Crawford's estimation, Seymour had compromised his sanctification because his attention had turned towards marrying Jennie Evans Moore, when it should have been on holy living in preparation for the Lord's return. Crawford generally frowned on marriage, encouraged young people to stay single, and stressed abstinence even among married couples.[273] Having suffered the casualty of divorce on two occasions, Florence believed that "sanctified" people should not be swayed by fleshly acts—and marriage,

271 Florence Louise Crawford, "Entire Sanctification," in *Sermons and Scriptural Studies*, comp. Raymond Robert Crawford, 33-34.
272 Florence Louise Crawford, "The Second Coming of Christ," in *Sermons and Scriptural Studies*, comp. Raymond Robert Crawford, 31.
273 "Camp Meeting: Apostolic Faith," *Time,* August 19, 1935, 34-35.

according to Crawford, was an act of the flesh.[274] The timeline evidence seems to support this as the reason for her departure, as Seymour married Moore on May 13, 1908, and Crawford's formal break from Seymour occurred in this same month.

However, Seymour was not quiet when it came to the issues of marriage and sexuality, but consistently argued that the Bible supported that sexual relations between married Christians were normal, and not merely for procreation. Therefore, according to Seymour, marriage was not sinful. Seymour's position on the matter was recorded in the *Apostolic Faith* in an article entitled, "Bible Teaching on Marriage and Divorce":

> It is no sin to marry. "Marriage is honorable and the bed undefiled, but whoremongers and adulterers God will judge." Heb. 13. 4. There are those today in the marriage life, since they have received sanctification and some the baptism with the Holy Ghost, who have come to think that it is a sin for them to live as husband and wife. Jesus said, in Matt. 19. 5-6, "For this cause shall a man leave father and mother, and shall cleave to his wife, and they twain shall be one flesh. Wherefore they are no more twain but one flesh." Dearly beloved, we cannot get outside of the Word. Paul writes a letter to the church on this subject in 1. Cor. 7. It is a letter that teaches husbands and wives how to live.[275]

Although this article was written in January 1907 (before Crawford's formal break from Seymour), the Azusa leader may have been trying to give a corrective measure to those at the mission (possibly including Crawford) who had begun to hold more extreme views of sanctification, as it relates to marriage.

274 "Camp Meeting," *Time*, 34-35.
275 William J. Seymour, ed., "Bible Teaching on Marriage and Divorce," *Apostolic Faith* 1, no. 5 (January 1907): 3.

Knowing that Crawford had unfortunate marriage experiences, Seymour may have had her in mind in describing those who had been sanctified and filled with Holy Spirit who came to believe that it was a sin to "live as husband and wife." He argued that these people were not holding to the biblical standard for marriage, which taught that husband and wife must unite to become one flesh.

The Azusa leader would take this teaching on marriage a step further the following January of 1908, just four months before he was to be wed, in a sermon entitled, "To the Married:"

> In these days, so many deceptive spirits are in the world, that we have felt impressed by the blessed Holy Spirit to write a letter on the seventh chapter of First Corinthians...He [Paul] says in the second and third verses, "Nevertheless, to avoid fornification, [sic] let every man have his own wife, and let every woman have her own husband. Let the husband render unto the wife due benevolence: and likewise also the wife unto the husband." This of course means conjugal intercourse between man and wife.[276]

Perhaps Seymour again had Crawford in mind in using Pauline theology pertaining to marriage. Though he did not mention her name, he was certainly more direct in his assessment of the importance of sex in marriage than his earlier corrective. Seymour stressed holiness in marriage, and insisted that sexual intimacy between a man and wife enabled the couple to maintain their sanctification, because they would not be tempted with incontinency.[277] Seymour argued from the Apostle Paul's stance that there was a "natural use" for a wife that was not based on lust, as Crawford had taught. To deny

276 William J. Seymour, "To the Married," *Apostolic Faith* 1, no. 12 (January 1908): 3.

277 Ibid.

this *use*, in Seymour's estimation, was to allow a "deceptive spirit or wrong teaching [to] creep in."[278]

A second possible reason for Crawford's charge against Seymour could have been related to financial impropriety, or a difference of opinion about the handling of church finances. Initially, there were no official offerings raised at the Azusa meetings. Seymour and the Azusa faithful had always relied on God, and the generosity of people, to meet their financial needs. However, the diary of Azusa participant George Studd records a controversy that had arisen at the mission over whether they should take up a formal offering.[279] In an entry dated February 2, 1908, Studd penned what he observed at the Azusa Street Mission: "What a Sunday at Azusa! Dispute as to taking collections. How the Devil tried to get in. How the Lord defeated him…"[280] Apparently, Studd was equating the decision by Seymour to collect a formal offering with allowing Satan to come in the Mission. This is supported through Studd's later diary entry, which explained that a man named Cecil Polhill gave £1,500 that day to clear Azusa's mortgage.[281] According to Studd, the Lord defeated the "Devil" (manifested through the fleshly desire to take offerings), by allowing Polhill to finance the mortgage. Rachel Sizelove, one of the organizers of the 1907 camp meeting, and fellow Azusa participant, would later support Studd's assessment of the situation:

> How well I remember the first time the flesh began to get in the way of the Holy Ghost, and how the burden came upon the saints that morning when Brother Seymore [sic] stood before the audience

278 Ibid.

279 Robeck, *Azusa Street Mission and Revival*, 289. While researching, Robeck apparently gained access to the diary of George Studd, who began attending the Azusa Street Mission in 1907.

280 Ibid.

281 Ibid. Polhill's gift of £1,500 amounted to $7, 317. The total mortgage at the time of the purchase was $15,000.

> and spoke of raising money to buy the Azusa Street Mission. The Holy Ghost was grieved. You could feel it all over the audience, when they began to ask for money and the Holy Ghost power began to leave.[282]

Perhaps this was the "rumor" that caused Crawford to question Seymour's sanctification. Though Crawford firmly advocated tithing and free will offerings at her meetings, she radically opposed asking for money or receiving formal offerings during worship services.[283] Crawford commented on her approach to finances in her ministry in Portland:

> Never once did we have the privilege of living on bread and water. Never once in the history of the work was a collection taken to carry on the work. God proved that He was abundantly able to provide.[284]

Like George Studd and Rachel Sizelove, Crawford may have felt that Seymour was acting in the flesh by not relying on the Holy Spirit to meet the financial needs of the mission.

A third possible reason for Crawford's accusation against Seymour may have been related to Seymour's treatment of one of Crawford's closest friends, the white Clara Lum. Before coming to Azusa Street, Lum had served in Charles Parham's house and had edited the *Firebrand*, the periodical of Charles Hanley's World Faith Missionary Association.[285] Like many early Pentecostals, Lum had come from a Holiness background, and had several years of experience as a Holiness preacher. She came to Azusa Street in search of the baptism of the Holy Spirit. After receiving her personal Pentecost, Lum was thrust into leadership at the Azusa Street Mission,

---

282 Ibid., 289-290.

283 "Camp Meeting," *Time*, 34-35; and Estrelda Alexander, *Limited Liberty: The Legacy of Four Pentecostal Women Pioneers* (Cleveland: Pilgrim Press, 2008), 45.

284 Raymond Robert Crawford, *Light of Life Brought Triumph*, 18.

285 Alexander, *Limited Liberty*, 45.

and served on the Mission's governing board. However, it was not long before her clerical skills were employed, as she was chosen to serve as the *Apostolic Faith* secretary and co-editor with Seymour and Crawford, from 1906 to 1908. Clara Lum's writing ability proved invaluable at Azusa, as she was integrally involved in every aspect of the newspaper.

Some scholars have even suggested that the initial idea of beginning a newspaper chronicling the events of the revival was Lum's, since she was the one person with the experience to edit periodicals.[286] She wrote several articles in the *Apostolic Faith,* and edited many more. More importantly, Lum was tasked with developing and maintaining a mailing list for local, national, and international constituencies. At its height, circulation of the paper reached over forty thousand recipients all over the world. Seymour, Crawford, and Lum developed a close friendship during this time, through their work relations, with Lum doing the bulk of the editing.

The relationship between Lum and Seymour, however, appeared to have the greatest depth to it. Reportedly, both had entertained the thought that their friendship might turn into a romantic relationship, and result in marriage. In a book entitled, *Bishop C. H. Mason and the Roots of the Church of God in Christ*, Ithiel Clemmons articulated a conversation that he had with Mason in 1948, regarding the relationship between William J. Seymour and Clara Lum.[287] According to Clemmons, Seymour confided to Mason that Clara Lum had fallen in love with him, and wanted the Azusa leader to propose. Reportedly, however, Mason counseled Seymour against marrying a white woman, given the strained racial relations of America in the Jim Crow era. Following this

286 Alexander, *Women of Azusa Street*, 51. Though Lum had editing experience, the idea for the paper may have come directly from Seymour, due to the fact that he sat under Charles Fox Parham, who was the first to name his paper the *Apostolic Faith*.

287 Ithiel Clemmons, *Bishop C. H. Mason and the Roots of the Church of God in Christ* (Bakersfield, CA: Pneuma Life Publishing, 1996), 50.

advice from his trusted friend, Seymour decided to marry Jennie Evans Moore, an African American woman.

One could only imagine the awkwardness and hurt that Lum may have felt. After ministering and working so closely with Seymour (who she reportedly loved) for over two years in one of the greatest revivals in American Church history, Lum may have been devastated, as Seymour would belong not to her, but to another woman. Perhaps Seymour had tried to let Lum down subtly while speaking to her about the racial discrimination that the two would have to confront if they decided to marry. Maybe Lum initially took Seymour's bad news well, but grew embittered while watching Seymour's relationship with Jennie Evans Moore blossom within this small Pentecostal community.

Since Crawford and Lum were close friends, Crawford may have viewed Seymour's refusal to marry Lum, a white woman, and his decision to marry Jennie Evans Moore, a black woman, as a compromise to the pressure of racism. Some scholars criticize early white Pentecostals by alleging that the Azusa Street Revival did not last longer because whites caved in to racial pressures, and went their separate ways.[288] Perhaps Crawford believed that Seymour had succumbed to the pressure of racism, unwilling to truly live out the "interracial miracle" that he had been espousing from the pulpit in his personal life, through a committed relationship with her friend Clara Lum.

While it is questionable whether Crawford's criticism of Seymour was related to his treatment of Lum, Seymour's marriage to Jennie Evans Moore did have adverse reactions. Both Florence Crawford and Clara Lum objected to Seymour's marriage; each for obviously different reasons. Lum decided to take the *Apostolic Faith* newspaper's national

288 Nelson, "For Such a Time as This," 255; and Iain MacRobert, *The Black Roots and White Racism of Early Pentecostalism* (New York: St. Martin's Press, 1988), 60-67.

and international mailing lists, and join her friend Florence Crawford's ministry in Portland, Oregon. This left Seymour with only the small Los Angeles list. The last edition of the paper that Lum helped produce from Los Angeles was the June 1908 issue. It was published a month after the marriage and the same month that Lum moved to Oregon.

After corroborating with Crawford to take the lists, Lum began working with Crawford's Portland Apostolic Faith Mission. The two women continued publishing the *Apostolic Faith* paper, producing the July to August 1908 edition, without a notification that a substantial change had been made, or that they were no longer affiliated with Seymour.[289] Crawford and Lum fashioned a short disclaimer that simply said, "We have moved the paper which the Lord laid on us to begin at Los Angeles to Portland, Oregon, which will now be its headquarters."[290] Most historians believe that the production of the *Apostolic Faith* paper was crippled in Los Angeles simply because Crawford and Lum were in possession of the mailing list. Possibly the technical expertise needed to produce the newspaper resided in Lum, and, upon her departure, Seymour struggled to find another person with the dexterity to create a regular periodical of the same quality.[291]

Ironically, while Crawford was busy accusing Seymour of compromising his sanctification, Seymour was convinced that Crawford and Lum were the unethical ones, as they stole the mailing list that was not rightfully theirs. He commented about the incident in the October to November 1908 issue of the *Apostolic Faith*:

> I must for the salvation of souls let it be known that the editor is still in Los Angeles and will not remove

289 Edith L. Blumhofer and Grant Wacker, "Who Edited the Azusa Mission's *Apostolic Faith*?" *Assemblies of God Heritage* 21, no. 2 (Summer 2001): 19.
290 Ibid.
291 Alexander, *Women of Azusa Street*, 54.

> 'The Apostolic Faith' from Los Angeles, without letting subscribers and field workers know. This is a sad thing to our hearts for a worker to attempt to take the paper which is the property of the Azusa Street Mission to another city without consent after being told not to do so.[292]

Apparently, before Seymour made this statement, he and his new bride, Jennie Evans, had visited Portland in an unsuccessful attempt to retrieve the lists. Moreover, it took Crawford and Lum several months before they were even willing to admit that the paper that they were now publishing was not a continuation of the Los Angeles' Azusa Street newspaper, but an entirely new endeavor.

In short, Florence Crawford was initially in doctrinal accord with Seymour, regarding sanctification. She came to Azusa Street in search of healing, and desiring a deeper level of holiness in her life. She believed that Seymour was the shepherd that would lead her to the "quiet waters" that her soul so desperately yearned for. The Oregon native received what she was looking for under Seymour's ministry, and was quickly placed in leadership. However, she began to disagree with Seymour and believed he had somehow compromised his sanctification. This led her to start her own ministry in Portland with the assistance of her close friend Clara Lum. Though they started out in agreement, the breach between Seymour and Crawford would never be fully repaired, even though Crawford would later recall fond memories of her days in Los Angeles.

Charles Fox Parham

Parham's influence on William J. Seymour has been well documented. There are however, still a few areas that need

292 William J. Seymour, *Apostolic Faith* (October to November 1908), as quoted in J. C. Vanzandt, *Speaking in Tongues* (Portland: Vanzandt Publications, 1926), 37.

to be examined. Because Parham played a significant role in shaping Seymour's theology, it is important to consider him in this discussion. For instance, though Parham was the one who introduced Seymour to Spirit baptism with the "Bible evidence" of speaking in tongues, the two men already had much in common through their close associations with the Wesleyan-Holiness movement. Both Parham and Seymour held a form of the Wesleyan-Holiness view of sanctification, and therefore each developed a doctrine of salvation which consisted of three separate experiences: justification, the "second blessing" of sanctification, and the "baptism in the Holy Spirit" with speaking in other tongues. Even though the two men would later disagree about whether speaking in tongues should be the ultimate verification of Spirit baptism, they each remained consistent in their soteriology comprised of two acts of grace and a third experience of Spirit baptism.

The dissimilarities between the two men's doctrines were exposed when Parham repudiated the revival at Azusa Street. Parham's theology of race was exposed in his bigoted comments about the interracial aspect of Azusa. He also criticized the lack of evidence of xenolalia among those who purported to speak in tongues, because he stressed the primacy of foreign tongues as evidence of genuine Spirit baptism. Parham's denunciation prompted Seymour to expand his theology through adding an ethical dimension to his understanding of the baptism of the Holy Spirit.

In essence, the rift between the two men disclosed some previously unspoken doctrinal items. They began to verbalize their true beliefs after each was offended by the other. Though Seymour had been a student in Parham's school before coming to Los Angeles, he never fully embraced all of Parham's teachings. Charles Parham's wife, Sarah, depicted Seymour as a faithful school attendant, and model student, who embraced all of the school's truths and teachings.[293] Mrs. Parham asserted that Seymour was so well versed in Parham's teachings that he could recite them verbatim. But she does not account for the fact that Seymour wholly rejected some of Parham's more extreme teachings, such as annihilation of the wicked, and the eighth day creation.[294] Apparently, while sitting under Parham's instruction, he kept his opinions on these issues to himself. But, after the friction in Los Angeles, his long held convictions surfaced. Seymour's opposing position on Parham's annihilation of the wicked doctrine was later recorded in the *Apostolic Faith*:

> Many people today do not believe in an everlasting hell; but we read in the precious Word of God that the Lord Jesus taught it...We can see that there is no annihilation in God's Word for the wicked, but there is a blazing and burning hell awaiting them. Their home will be in everlasting flames, where they will be tormented day and night forever and ever. Rev. 20, 10.[295]

293 Sarah E. Parham, *The Life of Charles F. Parham: Founder of the Apostolic Faith Movement* (Joplin, MO: Garland Publishing, 1985), 142.

294 Charles F. Parham, "Everlasting Gospel," in *The Sermons of Charles F. Parham*, ed. Donald W. Dayton (New York: Garland Publishing, 1985), 51; and Charles F. Parham, "A Voice Crying in the Wilderness," in *Sermons of Charles F. Parham*, ed. Dayton, 83. Parham disputed Christian orthodoxy in anticipating a final destruction for the wicked rather than an eternal punishment. Parham accredited the orthodox doctrine of eternal punishment to Roman Catholic absorption of pagan philosophy and Protestant preservation of Catholic teachings. The following excerpt from Parham's "Everlasting Gospel" helps to solidify his point of view: "He [God] will utterly destroy them, root and branch, soul and body, where they shall be the ashes under the soles of your feet, or, in other words, fertilizer to enrich the soil for the inheritance of the meek" (See Parham, "Everlasting Gospel," 51). In regard to eighth day creation, Parham was equally unorthodox in this manner by espousing a belief that God created two different species of humanity during two different epochs of creation. The first creatures on the earth were *created* on the sixth day, human beings in God's image who had dominion and authority, as well as everlasting life. On the eighth day, the Adamic race was *formed* from the dust of the ground. According to Parham, the Adamic race was the one that needed a savior. This would also explain where Cain got his wife. Parham believed that Cain, who was the first child of the eighth day creation, had intermarried with someone from the sixth day creation. For Parham, the consequences of this intermarriage was dreadful and "began the woeful inter-marriage of races for which cause the flood was sent in punishment" (Parham, "Voice Crying in the Wilderness," 83).

295 William J. Seymour, ed., "Annihilation of the Wicked," *Apostolic Faith* 1, no. 5 (January 1907): 2; and William J. Seymour, *Doctrines and Discipline of the Azusa Street Apostolic Faith Mission of Los Angeles, Cal.* (Los Angeles: 1915), 52. Seymour

Written three months after his mentor's stinging refutation of Azusa, in this passage, Seymour tackled Parham's teaching on annihilation, which asserted that the *wicked* would be utterly destroyed, and thereby, cease to exist. Importantly, this rejection provides early evidence of theological independence from Parham. Seymour was reacting to Parham's rejection of orthodox positions, which Parham understood to create a God who brought creatures into existence, only to take perverse pleasure in watching their eternal torment.[296] According to Parham:

> Catholics and Protestants have given us a God more impossible than Moloch, god of the ancient Canaanites, in whose arms human beings were burned, but we are supposed to believe in a God who, after bringing creatures into existence, will cast them into a lake of eternal torment; who is possessed with such a diabolical character that He is able to sit upon the throne of His glory, listen to their howling and screeching, and view them sizzling, stewing, frying, browning, without surcease throughout the countless cycles of Eternity.[297]

Obviously, Parham was distancing himself from the orthodox position of eternal punishment, to which Seymour and most Protestants held. Seymour elaborated further about his dissenting opinion in his *Doctrines and Discipline*:

> We don't believe in the doctrine of the Annihiation [sic] of the wicked. That is the reason why we could not stand for tongues being the evidence of the Baptism in

was so adamant about this heretical doctrine that he concluded that glossolalia was not the evidence of Spirit Baptism, because Parham spoke in tongues and still held to this erroneous view. Seymour could not understand how any person could be filled with the Holy Spirit and hold beliefs contrary to the teachings of the Holy Spirit.

296 Charles F. Parham, "Everlasting Gospel," in *Sermons of Charles F. Parham*, ed. Donald W. Dayton, 111.

297 Ibid.

> the Holy Ghost and fire. If tongues was the evidence of the gift of the Holy Spirit, then men and women that have received the gift of tongues could not [have] believed contrary to the teachings of the Holy Spirit.[298]

Seymour's logic becomes interesting at this point. Not only did he reemphasize his staunch opposition to his former mentor's position, but he made the connection that, in some way, Parham's radical stance further supported Seymour's pneumatological understanding that glossolalia was not the only, or primary, evidence that a person had received the baptism of the Holy Spirit. In effect, Seymour not only challenged Parham's annihilation theory, but he also used the opportunity to attack Parham's primary thesis that speaking in tongues was the "Bible evidence" that one had received the gift of the Holy Spirit. Seymour's premise was that the Spirit would not teach anything that was contrary to Scripture, which was inspired by the Spirit. Therefore, in Seymour's estimation, Parham's speaking in tongues hypothesis could not be true, since Parham could speak in tongues and still preach a heretical doctrine, while claiming to be led by the Spirit of *truth*.[299] Consequently, this pneumatological reasoning further strengthened Seymour's more nuanced position that tongues was *only one* of the signs that a person was Spirit-filled, rather than the sole evidence of Holy Spirit baptism.

Parham's earlier paternalistic racism had evolved into a more palpable and blatant bigotry, which affected Seymour's pneumatological approach. An understanding of Parham's radical "eighth day creation" theory helps one to understand the basis of his theology of race and its impact on Seymour. Though Parham was generally a biblical literalist, he believed that the days of creation were periods of time, rather than

298 Seymour, *Doctrines and Discipline*, 52.
299 Ibid.

twenty-four hour days.[300] Based on this belief, it was not difficult for Parham to espouse two distinct creation epochs: sixth-day creation, and eighth-day creation. According to Parham, God chose to save Noah from the flood not on the basis of his righteousness, but on the premise that Noah was "perfect in his generation; a pedigree without mixed blood in it, a lineal descendant of Adam."[301] Since Parham already believed that the flood was designed to destroy those who were part of the sixth-day creation because they had debased themselves by cohabitating with the eighth-day humans, he easily made a contemporary application by preaching against intermingling of the races. In his book, *A Voice Crying in the Wilderness*, Parham insisted that "were time to last and intermarriage continue between the white, the blacks, and the reds in America, consumption and other diseases would soon wipe the mixed bloods off the face of the earth."[302] In essence, he was insinuating that the "perfect person" is not the one of mixed races, but the one of pure blood. Parham's analogy likened the intermarriage of contemporary human races with the detestable intermarriage of sixth-day and eighth-day beings, whose origins differed from each other. Because of this, he presupposed unassailable differences among the races.[303] In her dissertation entitled, "Fleshly Manifestations: Charles Fox Parham's Quest for the Sanctified Body," Leslie Callahan elaborated further on Parham's ideology:

> Parham's comment [concerning creation unmasks a more profound inconsistency in his thinking. In one instance, miscegenation enabled Abraham's blood to mingle throughout the races to

300 Charles F. Parham, "A Voice Crying in the Wilderness," in *Sermons of Charles F. Parham*, ed. Donald W. Dayton, 81.
301 Ibid., 84.
302 Ibid., 83.
303 Leslie Callahan, "Fleshly Manifestations: Charles Fox Parham's Quest for the Sanctified Body" (PhD diss., Princeton University, 2002), 113.

> the end that it facilitates participation in the Body and Bride of Christ. In another, miscegenation's evils inspired the flood and threatened the destruction of humankind. These competing ideas are irreconcilable and illustrate that Parham was not a particularly systematic thinker. More importantly, they expose deep racial ambivalence about contemporary social interaction among the races and uncertainty about the means for including the "non-Israelite" people, Gentile and heathen, in the highest elevations of spiritual life. Even without a thoroughly coherent message, Parham's ideology and theology of race were formed and remained consistent over time. The ideology had Anglo-Saxon supremacy at its core and bespoke the hope for purity and perfection of the race.[304]

Comprehension of Parham's ideology helps provide the framework for understanding his treatment of people of color, and particularly his treatment of one person of color—William J. Seymour.

Seymour, on the other hand, did not believe that Parham, or any person of another race, was superior. In fact, one may argue that the primary distinctive at Azusa for Seymour was not glossolalia but the equality of all people under a sovereign God. To Seymour, tongues demonstrated the fact that all races and classes of people were indeed equal, because they were *all* able to partake of this gift of the Holy Spirit. Seymour's ideology of race was encapsulated in an article in the *Apostolic Faith*:

> All classes and nationalities meet on a common level. One who came for the first time said, "The thing that impressed me most was the humility of the people,

304 Ibid.

and I went to my room and got down on my knees and asked God to give me humility."[305]

Seymour's theology of race contradicted that of Parham's, because Seymour believed that God did not recognize color, flesh, or name;[306] instead, he believed God favored the contrite. The breach that resulted when Parham rejected Seymour's interracial vision further fueled Parham's racist theories. Seymour would later argue that extreme harshness, such as Parham demonstrated in his derogatory remarks against Azusa (and blacks in general), was an indication that a person was not truly baptized in the Spirit.[307]

Nevertheless, in spite of these major doctrinal differences, some scholars have credited these two men as co-founders of the Pentecostal movement[308] in America. Parham is considered to be formulator of the "initial evidence" doctrine, while Seymour is considered to be the catalyst for the perpetuation of global Pentecostalism. Though the two vehemently disagreed on issues concerning eternal punishment, the genuineness of Spirit baptism, and racial equality, both maintained a Wesleyan view of sanctification as a second work of grace for the remainder of their lives.

William H. Durham and the Finished Work Controversy

William H. Durham left Chicago in 1907, headed for the Azusa Street Mission, where he eventually received the baptism of the Holy Spirit during a late evening service. That night, Seymour prophesied that wherever Durham preached, there

305 William J. Seymour, ed., "Beginning of World Wide Revival," *Apostolic Faith* 1, no. 5 (January 1907): 1.
306 Ibid.
307 William J. Seymour, ed., "Character and Work of the Holy Ghost," *Apostolic Faith* 2, no. 13 (May 1908): 2
308 Vinson Synan, *The Holiness-Pentecostal Tradition: Charismatic Movements in the Twentieth Century* (Grand Rapids: William B. Eerdmans, 1997), 106.

would be an outpouring of the Holy Spirit upon the people. The incident was recorded in the *Pentecostal Testimony*:

> I heard Brother Seymour, the Pastor say, "He is through now, etc. He said that he had retired to rest early in the evening, and that the Spirit had spoken to him and said, "Brother Durham will get the baptism tonight," and that he had arisen and come down. Then he lifted up his hand and prophesied that where I should preach the Holy Spirit would fall on the people.[309]

The prophecy was quickly fulfilled when Durham returned to his Chicago church where his overcrowded meetings would often last far into the night. By the end of 1907, Durham's church had become a mecca for Midwestern Pentecostals. A contributing factor to his influence was his monthly periodical, the *Pentecostal Testimony.* Considered by some to be "a man of impressive personality,"[310] and somewhat of a "pulpit prodigy," Durham attracted thousands to his Pentecostal services at the North Avenue Mission, where a number of his followers partook of a strange shouting experience known as the "Durham jerks."[311] Moreover, it was Durham who gave Seymour probably the greatest compliment of any of his contemporaries in a 1907 statement:

> He is the meekest man I ever met. He walks and talks with God. His power is in his weakness. He seems to maintain a helpless dependence on God and is simple-hearted as a little child, and at the same time

309 William H. Durham, "The Great Crisis," *Pentecostal Testimony* 2, no. 2 (May 1912): 4.
310 Charles W. Shumway, "A Study of 'the Gift of Tongues'" (master's thesis, University of Southern California at Los Angeles, 1914), 179.
311 William H. Durham, "Personal Testimony of Pastor," *Pentecostal Testimony* 2, no. 3 (July 1912): 1-16.

> is so filled with God that you feel the love and power every time you get near him.[312]

However, the Durham that Seymour prophesied over in 1907 changed radically after receiving his personal Pentecost. Though the Chicago preacher had previously adhered to the Wesleyan view of sanctification, reportedly, after his trip to Los Angeles, he determined to never again preach sanctification as a second work.[313] Durham reflected on his transformation: "From that day to this, I could never preach another sermon on the second work of grace theory. I had held it for years, and continued to do so for some time, but could not preach on the subject again."[314]

Being firmly convinced that sanctification was an instantaneous work at conversion, which continued throughout the life of a believer, Durham denounced the "second blessing" doctrine promoted by Seymour and many others with Holiness leanings. Thus, Durham became a staunch advocate of the new doctrine, which he coined, "The Finished Work." Durham delineated his theology in his periodical, the *Pentecostal Testimony*:

> The doctrine of the Finished Work brings us back to the simple plan of salvation. Christ died for us. He became a substitute for every one of us; for He tasted death for every man. Here is a truth so simple and yet so great that it is wonderful. We are not saved simply because we are forgiven our sins. We are saved through our identification with our Savior Substitute, Jesus Christ.[315]

312 William H. Durham, "A Chicago Evangelist's Pentecost," *Apostolic Faith* 1, no. 6 (February to March 1907): 4.
313 Synan, *Holiness Pentecostal Tradition*, 150.
314 William H. Durham, "An Open Letter to My Brother Ministers in and out of the Pentecostal Movement. A Strong Appeal." *Pentecostal Testimony* 1, no. 8 (1911): 12-13.
315 William H. Durham, "The Finished Work of Calvary—It Makes Plain the Great Work of Redemption," *Pentecostal Testimony* 2, no. 2 (May 1912): 2.

Durham was careful to distinguish himself from Seymour and other Wesleyan-Holiness leaders by ensuring that his followers understood that salvation was *entirely complete* based upon the sacrificial death of Christ. Consequently, there was no need of a second experience to cleanse the individual of remaining inward sin. Durham emphatically added:

> No doubt the second work of grace theory has done more to blind the eyes of people to the simple truth of the Gospel than any other one theory that was ever taught. It has come to thousands of truly saved people declaring that they are not saved, and that, instead of men coming into Christ and receiving eternal life in conversion, all they get is pardon of their outward transgressions. They are told that when God pardoned them He left them full of sin and corruption, and that it requires a second work of grace to save them from hell...Such teaching is so unscriptural, unreasonable and damaging that by the grace of God we will show it up in its true light.[316]

Although Durham accented to the "finished work" doctrine shortly after his Azusa experience in 1907, the controversy began with a sermon that he preached at a Pentecostal convention in Chicago in 1910, in which he sought to nullify sanctification as a second definite work of grace.[317] Durham flatly denied the Wesleyan concept, which espoused that a "residue of sin" remained in the believer, and taught that a person was perfectly sanctified at conversion. Thus, the need for a later crisis experience, or second blessing, was unnecessary. Durham's teaching was in direct conflict with the accepted view of most Pentecostals (who had Holiness backgrounds), initiating a significant controversy that divided

316 Ibid., 3.

317 Synan, *Holiness Pentecostal Tradition*, 150.

the Pentecostal movement into two theological camps.[318]

Before the controversial teaching created a permanent breach in the Pentecostal movement, the issue came to a crisis when Durham returned to Los Angeles on a preaching mission in February of 1911. He first went to Elmer Fisher's Upper Room Mission, which had mushroomed into the largest Pentecostal church in the city by this time. When his doctrinal stance became known, however, he was asked to leave. Not only did the controversial doctrine appear to offend some people, but Durham's combative attitude seemed to inflame others. Durham then turned his attention to the place that served as a "birthing place" for many Pentecostals—the Azusa Street Mission, which had essentially become a small African American church, still led by Seymour. While Seymour was away from Los Angeles, touring the East, Durham was invited to preach at the Azusa Mission. The Chicago minister's dynamic personality and new-found message drew huge crowds from other Los Angeles missions. Eyewitness Frank Bartleman recalled that Azusa had become so congested under Durham's ministry that five hundred people had to be turned away.[319] As Durham preached the "finished work doctrine" with passion, Azusa began to resemble the earlier days of the revival. In spite of Durham's success, those at the mission who were loyal to Seymour, and his Wesleyan doctrine of sanctification, sent word for him to return to Los Angeles, and informed him that a different doctrine of sanctification was being preached at his church.[320] When Seymour returned,

318 Edith L. Blumhofer, "The Finished Work of Calvary: William H. Durham and a Doctrinal Controversy," *Assemblies of God Heritage* 3, no. 3 (Fall 1983): 9-11; and Synan, *Holiness Pentecostal Tradition*, 150.

319 Frank Bartleman, *Azusa Street* (South Plainfield, NJ: Bridge Publishing, 1980), 150.

320 Carl Brumback, *Suddenly from Heaven: A History of the Assemblies of God* (Springfield: Gospel Publishing House, 1961), 99-100, 103. Reportedly, Durham was attacked by a young Holiness woman at Azusa, who before her conversion, had worked as a prostitute. Though she had ceased to be prostitute, she struggled with smoking and had "prayed through" to be delivered from her habit. She became so upset with Durham for denouncing sanctification as a second work of grace that she

he confronted Durham, and insisted that he stop preaching the finished work doctrine at Azusa. Durham was unwilling to submit to Seymour's pastoral authority, so Seymour locked him and his followers out of the mission. Bartleman recounted the incident from his perspective:

> May 2 I went to Azusa Street after noon, as usual. But to our surprise we found the doors all locked with chain and padlock. Brother Seymour had hastened back from the East and with his trustees decided to lock Brother Durham out. But they locked God and the saints out also from the old cradle of power. It was Durham's message they objected to.[321]

Unfortunately for Seymour, Bartleman and several other key Pentecostal leaders threw their support behind Durham. Bartleman secured a mission on Kohler Street, as a temporary home for Durham; then his supporters secured a permanent mission in a large building on the corner of Seventh and Los Angeles Streets. On Sundays, one thousand would attend Durham's meetings in a large building in Los Angeles; meanwhile, Azusa became almost deserted.[322]

Eventually Durham left Los Angeles, but he did not leave quietly. The person that once complimented Pastor Seymour as being "the meekest man I ever met" now had some choice derogatory words for the Azusa leader. Having already nearly emptied the Azusa Street Mission, Durham next attacked Seymour through his periodical, the *Pentecostal Testimony*, asserting that Seymour was a failure, and that the power of God had entirely left him. To Durham, Seymour was no longer worthy of the respect of the saints.[323] Durham did not

---

went after the Chicago preacher with her hat pin.

321 Bartleman, *Azusa Street*, 151.

322 Ibid.

323 William H. Durham, "The Great Revival at Azusa Street—How It Began and How It Ended," *Pentecostal Testimony* 1, no. 8 (1911): 4.

consider his own actions vindictive, but sincerely believed that his critique of his former friend was his "unpleasant duty," because of Seymour's repudiation of what he believed was the God-revealed "finished work" doctrine.[324]

Though Seymour never attacked Durham verbally, Seymour's former mentor, Parham, did not hesitate to condemn Durham's doctrine. Reportedly, in January 1912, Parham prayed that God would show the world which teaching on sanctification was correct by taking the life of the teacher who was in error. When Durham died of tuberculosis that summer of 1912, Parham boasted that God had answered his prayer, and the "finished work" conflict was over.[325] However, Parham's statement proved presumptuous. Durham's message increased in popularity, and eventually became the predominant Pentecostal position, promulgated most heavily by the Assemblies of God, one of the largest Pentecostal denominations.

In summary, Seymour's relationships with his contemporaries, such as Crawford, Parham, and Durham, all had one thing in common. They began well, but ended in hurt and disappointment for the Azusa leader, because of schisms in the young Pentecostal movement over theological differences. Crawford's and Durham's relationships with Seymour were strained over disagreements on sanctification. Crawford accused Seymour of compromising his sanctification, while Durham accused Seymour of failing God through his unwillingness to accept Durham's stance on the timing of sanctification. Parham's situation was entirely different because the nature of the disagreement between the two was more complex. Seymour opposed Parham's position on eternal punishment and his theology of race. Furthermore, because of

324 Ibid.
325 James R. Goff Jr., *Fields White unto Harvest: Charles F. Parham and the Missionary Origins of Pentecostalism* (Fayetteville: University of Arkansas Press, 1988), 152.

these doctrinal errors, Parham's theory about glossolalia as the evidence of Spirit baptism was also suspect, because Seymour believed that a person truly baptized by the Holy Spirit would reject heretical doctrines devoid of truth. Therefore, since Parham could hold to a false doctrine like "annihilation of the wicked," and allege that his speaking in tongues was the evidence that he was Spirit-filled, Seymour concluded that glossolalia could not be the only evidence, but merely one of the signs that a person was baptized in the Holy Spirit.

CHAPTER FIVE

The Decline: How Did Seymour's Message Get Lost?

For several reasons, Seymour's influence began to decline fairly early in the Pentecostal movement. The decline began with the mailing list controversy when Seymour's friend, Clara Lum, left with her publishing expertise, and the *Apostolic Faith* newspaper's national and international mailing lists. Lum went to Portland, Oregon, where she joined the ministry of her long-time friend, Florence Crawford. This left Seymour with only the small Los Angeles mailing list. Because he was neither able to produce the paper without Lum's expertise, nor promulgate it without the national and international lists, Seymour's message could no longer be conveyed to his constituents. Though Lum's departure was an unfortunate setback for Seymour, there were other reasons that contributed to the loss of his influence in the Pentecostal movement. This chapter examines the other causes for Seymour's decline.

Durham Schism and Race Politics

The Durham schism of 1911 decreased Seymour's already deteriorating influence in the movement significantly. Durham commented in detail about the incident (Seymour's bolting of the door, which was in response to his finished work message) in the *Pentecostal Testimony*:

> Meantime Brother Seymour came, and instead of making the honest confession he owed the people, for the way he had compromised and denied the truth, and then taking a humble place, till such time as he had regained the confidence of the people, he attempted to push himself on the people, and preach to them against their will, and a little later, notified me that this was his work, and that he wanted his place... This last move was necessary to let all men see what manner of man he has come to be...I have been the last of all the brethren, that I know of, to give him up, and have always found an excuse for his failures and blunders; but now I am compelled to acknowledge that the brethren have been right, and that, though once a mighty man, he is such no longer.[326]

Clearly, Durham sacrificed fellowship with Seymour for the sake of theological correctness regarding sanctification. However, although Durham may not have been motivated by racial prejudice, his stance on sanctification eventually led to racial division, as the majority of whites embraced his view, and thereby rejected Seymour's. Though racism was obvious in Parham's vituperative remarks and repudiation of Azusa Street, these remarks were not enough to completely kill Seymour's popularity. But what Parham could not do through racial remarks, Durham accomplished through theological dispute. Durham's "Finished Work Controversy" not only divided the movement between those who held to the Wesleyan view of sanctification, and those who believed in the finished work message, but it also divided it between black and white. A. G. Osterburg, former trustee at Azusa and supporter of Durham, remembered the dispute as a racial issue:

326 William H. Durham, "The Great Revival at Azusa Street—How It Began and How It Ended," *Pentecostal Testimony* 1, no. 8 (1911): 4.

> ...The colored folks began to fight the whites because they said the whites were going to try to come in and take over Azusa...Seymour himself was very humble about it. She [Mrs. Seymour] antagonized all the colored people. The colored folks believed in an inter-racial church as long as they had a Negro pastor.[327]

Durham received overwhelming support from the white majority when he asked for a show of hands of those who wanted to continue the revival under his leadership.[328] Durham later accused Seymour of playing the race card, charging that he recruited black support to lock him out of the mission.

Because of his combative style, and blatant disregard for Seymour's pastoral authority, Durham abandoned the Azusa leader's concern for interracial equality and unity. Though the Chicago pastor died suddenly at the age of thirty-nine in 1912, his theology grew so popular that it became the basis for a new denominational organization.[329] Though unintentional, Durham's ideology reversed the direction of Seymour's interracial meetings, as the color line was re-drawn by whites' preference for Durham's Finished Work. Synan commented on the long-term effect that Durham's theology had on race relations:

---

327 A. G. Osterburg, "From the Personal," 4; "Notes from A. G. Osterberg, May 24, 1956," typescript, Flower Pentecostal Heritage Center, as cited in Larry Martin, *The Life and Ministry of William J. Seymour* (Joplin, MO: Christian Life Books, 1999), 288.

328 William H. Durham, "The Great Revival at Azusa Street," *Pentecostal Testimony* 1, no. 8 (1911): 4.

329 Vinson Synan, *The Holiness-Pentecostal Movement in the United States* (Grand Rapids: William B. Eerdmans, 1971), 170. In 1914 the Assemblies of God was founded in Hot Springs, Arkansas, when members of the white wing of the Church of God in Christ convened and sixty-eight people signed the charter of incorporation. The convention was dominated by those who held to Durham's "Finished Work" understanding of sanctification. Though several hundred Pentecostals attended, Synan noted: "As far as is known, no Negroes were invited to the convention." (Ibid., 170).

> The formation of the Assemblies of God was of the greatest importance to the future development of the Pentecostal movement. It represented the end of a notable experiment in interracial church development ...It also ended the period of doctrinal unity that existed from 1906.[330]

While he was still living, Durham not only radically opposed those who did not accept his view on sanctification, but he also ostracized those who did not hold that glossolalia was the evidence of Holy Spirit baptism. As time progressed, Durham's theology (with its focus on progressive sanctification and glossolalia as the evidence of Spirit baptism) became the dominant view in classical Pentecostal theology. With this in mind, it is easily surmised that Seymour's view of Pentecost (with its Wesleyan-Holiness understanding of sanctification, and emphasis on interracial harmony through divine love as evidence of the Spirit baptism) slowly began to fade away.

After Durham's death, his followers increased their momentum by announcing a large "World-Wide Camp Meeting at Los Angeles" in 1913 at Arroyo Seco, California. Internationally known evangelist, Maria B. Woodworth-Etter was the main speaker. The meeting attracted people from all over the United States, as well as Canada and Mexico.[331] Though the meeting was scheduled to only last a month, it continued for six weeks. Attendance numbered one thousand people, with as many as two hundred ministers on the platform at one time.[332] Seymour, however, attended as a mere spectator; he was not asked to participate in any way, and was not even recognized from the platform.[333]

330 Ibid., 153.
331 Charles W. Shumway, "A Study of 'the Gift of Tongues'," 191.
332 Ibid.
333 Ibid.

Seymour's snub was no surprise, since the organizers were those who had exited the Azusa Street Mission with Durham, under his assertion that "sanctification [was] not a second work of grace."[334] Although Woodworth-Etter desired that the meeting promote unity, it was perceived by some as only representing proponents of the "finished work" theology.[335] Racial lines were again drawn under the banner of ideological controversy, as the "finished work" appeared to be more attractive to whites.[336] Seymour's dream of equality of the races, based on the Spirit's sanction of divine love, was rejected; and with that rejection came the sobering reality of increasing white racism in the context of American religious life and society.[337] Anglican Vicar Alexander A. Boddy of Sunderland, England, who had visited Azusa in August of 1912, noted that American racial divisions were becoming "increasingly acute," because, "the whites [were] determined to keep their position as [the] dominant race."[338] By 1915, the Ku Klux Klan had been revived by an agenda to unite native-born white Christians in the preservation of American institutions and the supremacy of the white race. At the same time, the organization declared its opposition against African Americans, Japanese and other Asians, Roman Catholics, Jews, and all foreign-born persons.[339] Racial hostility climaxed a few years later in what James Weldon described as the "Red Summer" of 1919, which was a period of uninhibited interracial contention that resulted in twenty-five race riots.[340]

334 Ibid.
335 Ibid.
336 Iain MacRobert, *The Black Roots and White Racism of Early Pentecostalism in the USA* (New York: St. Martin's Press, 1988), 64-66. Most of the participants at Arroyo Seco that adhered to Durham's theology were white. By the end of the 1920s, two out of every three white Pentecostals became Finished Work believers, while only one out of eight blacks made the change.
337 Nelson, "For Such a Time as This," 255.
338 Alexander A. Boddy, *Confidence*, November 1912, 222.
339 John Hope Franklin, *From Slavery to Freedom: A History of Negro Americans*, 4th ed. (New York: Knopf, 1974), 356.
340 Nelson, "For Such a Time as This," 258.

Nelson reflected on the ever widening chasm of race, and its impact on Seymour's interracial vision:

> Seymour and the Azusa miracle gave birth to the Pentecostal movement in a transformation of prevailing white American racial attitudes of exclusiveness; now the movement began to conform to those attitudes. Dynamic power of the movement was released not simply by Seymour's leadership but by white acceptance of it, in repentance and humility. Now, with Seymour humiliated, rejected, and forgotten, whites openly embraced the old racial attitude, along with ideological controversy. Insofar as Seymour disappeared the color line reappeared.[341]

In short, though Durham's controversial teaching and divisive spirit contributed to Seymour's debacle, ultimately, it was Durham's followers who would propagate his teachings. Regardless of Durham's intentions, his doctrine did cause racial division, while Seymour's theology of racial inclusion (as evidenced by the Spirit's infusion of divine love) was increasingly ignored. To make matters worse, the Pentecostal movement began to succumb to the racial attitudes of the times in one of the greatest periods of interracial strife in American history.

Accusations of Racism in Seymour's Theology

Though Seymour sought interracial togetherness most of his life there are those who believe that the Azusa leader struggled with racism and may have alienated whites and Hispanics. A statement from Seymour in his *Doctrines and Discipline*, written in 1915, may help to explain why some may have been offended:

341 Ibid., 255.

> This Mission shall be composed of one Bishop, one Vice Bishop, one Secretary, one Treasurer, five Trustees, three Deacons, two Deaconesses, two Elders, one Superintendent of Sunday Schools, one Superintendent of Apostolic Endeavor. The Bishop, Vice-Bishop and Trustees must be people of Color.[342]

Though Seymour rationalized his decision to proscribe white leadership at the mission as a necessary adjustment to prevent the reoccurrence of earlier oppositions he endured from several white leaders, his statement requires further investigation. Some may see these revisions of the *Doctrines and Discipline* as giving credence to Durham's earlier accusation that Seymour had played the race card by recruiting people of his own color to unite with him to lock Durham out of the mission. Others might contend that Seymour's paranoia about losing the mission to another strong white personality might have driven him to proactively ensure that African Americans would always be in leadership, and have the authority to put down a "white rebellion," should the need ever arise. Some whites may have felt that Seymour was compromising on his stance of racial equality. The question is, had Seymour actually succumbed to the pressures of discrimination, thereby taking a hard line stance on race, or did he have a different reason for making the decision to intentionally place African Americans in leadership positions at the Mission? To answer this, it is necessary to critically analyze Seymour's thought within the racial context of the United States during this period. A statement from Seymour in *Doctrines and Discipline* provides some light:

> Now because we don't take them for directors it is not for discrimination, but for peace. To keep down

342 William J. Seymour, *Doctrines and Discipline*, 49.

> race war in the Churches and friction, so they can have greater liberty and freedom in the Holy Spirit. We are sorry for this, but it is the best now and in later years for the work. We hope every one that reads these lines may realize it is for the best: not for the worse. Some of our white brethren and sisters have never left us in all the division; they have stuck to us. We love our white brethrens [sic] and sisters and welcome them.[343]

Seymour's exclusion of whites from leadership at Azusa was not done vindictively, but reluctantly, and with an aim to stop racial divisiveness. He noted that both African Americans and whites had been guilty of prejudice, and had "caught the disease" of division.[344] However, though Seymour would implore both races to walk in love as Christ commanded, he made it clear that whites were the primary cause of the conflict. In his *Doctrines and Discipline*, Seymour gave a summary about the origins of the revival in Los Angeles, and insisted that:

> Very soon division arose through some of our brethren, and the Holy Spirit was grieved. We want all of our white brethren and white sisters to feel free in our churches and missions, in spite of all the trouble we have had with some of our white brethren in causing diversion [sic], and spreading wild fire and fanaticism.[345]

In essence, Seymour was never in favor of the removal of whites from Azusa, and its surrounding churches and missions. He strove for interracial fellowship until he died; however, he apparently believed that white leadership would somehow exacerbate racial division. Conversely, Seymour's decision to

343 Ibid., 12-13.
344 Ibid., 12.
345 Ibid.

ban whites from key leadership roles may have caused them to seek more favorable conditions and opportunities in other congregations. Since Seymour appeared to these whites as having abandoned his commitment to racial equality, they may have sensed that he was now a "respecter of persons," which he preached against since Azusa's inception.

Latino Contingency

Whites were not the only ones to walk out on Seymour. Reportedly, several Hispanics also took issue with the Azusa leader. Before conflict arose, however, Hispanics played an integral part at the Azusa Street Revival. An excerpt from the *Apostolic Faith* describes the interracial camaraderie that they enjoyed:

> If a Mexican or German cannot speak English, he gets up and speaks in his own tongue and feels quite at home for the Spirit interprets through the face and the people say 'Amen.' No instrument that God can use is rejected on account of color or dress or education.[346]

Rosa and Abundio de Lopez were prime examples of members of the Latino community that helped to create the multicultural fellowship at the Azusa Mission. Rosa and Abundio were Mexican immigrants who had migrated to California in 1902, the same year of their marriage.[347] Arriving at Azusa Street in May of 1906, just one month after Seymour and his followers moved there, the Lopez family members were among the first Hispanics to visit the mission. Their passion

346 William J. Seymour, ed., "Gracious Pentecostal Showers Continue to Fall," *Apostolic Faith* 1, no. 3 (November 1906): 1.

347 Estrelda Alexander, *Women of Azusa Street* (Cleveland: Pilgrim Press, 2005), 104.

for ministry was clearly evidenced in an *Apostolic Faith* article that was printed in Spanish, along with its English translation:

> We testify to the power of the Holy Spirit in forgiveness, sanctification, and the baptism with the Holy Ghost and fire. We give thanks to God for this wonderful gift which we have received from Him, according to the promise. Thanks be to God for the Spirit which brought us to the Azusa Street Mission, the Apostolic Faith, old-time religion, I and my wife, on the 29th of last May. I came for sanctification, and thank God also for the baptism with the Holy Ghost and fire which I received on the 5th of June, 1905. We cannot express the gratitude and thanksgiving which we feel moment by moment for what He has done for us, so we want to be used for the salvation and healing of both soul and body. I am a witness of His wonderful promise and marvelous miracles by the Holy Ghost, by faith in the Lord Jesus Christ. May God bless you all.[348]

Moreover, a report of the couples' efforts appeared in the November 1906 *Apostolic Faith,* declaring that both were filled with the Holy Spirit and that they were "being used of God in street meetings and in helping Mexicans at the altar at Azusa Street."[349] Seymour rewarded their efforts by ordaining Abundio to the ministry in 1909. Though there is no record of Rosa being ordained, she remained active with her husband in ministry. However, shortly after Abundio's ordination, the couple joined other Hispanics in a mass exodus from Azusa for reasons that are still clouded.

348 Abundio L. and Lopez and Rosa de Lopez, "Spanish Receive the Pentecost," *Apos \tolic Faith* 1, no. 2 (October 1906): 4.
349 Ibid.

According to Gaston Espinoza, in the beginning, Latinos had flocked to the Azusa Street Mission in search of a transcendent God; but "for reasons that are not entirely clear, their unbridled enthusiasm and desire to testify prompted the leader of the mission to 'ruthlessly crush' the Latino contingent in 1909."[350] Carmelo Alvarez first acknowledged the significant role of Hispanics at the Azusa Street Revival, but noted that the Hispanics were also victims of discrimination, as they were forced to fit into an American culture and language.[351] In "Borderlands Praxis: The Immigrant Experience in Latino Pentecostal Churches," Daniel Ramirez asserted that "Azusa's multicultural and multilingual promise proved illusory in the end."[352] Ramirez points to the testimony of Azusa participant and historian Frank Bartleman, who recorded the dissatisfaction of "some poor illiterate Mexicans" from the "old" Azusa Mission in late 1909, and compared their expulsion to "murdering the Spirit of God."[353]

Espinosa, Alvarez, and Ramirez all suggest that Seymour rejected the Hispanic contingency, either by not permitting them to speak, or through blatant discrimination. However, one has to question the source of their information—Frank Bartleman. Bartleman is an important figure, because of his effort to chronicle the Azusa events in his book, *How Pentecost Came to Los Angeles.*[354] His charge against Seymour, however, should be considered questionable, as it was couched in his

350 Gaston Espinosa, "The Silent Pentecostals," *Christian History and Biography,* Issue 58, vol. 17, no. 2 (1998): 23. In his article, Espinosa surmised that the conflict at Azusa gave birth to the Latino Pentecostal movement, "as scores left the mission and began preaching the Pentecostal message throughout barrios and migrant farm camps in the U.S., Mexico, and Puerto Rico."

351 Carmelo Alvarez, "Hispanic Pentecostals: Azusa Street and Beyond," *Encounter* 63, no. 1-2 (Winter to Spring 2002): 13-26.

352 Daniel Ramirez, "Borderlands Praxis: The Immigrant Experience in Latino Pentecostal Churches," *Journal of the American Academy of Religion* 67, no. 3 (September 1999): 575.

353 Bartleman, *Azusa Street,* 145.

354 Ibid.; and Frank Bartleman, *How Pentecost Came to Los Angeles: As It Was in the Beginning* (Los Angeles, 1925).

personal bias against formal church organization. This bias was reflected in the same work:

> Only God knows what this meant to those poor Mexicans. Personally I would rather die than to have assumed such a spirit of dictatorship. Every meeting was now programmed from start to finish. Disaster was bound to follow and it did so.[355]

As one reads Bartleman in context, it becomes clear that the treatment of the Mexican contingency was not the main reason for his diatribe. Rather, his tirade had more to do with the way that the services at Azusa were being conducted. Bartleman was against church committees and the organization of churches into associations. He even accused the Azusa leadership of failing God, simply because they placed a sign over the building that read, "Apostolic Faith Mission."[356]

Assuming that William J. Seymour was the leader that Bartleman indicated, his report must be viewed with suspicion, because it would have been totally out of character for Seymour to treat people in this manner, according to most other accounts and descriptions of the man. It would be inconsistent with Seymour's known character to espouse a view of equality for all, and then ruthlessly condemn his Mexican brothers and sisters. Nevertheless, Bartleman's report is still important because it confirms that something happened to cause the Mexicans to leave Azusa. The incident probably was not related to race or class, but to a theological difference.

The New Issue

The 1913 Arroyo Seco Camp Meeting led to the proliferation of the "Finished Work" theology, and another

355 Bartleman, *Azusa Street*, 145.
356 Ibid., 68.

subsequent division of the Pentecostal movement. This meeting was also the root of another major theological problem that came to be known as: the "New Issue," "Jesus only," "Jesus' name," or the "Oneness controversy." Canadian Pentecostal leader Robert E. McAllister's sermon on the subject hurled shockwaves through the fledgling Pentecostal movement, further dividing the "Finished Work" people over the issue.[357] While the Arroyo Seco Camp Meeting was the launching point for this "new issue," Ramirez cites several "Jesus' name" baptisms that preceded the 1913 event.[358] Of particular interest were the "Jesus' name" baptisms of Azusa participants Luis Lopez and Juan Navarro in 1909. Though Arlene Sanchez-Walsh believes that the origins of the Oneness movement are sketchy, she indicates that it may have started in 1909 in the vicinity of Los Angeles among the Mexicans who eventually converted Luis Lopez and Romanita Valenzuela in 1909.[359] If Ramirez and Sanchez-Walsh are correct about Lopez and several other Mexicans being re-baptized in Jesus' name, then Seymour's strong Trinitarian views (which espoused the view that the Godhead was made up of Father,

357 Arthur Clanton, *United We Stand* (Hazelwood, MO: Pentecostal Publishing House, 1970), 21-22; Gregory A. Boyd, *Oneness Pentecostals and the Trinity* (Grand Rapids: Baker Book House, 1992); and David A. Reed, "Oneness Pentecostalism," in *New International Dictionary of Pentecostal and Charismatic Movements,* rev. ed., ed. Stanley M. Burgess and Eduard M. Van Der Maas (Grand Rapids: Zondervan, 2002), 937. Oneness Pentecostals rejected the Trinitarian formula mentioned in Matthew 28:19 in favor of water baptism in Jesus name only, based on Acts 2:38. The message was embraced by several ministers who attended the camp meeting. This simple formula brought greater schism to an already divided Pentecostal movement as many "finished work" adherents adopted the Oneness formula. The "new issue" became so volatile that 156 Assemblies of God ministers embraced the teaching, and were expelled from the denomination at the 1916 General Council.

358 Ernesto S. Cantu and Jose A. Ortega, *Historia De La Asamblea Apostolica De La Fe En Cristo Jesus* (Mentone, CA: Sal's Printing Service, 1966), 12, as cited in Daniel Ramirez, "Borderlands Praxis: The Immigrant Experience in Latino Pentecostal Churches," *Journal of the American Academy of Religion* 67, no. 3 (September 1999): 575; and Arlene Sanchez-Walsh, *Latino Pentecostal Identity: Evangelical Faith, Self, and Society* (New York: Columbia University Press, 2003), 19. Luis Lopez, Juan Navarro and Francisco Llorente had all been baptized in Jesus name before the 1913 Arroyo Seco Camp Meeting.

359 Sanchez-Walsh, *Latino Pentecostal Identity*, 19.

Son and Holy Spirit) might have been the cause of the Mexican exodus. Perhaps several of the Mexicans decided that they wanted to share their newly found Oneness understanding, and were prohibited from doing so by Seymour or another Azusa leader.[360]

Sanchez-Walsh suggests a final theory for the Latino departure, explaining that the "color line being washed away in the blood" was simply rhetoric that emanated from Azusa Street. For her, white Pentecostals had never reconciled feelings of European American superiority over their African American and Latino brothers and sisters.[361] Borrowing from Joe Creech, who viewed Azusa Street as the central mythic event for early Pentecostals, Sanchez-Walsh saw Azusa as the location where God initiated an eschatological or end-times plan for the restoration of the church.[362] Sanchez-Walsh agreed with Creech that Azusa's rhetoric of interracial togetherness was romanticism, as the subservience of Latinos to their white overseers confirmed.[363]

In summary, though there were possibly several factors that contributed to the Hispanic departure from Azusa, such as discrimination from Seymour, ideological indifference, or white superiority, proponents of Seymour must accept the fact that he did write by-laws that prevented non-blacks from holding office in the mission. Though his decision to make this change was probably done with the intention of maintaining peace and preventing African Americans from being removed from power by whites, this policy also excluded the Latinos. Therefore, regardless of the reason for the Latino exodus, as pastor of the Azusa Street Mission, Seymour must be held partly responsible.

360 Seymour, *Doctrines and Discipline*, 82.

361 Sanchez-Walsh, *Latino Pentecostal Identity*, 6.

362 Ibid., 12; and Joe Creech, "Visions of Glory: The Place of the Azusa Street Revival in Pentecostal History," *Church History* 65, no. 3 (September 1996): 405–410.

363 Sanchez-Walsh, *Latino Pentecostal Identity*, 13.

Gender Equality

Another possible cause of Seymour's loss of influence may have been the lack of genuine gender equality. While Seymour led the Azusa Street Mission, it adhered to a message of equality, but some scholars question whether this was true of the women who were affiliated with it. Estrelda Alexander in *Women of Azusa Street* makes the argument that Florence Crawford's early departure from the mission and revival may have been related to the restrictions Seymour placed on her as a woman.[364] The Azusa leader's *Doctrines and Discipline* made a clear distinction between the roles of men and women, insisting that "all ordination must be done by men and not women."[365] Even though Seymour did not prohibit women from being ministers, they were not permitted to baptize or ordain others at the Azusa Street Mission.[366] Seymour's policy concerning women in ministry was obviously not in place at Azusa's inception, as six out of the initial twelve elders appointed to handle finances, communication, and ordination, were female.[367] Such a policy change possibly contributed to women leaving the mission.

Preoccupation with Tongues as Initial Evidence

Though Seymour's popularity may have declined from strained relationships over theological differences, the popularization of the doctrine of tongues as initial evidence may have been his greatest albatross. Again, Seymour had initially accepted Parham's thesis that speaking in tongues was the "Bible evidence" that one had received the baptism of the Holy Spirit, and promoted this teaching at Azusa Street.

364 Alexander, *Women of Azusa Street*, 66.
365 Seymour, *Doctrines and Discipline*, 91.
366 Ibid.
367 Estrelda Alexander, "Gender and Leadership in the Theology and Practice of Three Pentecostal Women Pioneers," PhD diss., Catholic University of America, 2003 (Ann Arbor: UMI Dissertation Services, 2003), 55.

However, shortly after Seymour's rift with Parham, he began to change his stance on the evidence of Spirit baptism to include an ethical dimension, based on the fruit of the Spirit.[368] For Seymour, speaking in tongues was to be considered as "one of the signs" that accompanied the baptism of the Holy Spirit, but not the "real evidence" of Spirit baptism in a person's everyday life.[369] While Seymour held to the belief that glossolalia should serve as a sign of Spirit baptism, he became convinced that divine love was the real evidence of baptism in the Holy Spirit.[370] This was evidenced in the racial harmony that Azusa Street enjoyed for a season, as races united under a black pastor in a loving atmosphere.

Seymour's understanding of Pentecost was quickly forgotten, however, as Pentecostals began to overemphasize tongues. Seymour had warned: "When people run out of the love of God, they get to preaching something else."[371] The infatuation with tongues made Seymour's expanded understanding of Pentecost more difficult to hear, as Pentecostal denominations based their beliefs about Spirit baptism on Parham's doctrinal formula.[372] Eventually, initial

368 William J. Seymour, ed., "To the Baptized Saints," *Apostolic Faith* 1, no. 9 (June to September 1907): 2.

369 Ibid.

370 William J. Seymour, ed., "Questions Answered," *Apostolic Faith* 1, no. 11 (October to January 1908): 2; and William J. Seymour, ed., Untitled article, *Apostolic Faith* 2, no. 13 (May 1908): 3. These two articles are examples of Seymour's view on love as proof of Spirit baptism.

371 William J. Seymour, ed., "The Church Question," *Apostolic Faith* 1, no. 5 (January 1907): 2.

372 Here are the doctrinal statements from four classical Pentecostal denominations that further demonstrate how the primacy of tongues overshadowed Seymour's understanding of Spirit baptism. Church of God, "Doctrinal Commitments," *Church of God*, http://www.churchofgod.org/index.php?page=doctrinal-commitments. Church of God (Cleveland, TN), **The speaking in tongues as the Spirit gives utterance as the initial evidence of the baptism in the Holy Ghost** (John 15:26; Acts 2:4, 10:44-46, 19:1-7). General Counsel of the Assemblies of God, "Baptism in the Holy Spirit," *Assemblies of God*, http://ag.org/top/Beliefs/gendoct_02_baptismhs.cfm. Assemblies of God: The baptism of Christians in the Holy Spirit is accompanied by the initial physical sign of speaking in other tongues (unlearned languages) as the Spirit of God gives them audible expression. (Luke 24:49; Acts 1:4,8, 2:4, 8:12-17, 10:44-46, 11:14-16, 15:7-9; 1 Cor. 12:1-31). International Pentecostal Holiness Church, "Articles of Faith," *International Pentecostal Holiness Church*, http://arc.iphc.org/theology/artfaith.

evidence became the "chief doctrinal" distinctive of classical Pentecostalism,[373] leaving Seymour's Pentecostal message far behind. Seymour had consistently admonished his followers at the Azusa Street Mission to not seek after tongues, but to focus on the giver of gifts and seek more of God.[374] Conversely, his advice was ultimately rejected by the entire Pentecostal movement, as tongues became the focal point of Pentecostal experience.

Neglect from Pentecostal Historians

Another probable contributing factor to Seymour's decline has been identified by ethicist Leonard Lovett. Lovett contends that previous Pentecostal historiography (the way in which Pentecostal history is recorded) has not viewed African American Pentecostalism in its proper historical context, having failed to appreciate the full spectrum of the heritage of African Americans who were numbered among early Pentecostals.[375] He believed that African American Pentecostalism "emerged out of the context of the brokenness of black existence. ...'God chose what [was] foolish in the

html. International Pentecostal Holiness Church: We believe that the Pentecostal baptism of the Holy Ghost and fire is obtainable by a definite act of appropriating faith on the part of the fully cleansed believer, and the initial evidence of the reception of this experience is speaking with other tongues as the Spirit gives utterance (Luke 11:13; Acts 1:5, 2:14, 8-17, 10:44-46, 19:6). Church of God in Christ, "The Doctrine of the Church of God in Christ," *Church of God in Christ*, http://www.cogic.com/doctrine.html. Church of God in Christ: We believe that the Baptism of the Holy Ghost is an experience subsequent to conversion and sanctification and that tongue-speaking is the consequence of the baptism in the Holy Ghost with the manifestations of the fruit of the spirit (Gal. 5:22-23; Acts 10:46, 19:1-6). Interestingly, out of the four denominations, the COGIC is the only one that added the phrase, "with the manifestations of the fruit of the spirit" to their doctrinal formula. Perhaps their founder, C. H. Mason was responsible for this due to his close friendship with Seymour.

373 Gary B. McGee, "Initial Evidence," in Burgess and Van Der Maas, *New International Dictionary of Pentecostal and Charismatic Movements*, 784-791.

374 William J. Seymour, ed., Untitled article, *Apostolic Faith* 1, no. 11 (October to January 1908): 4.

375 Leonard Lovett, "Black Origins of the Pentecostal Movement," in *Aspects of Pentecostal-Charismatic Origins*, ed. Vinson Synan (Plainfield, NJ: Logos International, 1975), 127.

world to shame the wise'" (1 Cor. 1:27, RSV).[376] Lovett made the following observation:

> Black Pentecostalism is what it is, for the most part, because of its own unique experience in America. Attempts to objectively evaluate black Pentecostalism have been hampered by preconceived notions about such things as illiteracy, religious fanaticism, unrestrained emotionalism, and exhibitionism.[377]

In Lovett's estimation, early historical accounts made little or no mention of Seymour, because white historians simply did not give African American Pentecostalism a fair hearing. For Lovett, one could not even have a meaningful conversation about the origins of contemporary Pentecostalism unless the role of African Americans was clearly defined.[378] In essence, Lovett believed that some of the classical Pentecostal historians' lack of attention to Seymour was so obvious that it should have been considered as a "form of judgment on [their] ethnic and racial pride."[379] Klaud Kendrick's 1961 work, *The Promise Fulfilled: A History of the Modern Pentecostal Movement*, serves as an example. Kendrick was commended for willing to break with a certain defensiveness, which was indicative of some earlier Pentecostal historians who tended to omit things that could potentially hurt the movement (such as Parham's alleged homosexual liaison).[380] Yet, Kendrick's

376 Ibid., 138-139.
377 Ibid., 139.
378 Ibid., 138.
379 Ibid., 131.
380 An example of the defensiveness in early Pentecostal writing is Stanley H. Frodsham, *With Signs Following*: *The Story of the Pentecostal Revival in the Twentieth Century*, rev. ed. (1926; repr., Springfield: Gospel Publishing House, 1946), 19-29. In his monograph, Frodsham managed to write two whole chapters about Parham's schools without ever mentioning his name. Interestingly, Frodsham mentioned Seymour's name seven times noting Seymour's concern for salvation as more important than glossolalia. However, Frodsham paid little attention to the miracle of interracial fellowship other than quoting Bartleman who said, "We had no respect of persons," and "...all were equal" (Ibid. 36).

work stressed the role of Parham, and hailed him as the father of contemporary Pentecostalism.[381] And, although Kendrick acknowledged the importance of the Azusa Street Revival for the propagation of Pentecostalism, he gave little attention to the revival's leader: Seymour.[382] According to Kendrick, Seymour was the recognized leader in the early months, but eventually was "superseded by men of greater natural ability, and after a while the races no longer mixed in services."[383] One must wonder who the "men of greater natural ability" were that Kendrick referred to.

Kendrick, however, was not the only modern classical Pentecostal historian to ignore Seymour. In Carl Brumback's work, *Suddenly from Heaven: A History of the Assemblies of God*, he described Pentecostal origins as being supernaturally initiated by the Holy Spirit, rather than a result of any human efforts.[384] Brumback argued that founding Pentecostal figures such as A. J. Tomlinson, Charles F. Parham, and William J. Seymour should not be credited with the founding of the movement, because of its sudden and explosive nature. But he appears to send a mixed message in his assertion that "[t]he Pentecostal outpouring did not begin in a back alley mission but in a mansion!"[385] Obviously, Brumback was referring to Parham's Topeka Bible School known as Stone's Mansion by the citizens of Topeka, Kansas. Brumback devoted considerable attention to Parham without ever mentioning his racial tenets or his fall from grace. Yet, he portrayed Seymour as a man who was "in over his head," and in desperate need of Parham's help to discern between genuine and false manifestations at Azusa

381 Klaud Kendrick, *The Promise Fulfilled: A History of the Modern Pentecostal Movement* (Springfield: Gospel Publishing House, 1961), 36.
382 Ibid., 64-68. Kendrick only devoted four pages to Seymour and the Azusa Street Revival.
383 Ibid., 66-67.
384 Carl Brumback, *Suddenly from Heaven: A History of the Assemblies of God* (Springfield: Gospel Publishing House, 1961), 57-63.
385 Ibid., 21.

Street. Further, he adopts Parham's inflammatory rhetoric in asserting that:

> Seymour had reason for concern, for the work was getting beyond him and he needed help from someone who was more experienced than himself. Therefore he urged Parham to come, because "hypnotic forces and fleshly contortions as known in the colored Camp Meetings in the South had broken loose in the meeting." He urged Mr. Parham to come quickly to help discern between that which was real and that which was false.[386]

This assertion by Brumback was based on Parham's unsupported allegations about Seymour, though it was presented as though Seymour was the one who was actually speaking.

Robert Mapes Anderson's *Vision of the Disinherited*: *The Making of American Pentecostalism* referred to Seymour by name over fifty-five times. Yet, although Anderson also noted Charles Fox Parham's racial attitudes in his comprehensive survey, he presented the Pentecostal movement as originating from the whites in Topeka under Parham's leadership, and thereby minimized the role of African Americans.[387] Furthermore, Anderson spoke positively of Azusa, describing it as a miracle of equality in Christ that overcame barriers of race, sex, and class. Seymour's theological input was overlooked, however, as Anderson viewed the Azusa leader as someone who merely introduced a "simplified version" of Parham's thesis in Los Angeles.[388] In short, although Anderson repudiated Parham's racism by describing it as, "one facet of the white supremacist thinking underlying the wholesale

386 Ibid., 60.

387 Robert Mapes Anderson, *Vision of the Disinherited: The Making of American Pentecostalism* (Peabody: Hendrickson, 1992), 257.

388 Ibid., 47.

degradation of the Negro,"[389] he missed the essence of Seymour's message by fixating on his argument that Seymour was ultimately unsuccessful in "inducing tongues."[390] The notion that Seymour narrowly focused on "inducing tongues" is based on the assumption that glossolalia was his primary concern, and ignores Seymour's profound quest for a new community of true Christian equality and fellowship.[391]

These examples are not intended to be exhaustive, but representative, of the failure of some Pentecostal historians to recognize the import of Seymour's pivotal role in shaping Pentecostal theology. Whether through racial indifference, denominational triumphalism, a certain tendency to minimize the Azusa leader's teachings, or by focusing too much on speaking in tongues as evidence of Spirit baptism, Seymour's reconciling message of Pentecost, with its emphasis on divine love and interracial equality, became more difficult to hear over all the other voices.

Implications of the Loss

Regardless of the causes of Seymour's loss of position in the Pentecostal movement, this loss does have implications for the Pentecostal/Charismatic movement today. Nelson argues that the rejection of Seymour's reconciling vision of interracial unity, coupled with an overemphasis on tongues by white leaders in the movement, caused the subsequent trivialization of Pentecostalism.[392]

By the end of the Azusa era, the Pentecostal movement had divided along ideological and racial lines.[393] White Pentecostals became overly concerned with speaking in tongues, perhaps thinking that glossolalia was the essential

389 Ibid., 88.
390 Ibid., 65.
391 Nelson, "For Such a Time as This," 148.
392 Nelson, "For Such a Time as This," 13-14.
393 Ibid., 13.

uniting factor. But they failed to view tongues as an outward sign, based on an inward reality of the love of God infused into people's hearts, making them all one. Unfortunately, because of the preoccupation with speaking in tongues, the movement began to be defined merely as a behavioral phenomenon.[394] Seymour had consistently cautioned Azusa participants not to simply focus on tongues, or any other particular manifestation, but he instructed them to seek God with all their hearts.[395] However, as the Pentecostal movement began to unite around this distorted emphasis on an outward glossolalia manifestation (making this initial evidence of Spirit baptism its distinctive mark), it became widely attacked as the "tongues movement."[396] In fact, the primacy of glossolalia as evidence of Spirit baptism grew to such popularity that it became a doctrinal requirement in several Pentecostal denominations.[397] Although Pentecostals and Charismatics have become more nuanced today in their interpretations of what it means to be Spirit-filled,[398] Seymour's understanding

394 Ibid., 14.

395 William J. Seymour, ed., "The Baptism with the Holy Ghost," *Apostolic Faith*, 1, no. 11 (October to January 1908): 4.

396 Nelson, "For Such a Time as This,"53. Though early critics coined the term, "tongues movement," glossolalia is still very much the identity of Pentecostalism today. However, one must not overlook the overall role that tongues have played in the proliferation of Pentecostalism. For a more thorough discussion on the impact of tongues toward the growth of Pentecostalism globally, see Vinson Synan, "Role of Tongues as Initial Evidence," in *Spirit and Renewal: Essays in Honor of J. Rodman Williams*, ed. Mark Wilson (Sheffield, UK: Sheffield Academic Press, 1994), 67-82.

397 Brumback, *Suddenly from Heaven*, 216-225; and General Counsel of the Assemblies of God, "Baptism in the Holy Spirit," *Assemblies of God*, http://ag.org/top/Beliefs/gendoct_02_baptismhs.cfm. For example, the in its 1918 General council meeting in Springfield, Missouri, the Assemblies of God decided that glossolalia was the initial evidence of every recipient of Spirit baptism. Although there was an intense debate between F. F. Bosworth and D. W Kerr, Kerr's position (which argued that baptism in the Holy Spirit was regularly accompanied by the initial physical sign of speaking in tongues), was unanimously accepted. Though today the Assemblies of God stance on Spirit baptism appears to be a bit more nuanced (with emphases on the provision of power for victorious Christian living and productive service, as well as the endorsement of specific spiritual gifts for more effective ministry), one of its four cardinal doctrines asserts that baptism of Christians in the Holy Spirit is accompanied by the initial physical sign of speaking in other tongues.

398 Vinson Synan, *The Holiness-Pentecostal Tradition: Charismatic Movements in the Twentieth Century* (Grand Rapids: William B. Eerdmans, 1997), 220-278. As Pentecost spread to mainline denominations, the Catholic Church, and Third

of Pentecost (with its unifying vision of equality, as evidenced by divine love) is still not considered the primary mark of Spirit baptism; rather, speaking in tongues often takes center stage.[399]

Wavers, these groups developed a more nuanced position on Spirit baptism. For instance, Third Wavers, composed of evangelicals in major traditional churches, exercised the gifts of the Spirit without accepting labels such as "Spirit-filled," or "Pentecostal." Though they accepted glossolalia as a genuine gift of the Spirit, it was not considered to be the initial evidence of Spirit baptism, but was only one among many gifts.

399 Gary B. McGee, "Initial Evidence," in Burgess and Van Der Maas, *New International Dictionary of Pentecostal and Charismatic Movements,* 784-791; and Gary B. McGee, ed., *Initial Evidence: Historical and Biblical Perspectives on the Pentecostal Doctrine of Spirit Baptism* (Peabody: Hendrickson, 1991). According to these sources, the doctrine of initial evidence is considered to be the "chief doctrinal" distinctive of classical Pentecostalism.

CHAPTER SIX

Conclusion: Implications of Recovering Seymour

The goal of this work is to recover William J. Seymour's message in order to recapture the essence of Pentecost and to mine its implications for the ongoing process of reshaping the way that we as Pentecostal/Charismatics define the "Spirit-filled life." In order to accomplish this task, the past five chapters examined Seymour's historical roots, traced his connections with key personalities, explained his theology, placed him in dialogue with fellow contemporaries, and articulated the reasons for his loss of influence.

This section of the book, *William J. Seymour: Pioneer of the Azusa Street Revival,* sought to recover Seymour's Pentecostal message by first examining the historical context in his original home of Centerville, Louisiana. This context helped form the Azusa leader's worldview through his exposure to various local religions; often these were of African origin, interwoven into mandated Catholicism. Seymour's exposure to the African slave tradition, where dreams, visions, and the supernatural were common, may have made him more open to seek-out the supernatural after his conversion in the Methodist Episcopal Church. It was this openness that prepared him for, and eventually led him to, 312 Azusa Street.

A second aspect to reclaiming Seymour's message was to trace his connections to personalities and movements that may have shaped his theology, such as the teachings of the "Evening Light Saints," Martin Wells Knapp, Charles Harrison Mason, Charles Price Jones, and Charles Fox Parham. Seymour's theology continued to mature over time, based on his experiences with various personalities within the Pentecostal movement, and his life circumstances. Seymour's early influences were also paramount his formation in the areas of soteriology, pneumatology, and ecclesiology.

Although the antecedents that helped shape Seymour's theology were important to his development in his more formative years, a more mature Seymour put his theology into practice at the Azusa Street Mission. Seymour viewed justification, sanctification, and the baptism of the Holy Spirit as the "full blessing" of Christ, as symbolized by his utilization of tabernacle imagery. According to the Azusa leader, these three experiences were obtained through the sacrificial death of Jesus on the Cross, and Spirit baptism was accessible for every believer.

Seymour's soteriology embraced the two central assertions about the mature Christian life: justification and sanctification. In Seymour's understanding of justification, God offered the individual forgiveness from sins, as well as acquittal from the punishment of those sins. Justification occurred at a specific moment in time, and was experienced by the individual at conversion. Seymour explained his view of sin and salvation in the *Apostolic Faith*:

> A sinner comes to the Lord all wrapped up in sin and darkness. He cannot make any consecration because he is dead. The life has to be put into us before we can present any life to the Lord. He must get justified by faith. There is a Lamb without spot

> and blemish slain before God for him, and when he repents toward God for his sins, the Lord has mercy on him for Christ's sake, and put [*sic*] eternal life in his soul, pardoning him of his sins, washing away his guilty pollution, and he stands before God justified as if he had never sinned.[400]

According to Seymour, after justification there was sanctification, which dealt with sin in the singular, or the "sin nature," or "original sin." Seymour said:

> Sanctification makes us holy and destroys the breed of sin, the love of sin and carnality. It makes us pure and whiter than snow. ...Any man that is saved and sanctified can feel the fire burning in his heart, when he calls on the name of Jesus.[401]

For Seymour, the second work, or "second blessing," was an act of cleansing, rather than an act of forgiveness. With this, the justified person had the ability to feel a heightened sense of God's presence after having their request for sanctification answered. Sanctification made it possible for a person to live free from sin, and made them prime candidates receive the baptism of the Holy Spirit.

In sum, Seymour's two-stage view of grace was essential for his theology of the mature Christian life. Justification and sanctification were absolutely necessary if a person would ever partake of the third experience, the baptism of the Holy Spirit. Spirit baptism was not considered as a third work of grace, but was a "gift of power" to help the justified and sanctified believer in the ministry of the gospel to others.[402]

---

400 William. J. Seymour, "The Way into the Holiest," *Apostolic Faith* 1, no. 2 (October 1906): 4.

401 William J. Seymour, "Sanctified on the Cross," *Apostolic Faith* 2, no. 13 (May 1908): 2.

402 William J. Seymour, ed., "The Apostolic Faith Movement," *Apostolic Faith* 1, no. 1 (September 1906): 2.

In his pneumatology or doctrine of the Holy Spirit, Seymour initially linked speaking in tongues with proof of Spirit baptism, because of the influence of Parham. However, the Azusa leader was always careful to maintain a sense of balance in regard to the goal of having this experience. Seymour admonished his followers, even in the earlier stages of the revival, that glossolalia was not something to be sought as an end in itself. According to Seymour, individuals who came to Azusa seeking tongues did not really understand the baptism of the Holy Spirit. At one point, Seymour wrote:

> Beloved...we are not seeking for tongues, but we are seeking the baptism with the Holy Ghost and fire. And when we receive it, we shall be so filled with the Holy Ghost, that He Himself will speak in the power of the Spirit.[403]

Seymour made it clear that the ultimate goal was not speaking in tongues, but the baptism of the Holy Spirit. Glossolalia was something that God would "throw in" as an extra blessing.[404]

Seymour's view of the Holy Spirit would become more nuanced over time, probably because of what he observed from those who claimed to be Spirit-filled, yet did not have the character to support their words.[405]

> Tongues are one of the signs that go with every baptized person, but it is not the real evidence of the baptism in the every day life. Your life must measure with the fruits of the Spirit. If you get angry, or speak

403 William J. Seymour, "The Baptism with the Holy Ghost," *Apostolic Faith* 1, no. 6 (February to March 1907): 7.

404 Ibid.

405 This statement refers primarily to Charles Parham's questionable actions at Azusa in October of 1906. He repudiated the revival and later criticized Seymour, using racial slurs. Parham's behavior was the primary factor in Seymour change in pneumatology.

> evil, or backbite, I care not how many tongues you may have, you have not the baptism of the Holy Spirit.[406]

For Seymour, the ability to speak in tongues was good, but it was not the standard for Christian spirituality. Seymour wanted to ensure that his followers were balanced in their Christianity. He supported spiritual manifestations, but did not promote them. He constantly admonished his followers to "keep their eyes on Jesus and not on manifestations," or they might get a counterfeit manifestation.[407]

In short, Seymour's pneumatology encouraged people to seek the baptism of the Holy Spirit by focusing on the giver of the gifts, rather than on one particular gift, and to use the gifts of the Holy Spirit for the glory of God. For Seymour, glossolalia as evidence for the baptism of the Holy Spirit on "all flesh" implicitly served to demonstrate the equality of all races; the fact that all *races* received this experience at Azusa was proof of the equality of all people.

In his ecclesiology or doctrine of the church, Seymour argued for the practice of divine love that allowed believers the freedom to live in unity, rather than in the adaptation of creeds and confessions, which in his mind, divided Christians. The Azusa leader's vision even extended to those who were considered outsiders by the Pentecostal movement. His intention was never to cause division, or fight against other churches or denominations, but to simply live-out practical Christianity through "love, faith and unity."[408] Seymour became convinced that the secret to the success of the Azusa Revival was that believers were united in purpose, similar to the day of Pentecost in the book of Acts.

406 William J. Seymour, ed., "To the Baptized Saints," *Apostolic Faith* 1, no. 9 (June to September 1907): 2.
407 William J. Seymour, ed., untitled article, *Apostolic Faith* 1, no. 11 (October to January 1908): 4.
408 William J. Seymour, ed., "The Apostolic Faith Movement," *Apostolic Faith* 1, no. 1 (September 1906): 2.

Seymour not only emphasized unity in the body of Christ, but he also believed that the duty of the Church was to fulfill the great commission. This was evidenced by the missionaries sent out from Azusa Street, who eventually spread the message of Pentecost around the world, as Azusa missionaries were responsible for Pentecostal outbreaks in places such as: Jerusalem, India, China, Europe, South America, Africa, and the islands of the sea.[409]

Essential to Seymour's ecclesiology was his understanding of divine love. Again, the theological transformation that Seymour underwent moved him from the assertion that speaking in tongues was the evidence of Spirit baptism, to the belief that divine love was the sign of baptism in the Holy Spirit. According to Seymour, the "Pentecostal power," or the baptism of the Holy Spirit, was simply more of God's love.[410] In Seymour's estimation, Pentecost enabled people to love God more, in addition to giving them an increased love for their brothers and sisters, for the purpose of bringing all into one common family.[411]

Though Seymour stressed the importance of a loving church, he also believed that God could only use vessels who were dedicated to live free from sin and all uncleanness.[412] Seymour often implored followers to prepare themselves for the return of Christ by referring to the sanctified church motif throughout the *Apostolic Faith*.[413] According to Seymour, the

409 William J. Seymour, ed., "Good News from Danville, VA," *Apostolic Faith* 1, no.1 (September 1906): 4; William J. Seymour, ed., "Missionaries to Jerusalem," *Apostolic Faith* 1, no. 1 (September 1906): 4; G. W. Batman and Daisy Batman, "En Route to Africa," *Apostolic Faith* 1, no. 4 (December 1906): 4; and William J. Seymour, ed., "Revival in India," *Apostolic Faith* 1, no. 4 (December 1906): 4. For more examples of missionary activity among Azusa participants, see *Apostolic Faith* (September 1906 through May 1908).

410 William J. Seymour, ed., Untitled article, *Apostolic Faith* 2, no. 13 (May 1908): 3.

411 Ibid.

412 Seymour, *Doctrines and Discipline*, 10.

413 William J. Seymour, "Rebecca; Type of the Bride of Christ-Gen. 24," *Apostolic Faith* 1, no. 6 (February to March 1907): 2.

only people eligible to meet Jesus at His coming were the sanctified ones.

Perhaps the greatest example of Seymour's ecclesiology was his stance on racial inclusion. Though the fact that blacks and whites were able to come together and worship under the leadership of an African American pastor in 1906 should be considered a miracle, Seymour's theology of race did play a significant role, in that he had sought interracial togetherness for most of his life. Seymour himself suggested that racial togetherness was one of the prime reasons why the Azusa Street work was so successful.[414] For Seymour, racial inclusiveness was the sign of the true Church that was birthed on the day of Pentecost, as various ethnic groups gathered to hear the gospel in their own native language.

Seymour's ecclesiology implored the church to abandon its denominationalism and racial indifference, to allow the Holy Spirit to bring it into true Christian fellowship. According to Seymour, the chief task of the Holy Spirit was not to produce glossolalia as the distinctive mark of Pentecostal unity. Instead, the work of the Holy Spirit was to make all races and nations into one global family through divine love.

Seymour's theology was also articulated through dialogue with his contemporaries in the early Pentecostal movement, such as Florence Crawford, Charles Fox Parham, and William H. Durham. The comparison and contrast between Seymour and these early Pentecostal pioneers demonstrated how Seymour was viewed by his peers, and also showed how Seymour responded to their criticisms.

In sum, Seymour's relationships with his contemporaries all had one thing in common: they started well, yet, because of theological differences, they ended in hurt and disappointment for the Azusa leader. His relationships with Crawford

414 William J. Seymour, ed., "Gracious Pentecostal Showers Continue to Fall," *Apostolic Faith* 1, no. 3 (November 1906): 1.

and Durham were strained because of disagreements over sanctification, while Seymour and Parham argued over eternal punishment, race, and Spirit baptism.

Finally, in order to recover someone or something, it is important to first know exactly what the search is for, as well as what may have initially caused the loss of the person or thing. An important part of this first section examined the possible causes for Seymour's loss of influence, as well as the implications of that loss for the current Pentecostal/Charismatic movement. The purpose of this exercise was not merely to assert blame to those responsible for the decline of Seymour's place in Pentecostal history. The purpose was to critically appraise Seymour, and determine whether his own actions contributed to his decreasing popularity in the Pentecostal movement through the years.

Regardless of where ultimate responsibility lay for the decline of Seymour's influence, the implications for this loss meant that Seymour's reconciling message of Pentecost, which highlighted love and interracial unity, would remain unknown for many years. Meanwhile the Pentecostal movement would be trivialized by outsiders, and gain notoriety as a behavioral phenomenon, because of its preoccupation with tongues.

After spending several years studying the life of this humble man from Louisiana, I have concluded that Seymour had an understanding of the Spirit-empowered life that was based on divine love, interracial equality, and unity. However, Seymour's reconciling understanding of Pentecost was quickly forgotten for such reasons as theological schism, race politics, and preoccupation with speaking in tongues as the defining mark of Spirit baptism. Although Seymour died of a heart attack in 1922 at the young age of fifty-two while dictating a letter, one questions if the cause of death was not from a "broken heart" because his understanding of the essence of Pentecost (which consisted of a multi-ethnic, multi-cultural and multi-gifted church, under the banner of love) was never fully embraced by his contemporaries. Although we celebrate the impact that William J. Seymour and Azusa Street had on the proliferation of the Pentecostal/Charismatic movement, which has grown to over 600 million adherents globally, one can only imagine the kind of legacy that Pentecostals could have had if they had adhered to his message of love and racial harmony. Perhaps they would have been known more for helping take the lead in breaking down racial barriers in the United States even before Dr. Martin Luther King, Jr. and the Civil Rights Movement; or maybe the "evidence" of love would have been the primary distinctive of Pentecostal/ Charismatic spirituality.

Section Two

Part A

William J. Seymour's

Signed Articles

in

The Apostolic Faith

(1906-1908)

THE FIVE-FOLD GOSPEL OF AZUSA STREET

Although the Azusa Street statement of faith was not signed by Seymour, it was obviously written by him in order to inform his readers exactly what doctrines were upheld at the Mission. This is now called the "five-fold gospel" of Azusa Street, which was the universal position of the first Pentecostals as taught by both Parham and Seymour. This doctrinal scheme was also adopted by the first wave of Pentecostal denominations including the Church of God in Christ, the Church of God (Cleveland, Tennessee), the Pentecostal Holiness Church, the Fire-Baptized Holiness Church, and the Pentecostal Free Will Baptist Church.

The five doctrinal points were: 1. Justification by faith (as taught by Martin Luther; 2. Entire sanctification as taught by John Wesley and the Methodist-Holiness movement; 3. The baptism in the Holy Spirit with the "Bible evidence" of speaking in tongues as taught by Seymour's mentor Charles Parham; 4. Divine healing as in the atonement as taught by Charles Cullis. A.J. Gordon, and A.B. Simpson; and 5. The imminent second coming of Christ as taught by John Nelson Darby and Edward Irving.

Interestingly, the statement of faith did not include a paragraph on the second coming. One can only guess why it was left out since those who were baptized in the Holy Spirit at Azusa Street felt a great urgency to evangelize the world in the power of the Holy Spirit before the soon expected rapture of the church.

Four of the above doctrines had already been in place throughout much of the Holiness movement by 1906. The "Fourfold gospel" of A.B. Simpson's Christian and Missionary Alliance was the platform that led to the "five-fold gospel" of Azusa Street.

By separating the second blessing into two separate

experiences, one a sanctification crisis followed by a baptism in the Holy Spirit, Seymour was following the "third blessing" tradition established in the 1890s by Benjamin Hardin Irwin's Fire-Baptized Holiness movement, the first to make such a distinction. Asserting that tongues was the "evidence" of the third blessing baptism was the most startling and original doctrinal innovation in Seymour's five-fold gospel. Vinson Synan

THE APOSTOLIC FAITH MOVEMENT

Stands for the restoration of the faith once delivered unto the saints—the old time religion, camp meetings, revivals, missions, street and prison work and Christian Unity everywhere.

Teaching on Repentance—Mark 1:14, 15.

Godly Sorrow for Sin, Example—Matt. 9:13; 2 Cor. 7, 9, 11; Acts 3:19; Acts 17:30, 31.

Of Confessions of Sins—Luke 15:21 and Luke 18:13.

Forsaking Sinful Ways—Isa. 55:7; Jonah 3:8; Prov. 28; 13.

Restitution—Ezek. 33; 15; Luke 19:8.

And faith in Jesus Christ.

First Work—Justification is that act of God's free grace by which we receive remission of sins. Acts 10:42, 43; Rom. 3:25.

Second Work—Sanctification is the second work of grace and the last work of grace. Sanctification is that act of God's free grace by which He makes us holy. John 17:15, 17—"Sanctify them through Thy Truth; Thy word is truth." 1 Thess. 4:3; 1 Thess. 5:23; Heb. 13:12; Heb. 2:11; Heb. 12:14.

Sanctification is cleansing to make holy. The Disciples were sanctified before the Day of Pentecost. By a careful study of Scripture you will find it is so now. "Ye are clean through the word which I have spoken unto you" (John 15:3; 13:10); and Jesus had breathed on them the Holy Ghost (John 20:21, 22).

You know, that they could not receive the Spirit if they were not clean. Jesus cleansed and got all doubt out of His Church before He went back to glory.

The Baptism with the Holy Ghost is a gift of power upon the sanctified life; so when we get it we have the same evidence as the Disciples received on the Day of Pentecost (Acts 2:3, 4), in speaking in new tongues. See also Acts 10:45, 45; Acts 19:6; 1 Cor. 14:21. "For I will work a work in your days which ye will not believe though it be told you"—Hab. 1:5.

Seeking Healing—He must believe that God is able to heal.—Ex. 15:26: "I am the Lord that healeth thee." James 5:14; Psa. 103:3; 2 Kings 20:5; Matt. 8:16, 17; Mark 16:16, 17, 18.

He must believe God is able to heal. "Behold I am the Lord, the God of all flesh; is there any thing too hard for Me?"—Jer. 32:27.

Too many have confused the grace of Sanctification with the enduement of Power, or the Baptism with the Holy Ghost; others have taken "the anointing that abideth" for the Baptism, and failed to reach the glory and power of a true Pentecost.

The blood of Jesus will never blot out any sin between man and man they can make right; but if we can't make wrongs right the Blood graciously covers. (Matt. 5:23, 24.)

We are not fighting men or churches, but seeking to displace dead forms and creeds and wild fanaticisms with living, practical Christianity. "Love, Faith, Unity" are our watchwords, and "Victory through the Atoning Blood" our battle cry. God's promises are true. He said: "Be thou faithful over a few things, and I will make thee ruler over many." From the little handful of Christians who stood by the cross when the testings and discouragements came, God has raised a mighty host.

SEYMOUR'S THEOLOGY OF HEALING

This article on healing was the first article in *Apostolic Faith* signed by William J. Seymour. It appeared in the September 1906 edition on p. 2. In this article, Seymour presents a standard view of healing that was already popular in the Holiness movement. Called "divine healing as in the atonement," this theology was popularized in the late 19th Century by such writers as Charles Cullis in his *Faith Cures* (1879), by A.J. Gordon in his *The Ministry of Healing* (1882), and by A. B. Simpson in his *The Gospel of Healing* (1996).

Here Seymour sees the new birth, sanctification, divine healing, and baptism in the Holy Spirit as benefits of the atonement. Although this view was criticized by some as placing healing of the body on the same level as salvation of the soul, Seymour, as well as almost all early Pentecostals, continued to hold this view all his life. Seymour also joined with many other Pentecostals in refusing to use doctors and medicine, following the lead of John Alexander Dowie of Zion City, Illinois. In the December 1906 issue, he stated, "many Christians will take a doctor before Jesus. They put a doctor between them and the atonement....The doctor gives you poison and you die because you dishonor the atonement." VS

THE PRECIOUS ATONEMENT

Children of God, partakers of the precious atonement, let us study and see what there is in it for us.

First. Through the atonement we receive forgiveness of sins.

Second. We receive sanctification through the blood of Jesus. "Wherefore Jesus also that He might sanctify the people with His own blood, suffered without the gate." Sanctified from all original sin, we become sons of God. "For both He that sanctifieth and they who are sanctified are all of one: for which cause He is not ashamed to call them brethren" (Heb. 2:11) (it seems that Jesus would be ashamed to call them brethren, if they were not sanctified). Then you will not be ashamed to tell men and demons that you are sanctified, and are living a pure and holy life free from sin, a life that gives you power over the world, the flesh and the devil. The devil does not like that kind of testimony. Through this precious atonement, we have freedom from all sin, though we are living in this old world, we are permitted to sit in heavenly places in Christ Jesus.

Third. Healing of our bodies. Sickness and disease are destroyed through the precious atonement of Jesus. O how we ought to honor the stripes of Jesus, for "with his stripes we are healed." How we ought to honor that precious body which the Father sanctified and sent into the world, not simply set apart, but really sanctified, soul, body and spirit, free from sickness, disease and everything of the devil. A body that knew no sin and disease was given for these imperfect bodies of ours. Not only is the atonement for the sanctification of our souls, but for the sanctification of our bodies from inherited disease. It matters not what has been in the blood. Every drop of blood we received from our mother is impure. Sickness is born in a child just as original sin is born in the child. He was manifested to destroy the works of the devil. Every sickness is of the devil.

Man in the garden of Eden was pure and happy and knew no sickness till that unholy visitor came into the garden, then his whole system was poisoned and it has been flowing in the blood of all the human family down the ages until God spoke to His people and said, "I am the Lord that healeth thee."

The children of Israel practiced divine healing. David after being healed of rheumatism, (perhaps contracted in the caves where he hid himself from his pursuers), testified saying, "Bless the Lord, O my soul and all that is within me bless His holy name, who forgiveth all thine iniquities, who healeth all thy diseases." David knew what it was to be healed. Healing continued with God's people till Solomon's heart was turned away by strange wives, and he brought in the black arts and mediums, and they went whoring, after familiar spirits. God had been their healer, but after they lost the Spirit, they turned to the arm of flesh to find something to heal their diseases.

Thank God we have a living Christ among us to heal our diseases. He will heal every case. The prophet had said, "With His stripes we are healed," and it was fulfilled when Jesus came. Also, "He hath borne our griefs," (which means sickness, as translators tell us). Now if Jesus bore our sicknesses, why should we bear them? So we get full salvation through the atonement of Jesus.

Fourth. And we get the baptism with the Holy Ghost and fire upon the sanctified life. We get Christ enthroned and crowned in our hearts. Let us lift up Christ to the world in all His fullness, not only in healing and salvation from all sin, but in His power to speak all the languages of the world. We need the triune God to enable us to do this.

We that are the messengers of this precious atonement ought to preach all of it—justification, sanctification, healing, the baptism with the Holy Ghost and signs following. "How shall we escape if we neglect so great salvation?" God is now confirming His Word by granting signs and wonders to follow the preaching of the full gospel in Los Angeles.

September, 1906

SEYMOUR'S NEW VIEW OF SANCTIFICATION

Coming from the second blessing Wesleyan movement, Seymour for years had taught the standard Holiness view that entire sanctification was a cleansing brought about by the fire of the baptism in the Holy Spirit which was part of the second blessing. Now with the Pentecostal view of baptism in the Holy Spirit as a "third blessing" after salvation and sanctification, Seymour explains that sanctification now prepares the seeker by cleansing the temple before the tongues attested baptism in the Holy Spirit. He often repeated the phrase, "the baptism with the Holy Ghost. It is a free gift upon the sanctified, cleansed heart." This became the universal theology of the first wave of American Pentecostals before William H. Durham introduced the "finished work of Calvary" theology after 1911.

In all of Seymour's signed articles, there is more attention given to sanctification than to speaking in tongues, which he tended to de-emphasize as time went on. But his devotion to the sanctification experience never wavered. In his book, *The Azusa Street Mission*, Mel Robeck records many testimonies of Azusa people receiving the sanctification experience, many in quite colorful language. VS

THE WAY INTO THE HOLIEST

A sinner comes to the Lord all wrapped up in sin and darkness. He cannot make any consecration because he is dead. The life has to be put into us before we can present any life to the Lord. He must get justified by faith. There is a Lamb without spot and blemish slain before God for him, and when he repents toward God for his sins, the Lord has mercy on him for Christ's sake, and puts eternal life in his soul, pardoning him of his sins, washing away his guilty pollution, and he stands before God justified as if he had never sinned.

Then there remains that old original sin in him for which he is not responsible till he has the light. He hears that "Jesus, that He might sanctify the people with His own blood, suffered without the gate," and he comes to be sanctified. There is Jesus, the Lamb without blemish, on the altar. Jesus takes that soul that has eternal life in it and presents it to God for thorough purging and cleansing from all original and Adamic sin. And Jesus, the Son of God, cleanses him from all sin, and he is made every whit whole, sanctified and holy.

Now, he is on the altar ready for the fire of God to fall, which is the baptism with the Holy Ghost. It is a free gift upon the sanctified, cleansed heart. The fire remains there continually burning in the holiness of God. Why? Because he is sanctified and holy and on the altar continually. He stays there and the great Shekinah of glory is continually burning and filling with heavenly light.

October, 1906

SEYMOUR REJECTS CESSATIONISM

The key phrase in this teaching that Jesus gave to the woman at the well was the key to the beginnings of Pentecostalism, that the miracles of the New Testament never ceased but will continue to be manifested until the second coming of Christ. "The promise is unto you, and to your children, and to all that are afar off, even as many as the Lord our God shall call." This phrase summarizes the Pentecostal belief that signs, wonders and miracles would be abundantly manifested in the last days as in the beginning of the church. This is the most important point made by the Pentecostals, that the miracles of the New Testament did not cease with the death of the last apostle, but continue until Jesus returns. "Cessationism" is a teaching that had been broadly accepted in the Western church since the days of St. Augustine in the fourth century. The Pentecostals have done the most to demolish that theory, so much so that only a tiny fraction of today's Christians hold that view. Seymour here clearly stands against the cessationists and with the Pentecostals on the question of signs and wonders and miracles in modern times. VS

RIVER OF LIVING WATER

In the fourth chapter of John, the words come, "Jesus answered and said unto her, If thou knewest the gift of God and who it is that saith to thee Give me to drink, thou wouldest have asked of Him and He would have given thee living water." Praise God for the living waters today that flow freely, for it comes from God to every hungry and thirsty heart. Jesus said, "He that believeth on me, as the scripture hath said, out of his inmost being shall flow rivers of living waters." Then we are able to go in the mighty name of Jesus to the ends of the earth and water dry places, deserts and solitary places until these parched, sad, lonely hearts are made to rejoice in the God of their salvation. We want the rivers today. Hallelujah! Glory to God in the highest!

In Jesus Christ we get forgiveness of sin, and we get sanctification of our spirit, soul and body, and upon that we get the gift of the Holy Ghost that Jesus promised to His disciples, the promise of the Father. All this we get through the atonement. Hallelujah!

The prophet said that He had borne our griefs and carried our sorrows. He was wounded for our transgressions, bruised for our iniquities, the chastisement of our peace was upon Him and with His stripes we are healed. So we get healing, salvation, joy, life—everything in Jesus. Glory to God!

There are many wells today, but they are dry. There are many hungry souls today that are empty. But let us come to Jesus and take Him at His Word and we will find wells of salvation, and be able to draw waters out of the well of salvation, for Jesus is that well.

At this time Jesus was weary from a long journey, and He sat on the well in Samaria, and a woman came to draw water. He asked her for a drink. She answered, "How is it that thou being a Jew askest drink of me who am a woman of Samaria, for the Jews have no dealings with the Samaritans?" Jesus said, "If thou knewest the gift of God, and who it is that saith to thee, give me to drink, thou wouldest have asked of Him and He would have given thee living water."

O, how sweet it was to see Jesus, the Lamb of God that takes away the sin of the world, that great sacrifice that God had given to a lost, dying and benighted world, sitting on the well and talking with the woman; so gentle, so meek and so kind that it gave her an appetite to talk further with Him, until He got into her secret and uncovered her life. Then she was pricked in her heart, confessed her sins and received pardon, cleansing from fornication and adultery, was washed from stain and guilt of sin and was made a child of God, and above all, received the well of salvation in her heart. It was so sweet and joyful and good. Her heart was so filled with love that she felt she could take in a whole lost world. So she ran away with a well of salvation and left the old water pot on the well. How true it is in this day, when we get the baptism with the Holy Spirit, we have something to tell, and it is that the blood of Jesus Christ cleanseth from all sin. The baptism with the Holy Ghost gives us power to testify to a risen, resurrected Saviour. Our affections are in Jesus Christ, the Lamb of God that takes away the sin of the world. How I worship Him today! How I praise Him for the all-cleansing blood.

Jesus' promises are true and sure. The woman said to Him, after He had uncovered her secret, "Sir I perceive that Thou art a prophet." Yes, He was a prophet. He was that great prophet that Moses said the Lord would raise up. He is here today. Will we be taught of that prophet? Will we hear Him? Let us accept Him in all His fullness.

He said, "He that believeth on me, the works that I do shall he do also, and greater works than these shall ye do, because I go unto my Father." These disciples to whom He was speaking, had been saved, sanctified, anointed with the Holy Spirit, their hearts had been opened to understand the scriptures, and yet Jesus said, "Tarry ye in the city of Jerusalem, until ye be endued with power from on high." "John truly baptized with water, but ye shall be baptized with the Holy Ghost not many days hence." So the same commission comes to us. We find that they obeyed His commission and were all filled with the Holy Ghost on the day of Pentecost, and Peter standing up, said, "This is that which was spoken by the prophet Joel." Dear loved ones, we preach the same sermon. "This is that which was spoken by the prophet Joel, I will pour out my Spirit upon all flesh, and your sons and your daughters shall prophesy, and your young men shall see visions, and your old men shall dream dreams; and on my servants and on my handmaidens I will pour out in those days of my Spirit, and they shall prophesy...The promise is unto you, and to your children, and to all that are afar off, even as many as the Lord our God shall call." That means until now and to last until Jesus comes.

There are so many people today like the woman. They are controlled by the fathers. Our salvation is not in some father or human instruments. It is sad to see people so blinded, worshiping the creature more than the Creator. Listen to what the woman said, "Our fathers worshiped in this mountain, and ye say Jerusalem is the place where men ought to worship." So many today are worshiping in the mountains, big churches, stone and frame buildings. But Jesus teaches that salvation is not in these stone structures—not in the mountains—not in the hills, but in God. For God is a Spirit. Jesus said unto her, "Woman, believe Me, the hour cometh and now is when ye shall neither in this mountain nor yet at Jerusalem worship the Father." So many people today are controlled by men. Their salvation reaches out no further than the boundary line of human creeds, but praise God for freedom in the Spirit. There are depths and heights and breadths that we can reach through the power of the blessed Spirit. "Eye hath not seen, nor ear heard, neither have entered into the hearts of man the things that God hath prepared for them that love Him."

The Jews were the religious leaders at this time, and people had no more light upon salvation than the Jews gave them. The Jews were God's chosen people to evangelize the world. He had entrusted them to give all nations the true knowledge of God, but they went into traditions and doctrines of men, and were blinded and in the dark. Jesus came as the light of the world, and He is that light. "If we walk in the light as He is in the light, we have fellowship one with another, and the blood of Jesus Christ His Son cleanseth us from all sin." Let us honor the Spirit, for Jesus has sent Him to teach and lead us into all truth.

Above all, let us honor the blood of Jesus Christ every moment of our lives, and we will be sweet in our souls. We will be able to talk of this common salvation to everyone that we meet. God will let His anointing rest upon us in telling them of this precious truth. This truth belongs to God. We have no right to tax anyone for the truth, because God has entrusted us with it to tell it. Freely we receive, freely we give. So the gospel is to be preached freely, and God will bless it and spread it Himself, and we have experienced that He does.

We have found Him true to His promise all the way. We have tried Him and proved Him. His promises are sure.

November, 1906

A PRACTICAL FINANCIAL MESSAGE FOR EAGER WITNESSES

In the early days of the Azusa Street revival, hundreds of newly Spirit-filled believers felt an unquenchable urge to go out and witness to the lost in the United States and around the world. Azusa Street became for all practical purposes a missions sending agency as offerings were taken for those who felt the call to evangelize. These Azusa Street "pilgrims" were soon departing for various parts of the world. I have called them the "Missionaries of the One Way Ticket" because they often went out with little support and usually no money to return home (which is now required by most missions boards).

Although no offerings were received in the Azusa Street services, as suggested by Charles Parham, a box hung from a wall that announced "settle with the Lord." Despite the lack of offerings and requests for money, the money poured in. These new Pentecostals were extremely generous in supporting the *Apostolic Faith* newspaper which was sent free to 50,000 subscribers. Also, money was given to many eager missionaries who could not wait to get onto the field and preach in their new found tongues without learning the languages in the normal manner.

Sometimes the over zealous ones would sell all their worldly goods in order to buy tickets and abandon the support of their wives and children in their eagerness to get on the field. Often they would come to Seymour and the Azusa Street saints for support. In order to bring order out of this financial chaos,

Seymour felt it was necessary to write this very practical message on money matters. VS

IN MONEY MATTERS

There have been teachers who have told all the people to sell out, and many of them have gone into fanaticism. We let the Spirit lead people and tell them what they ought to give. When they get filled with the Spirit, their pocket books are converted and God makes them stewards and if He says, "Sell out," they will do so. But sometimes they have families. God does not tell you to forsake your family. He says if you do not provide for your own you are worse than an infidel. Some are not called to go out and teach. We find some who have no wisdom nor faith, and the devil takes them to disgrace the work. Under false teaching, children have been left to go half naked, women have left their husbands, and husbands leave their wives to wash and scrub and the Bible says that is worse than infidelity. Then they will go and borrow and cannot pay back. That person ought to go to work. The Bible says, "Let him labor, working with his hands the thing which is good, that he may have to give to him that needeth."

He sent those that were called out to preach the gospel, to "take no thought what ye shall eat or drink." Get down and pray. Make your wants known unto God and He will send it in.

God does not expect all to sell out for He says in 1 Cor. 16:1, "Now concerning the collection for the saints, upon the first day of the week, let everyone of you lay by him in store, as God hath prospered him." It does not mean for you to have great real estate and money banked up while your brothers and sisters are suffering. He means for you to turn loose because all that money is soon going to be thrown to the moles and bats. So it is better to spread the gospel and get stars in your crown than to be holding it. But for us to go and tell you to do it, pick out somebody that has money and read the Word to them, would not be the Spirit of the Lord. The Spirit will tell you what to do. He makes you do it. When He wakes you up at night and tells you what to do, you cannot sleep till you obey. He says everyone shall be taught of God from the least to the greatest. God wants a free giver.

Ananias wanted to have a reputation that he sold out like the rest, so he plotted that he should give a portion and say he had sold out for the Lord. But the Holy Ghost told Peter that Ananias had told a lie. Peter told him the property was his. The Lord allows you to be the steward over it. The property was his and the sin was in lying to the Holy Ghost. It is right for you to have property, but if the Lord says, take $200 or $500 or $1,000 and distribute here or there, you do it.

We must know our calling. We can work when baptized with the Holy Ghost. Some think they have got to preach. Well, we do preach in testifying. Some think they must go out because they have the tongues but those are good for Los Angeles or anywhere else. The Lord will lead you by His small voice.

November, 1906

SEYMOUR DISCERNS THE FALSE FROM THE TRUE

When word spread around Los Angeles that people were speaking in tongues at Azusa Street, thousands of curious people flocked to the mission to see and hear what was happening. The Los Angeles newspapers were full of lurid and racist reports that only resulted in drawing even larger crowds. Los Angeles was referred to by Frank Bartleman as the "American Jerusalem" because of the numerous sects and cults that were attracted to the city. Soon after the services started in April of 1906, many spiritualists as well as Christian Scientists and Theosophists came and tried to imitate the tongues speech that was attracting so much attention. Seymour called them "the spirits." When the "Spirits" were manifested, the Azusa Street saints would cast out the "demons" as a matter of course.

Since services continued three times a day for over three years, Seymour could not be physically present in each service, sometimes resting upstairs while his workers were in charge downstairs. Many times, he would discern the counterfeit spirits in the service and would come running down the stairs to set things in order. He would then cast out the "Christian Science demons" and others as the occasion arose. The congregation seemed to be able to discern false spirits instantly and, led by Seymour, begin to exorcise them on the spot. In this article, Seymour points out biblical "counterfeits" that were to be avoided. They included Ananias and Sapphira, and the Egyptian magicians that Pharaoh used to withstand Moses. VS

COUNTERFEITS

God has told us in His precious Word that we should know a tree by its fruit. Wherever we find the real, we find the counterfeit also. But praise God for the real. We find in the time of Peter, when men and women were receiving the power of the Holy Ghost, the counterfeit appeared in Ananias and Sapphira. But God's power was mightier than all the forces of hell, so their sin found them out. Be careful, dear loved ones for your sin will surely find you out. But if we walk in the light as He is in the light, we have fellowship one with another and the blood of Jesus Christ, His Son cleanseth us from all sin.

In our meetings, we have had people to come and claim that they had received the baptism with the Holy Spirit, but when they were put to the test by the Holy Spirit, they were found wanting. So they got down and got saved and sanctified and baptized with the Holy Spirit and spoke in other tongues by the Holy Spirit. And again people have imitated the gift of tongues, but how quickly the Holy Spirit would reveal to every one of the true children that had the Pentecostal baptism. (Not legible in original) heavy (not legible in original) till the counterfeits were silenced and condemned. God's promises are true and sure.

People are trying to imitate the work of the Holy Ghost these days, just as they did when the Lord sent Moses to Pharaoh in Ex. 7:8, and gave him a miracle or sign to show before Pharaoh, that when Aaron should cast his rod before Pharaoh, it should become a serpent. So when Pharaoh saw that Aaron's rod, had become a serpent, he called for his wise men and the counterfeit sorcerers and magicians of Egypt. They also did in like manner with their enchantments, for they cast down every man his rod, and they became serpents but Aaron's rod swallowed up their rods. So the power of the Holy Ghost in God's people today condemns and swallows up the counterfeit. It digs up and exposes all the power of Satan—Christian Science, Theosophy and Spiritualism—all are uncovered before the Son of God. Glory to God.

Spiritualists have come to our meetings and had the demons cast out of them and have been saved and sanctified. Christian Scientists have come to the meetings and had the Christian Science demons cast out of them and have accepted the blood. Every plant that my heavenly Father hath not planted shall be rooted up.

People have come to this place full of demons and God has cast them out, and they have gone out crying with loud voices. Then when all the demons were cast out, they got saved, sanctified and baptized with the Holy Ghost, clothed in their right minds and filled with glory and power.

Dear loved ones, it is not by might nor by power but by my Spirit saith the Lord. "Tarry ye in the city of Jerusalem, until ye be endued with power from on high. John truly baptized with water, but ye shall be baptized with the Holy Ghost not many days hence." These were Jesus' departing words. May you tarry until you receive your personal Pentecost. Amen.

December, 1906

SEYMOUR'S DOCTRINE OF LAST THINGS

This article reveals several things about Seymour's eschatology which means the Biblical understanding of last things, including the rapture of the saints and the tribulation. His teachings on the second coming had gained wide acceptance among evangelicals and Holiness people by the turn of the century. First taught by John Nelson Darby and the Plymouth Brethren, this view of the end times included the pre-millennial sudden rapture of the church for those who were prepared and watching, followed by a three-and-a-half year tribulation that those left behind would have to endure. After this the thousand year millennium would bring the saints into control of the world before Satan returned to attempt a comeback. These teachings placed Seymour in the camp called "pre-millenialists" and "pre-tribulationists." The "post-millennialists" believed that the world would be gradually converted and that after the thousand years of peace Christ would return to set up his kingdom on a Christianized earth. Almost all of the early Pentecostals agreed with Seymour's theology of last things.

What made Seymour's theology different from that of

the evangelicals and Holiness teachers was that the "third-blessing" baptism in the Holy Spirit with tongues was now seen as necessary to qualify for the rapture. In Seymour's theology, the five foolish virgins represented the pure and sanctified saints, who like these virgins lacked enough oil in their lamps to meet the bridegroom. To Seymour, these were saved and sanctified, but not sealed by the Holy Spirit due to their lack of oil, a pervasive symbol of the Holy Spirit in Scripture. Therefore, those who had not been baptized in the Holy Spirit with the sign of speaking in tongues would not be qualified for the bridehood saints.

This view was given theological form in one of the earliest books defending Pentecostalism, *The Spirit and the Bride*, written by George Floyd Taylor in 1907. In his book, Taylor elaborated on the position that tongues were necessary to go up in the rapture. This became a widely accepted article of faith among most of the early Pentecostals. VS

BEHOLD THE BRIDEGROOM COMETH

Then shall the kingdom of heaven be likened unto ten virgins, which took their lamps, and went out to meet the bridegroom. And five of them were wise and five were foolish. They that were foolish took their lamps and took no oil with them; but the wise took oil in their vessels with their lamps.

"While the bridegroom tarried, they all slumbered and slept. And at midnight, there was a cry made, Behold the bridegroom cometh: go ye out to meet him.

"Then all those virgins arose and trimmed their lamps. And the foolish said unto the wise, Give us of your oil for our lamps are gone out. (Revised Version, "going out"). But the wise answered saying, Not so; lest there be not enough for us and you; but go ye rather to them that sell, and buy for yourselves.

"And while they went to buy the bridegroom came; and they that were ready went in with him to the marriage: and the door was shut. Afterward the other virgins came saying, Lord, Lord, open to us. But he answered and said, Verily I say unto you, I know you not. Watch therefore, for ye know neither the day nor the hour wherein the Son of Man cometh" (Matt. 25: 1-13).

You know "virgin" in the Scripture is a type of purity. Christ is speaking in this parable about the church and its condition at His coming. Many precious souls today are not looking for the return of their Lord, and they will be found in the same condition as the five foolish virgins. They started out to meet the bridegroom, and had some oil in their lamps but none in their vessels with their lamps. So when the cry was made to go forth, they were found wanting in oil, which is the real type of the Holy Ghost. Many of God's children are cleansed from sin and yet fight against getting more oil. They think they have enough. They have some of God's love in their souls, but they have not the double portion of it. The thing they need is oil in their vessels with their lamps. It is just as plain as can be.

Dearly beloved, the Scripture says, "Blessed are they which are called to the marriage supper of the Lamb: (Rev. 19:9). So they are blessed that have the call. Those that will be permitted to enter in are those who are justified, sanctified and baptized with the Holy Ghost—sealed unto the day of redemption. O may God stir up His waiting bride everywhere to get oil in their vessels with their lamps that they may enter into the marriage supper. The Holy Ghost is sifting out a people that are getting on the robes of righteousness and the seal in their foreheads. The angels are holding the winds now till all the children of God are sealed in their foreheads with the Father's name. Then the wrath of God is going to be poured out.

"Behold the Bridegroom cometh!" O the time is very near.

All the testimonies of His coming that have been going on for months are a witness that He is coming soon. But when the trumpet sounds, it will be too late to prepare. Those that are not ready at the rapture will have to go through the awful tribulation that is coming upon the earth. The wise virgins will be at the marriage supper and spend the time of the great tribulation with the Lord Jesus. They will have glorified bodies. For we which remain unto the coming of the Lord will be changed in the twinkling of an eye.

Many precious souls believe today that in justification they have it all, that they have already the baptism with the Holy Ghost or enduement of power; but in that day, they will find they are mistaken. They say, away with this third work. What is the difference, dear one, if it, takes 300 works? We want to be ready to meet the bridegroom. The foolish virgins said to the wise, "Give us of your oil." This thing is going to happen. Many that are saying they have enough and are opposing, will find their lamps going out and ask the prayers of God's people. God is warning you through His servants and handmaidens to get ready; but many are going to come back to get the oil from others. Dear ones, we cannot get more than enough for ourselves. You can grasp the saints' hands but you cannot squeeze any oil out. You have to get the vessel filled for yourself. Many are going to be marrying and giving in marriage, buying and selling, and the cares of this world are going to get in the way. Above all, we want to get the oil, the Holy Ghost. Every Christian must be baptized with the Holy Ghost for himself. Many poor souls in that day will be awfully disappointed. May we seek Him today, the baptism with the Holy Ghost and fire. Now is the time to buy the oil; that is, by tarrying at the feet of the Lord Jesus and receiving the baptism with the Holy Spirit.

It seems that people will be able to buy oil during the rapture. It seems that the Spirit will still be here on earth and that they could get it, but it will be too late for the marriage supper. So the Lord warns us to be ready, for we know not the day nor the hour.

Those that get left in the rapture and still prove faithful to God and do not receive the mark of the beast, though they will have to suffer martyrdom, will be raised to reign with Christ. Antichrist will reign during the tribulation and everything will be controlled by him and by the false prophet, when they have succeeded in uniting the whole world in acknowledging the Antichrist. Those that acknowledge him will be permitted to buy and sell, but those that stand faithful to the Lord Jesus and testify to the blood will be killed for the word of their testimony. But by proving faithful to death, they will be raised during the millennium and reign with Christ. But we that are caught up to the marriage supper of the Lamb will escape the plagues that are coming on the earth.

May God fit every one of us for the coming of the Lord, that we may come back with Him on white horses and help Him to execute judgment on the earth and make way for the millennial kingdom, when He shall reign from shore to shore, and righteousness shall cover the earth as waters cover the sea.

That is the time that Enoch prophesied of, "Behold the Lord cometh with ten thousand of His saints" (Jude 14). "Then shall the Lord go forth and fight against those nations, as when He fought in the day of battle. And His feet shall stand in that day upon the mount of Olives" (Zec. 14: 3, 4). The mountain shall be parted in two. Then shall the Antichrist and the false prophet be cast into the lake of fire and brimstone and Satan shall be bound a thousand years (Rev. 19, 20 and 22).

We shall be priests and kings unto God, reigning with Him a thousand years in a jubilee of peace. Our Christ will be King of kings and Lord of lords over the whole earth. We shall reign with Him over unglorified humanity. Some will be appointed over ten cities and some over two, and the twelve apostles will be over the twelve tribes of Israel. "To him, that overcometh will I grant to sit with me in My throne, even as I also overcame and am set down with my Father in His throne" (Rev. 3:21).

January, 1907

SEYMOUR'S THREE BLESSING THEOLOGY

In this article, Seymour again explains his doctrine of the three blessings as taught by his mentor Charles Parham, and the saints at Azusa Street. He explains what the first work was as taught by Martin Luther. It is at one and the same time justification and regeneration. After this, following John Wesley, comes the second blessing of sanctification which is "wrought in our hearts "by the power of the Blood and the Holy Ghost." The first two experiences, justification and sanctification, were works of grace that dealt with the question of sin, while the third work was a gift of the Spirit and not a work of grace.

This gift or "third blessing" was the baptism in the Holy Spirit with tongues, (although tongues were not mentioned), which qualified the recipient to go up in the rapture at the second coming of Christ. He ends the article with a Pentecostal style altar call: "O worship, get down on your knees and ask the Holy Ghost to come in, and you will find Him right at your heart's door, and He will come in. Prove Him now. Amen." VS

RECEIVE YE THE HOLY GHOST

The first step in seeking the baptism with the Holy Ghost, is to have a clear knowledge of the new birth in our souls, which is the first work of grace and brings everlasting life to our souls. "Therefore, being justified by faith, we have peace with God." Every one of us that repents of our sins and turns to the Lord Jesus with faith in Him, receives forgiveness of sins. Justification and regeneration are simultaneous. The pardoned sinner becomes a child of God in justification.

The next step for us, is to have a clear knowledge, by the Holy Spirit, of the second work of grace wrought in our hearts by the power of the blood and the Holy Ghost. "For by one offering, He hath perfected forever them that are sanctified, whereof the Holy Ghost also is a witness to us" (Heb. 10:14, 15). The Scripture also teaches, "For both He that sanctifieth and they who are sanctified are all of one; for which cause He is not ashamed to call them brethren" (Heb. 2:11). So we have Christ crowned and enthroned in our heart, "the tree of life." We have the brooks and streams of salvation flowing in our souls, but praise God, we can have the rivers. For the Lord Jesus says, "He that believeth on me as the Scripture hath said, out of his innermost being shall flow rivers of living water. This spake He of the Spirit, for the Holy Ghost was not yet given." But, praise our God, He is now given and being poured out upon all flesh. All races, nations and tongues are receiving the baptism with the Holy Ghost and fire, according to the prophecy of Joel.

When we have a clear knowledge of justification and sanctification, through the precious blood of Jesus Christ in our hearts, then we can be a recipient of the baptism with the Holy Ghost. Many people today are sanctified, cleansed from all sin and perfectly consecrated to God, but they have never = obeyed the Lord according to Acts 1, 4, 5, 8 and Luke 24: 39, for their real personal Pentecost, the enduement of power for service and work and for sealing unto the day of redemption. The baptism with the Holy Ghost is a free gift without repentance upon the sanctified, cleansed vessel. "Now He which stablisheth us with you in Christ, and hath anointed us, is God, who hath also sealed us, and given the earnest of the Spirit in our hearts" (2 Cor. 1:21-22). I praise our God for the sealing of the Holy Spirit unto the day of redemption.

Dearly beloved, the only people that will meet our Lord and Savior Jesus Christ and go with Him into the marriage supper of the Lamb, are the wise virgins—not only saved and sanctified, with pure and clean hearts, but having the baptism with the Holy Ghost. The others we find will not be prepared. They have some oil in their lamps but they have not the double portion of His Spirit.

Before Pentecost, the disciples were filled with the unction of the Holy Spirit that sustained them until they received the Holy Ghost baptism. Many People today are filled with joy and gladness, but they are far from the enduement of power. Sanctification brings rest and sweetness and quietness to our souls, for we are one with the Lord Jesus and are able to obey His precious Word, that "Man shall not live by bread alone but by every word that proceedeth out of the mouth of God," and we are feeding upon Christ.

But let us wait for the promise of the Father upon our souls, according to Jesus' Word, "John truly baptized with water, but ye shall receive the Holy Ghost not many days hence... Ye shall receive power after that the Holy Ghost is come upon you: and ye shall be witnesses unto me, both in Jerusalem and in all Judea, and in Samaria, and unto the uttermost part of the earth" (Acts 1:5, 8). Glory! Glory! Hallelujah! O worship, get down on your knees and ask the Holy Ghost to come in, and you will find Him right at your heart's door, and He will come in. Prove Him now. Amen

January, 1907

SEYMOUR SITUATES TONGUES AS A GIFT OF THE SPIRIT

The primary attraction at Azusa Street was the demonstration of speaking in other tongues. People came from many states and nations to hear this manifestation which had lain dormant in the church for so many centuries. Everything else at Azusa Street, i.e. salvation, sanctification, divine healing, and the second coming of Jesus were emphasized in the broader Holiness movement. The new thing was the actual sound of tongues speech and the doctrine that it was the "Bible evidence" of the baptism in the Holy Spirit.

Here, Seymour situates tongues as one of the gifts of the Spirit and answers his critics who said that at best tongues were the least of the gifts and at worst, were useless and confusing. As usual, Seymour uses Scripture to answer his critics. He agrees with Paul that prophecy is the most useful gift for the edification of the church, but he also says that tongues with interpretation is equal to prophecy. He warns against an over emphasis on tongues, but argues that the church accept the valid use of tongues in the life of the believer and the church.

He also makes an interesting point concerning how the use of tongues had changed at Azusa Street. In the beginning at Azusa Street tongues were spoken almost all the time, but as the church matured, he said that "we have learned to be quieter with the gift" especially during the preaching of the Word. VS

GIFTS OF THE SPIRIT

"Now concerning spiritual gifts brethren, I would not have you ignorant."

Paul was speaking to the Corinthian church at this time. They were like Christ's people everywhere today. Many of

His people do not know their privileges in this blessed gospel. The gospel of Christ is the power of God unto salvation to everyone that believeth. And in order that we might know His power, we must forever abide in the Word of God that we may have the precious fruits of the Spirit, and not only the fruits but the precious gifts that the Father has for His little ones.

Dearly beloved, may we search the Scriptures and see for ourselves whether we are measuring up to every word that proceedeth out of the mouth of God. If we will remain in the Scriptures and follow the blessed Holy Spirit all the way, we will be able to measure up to the Word of God in all of its fullness. Paul prayed in Eph. 3:16-20, "That He would grant you, according to the riches of His glory, to be strengthened with might by His Spirit in the inner man; that Christ may dwell in your hearts by faith; that ye being rooted and grounded in love, may be able to comprehend with all saints, what is the breadth, and length, and depth and height, and to know the love of Christ which passeth knowledge; that ye might be filled with all the fullness of God. Now unto Him that is able to do exceeding abundantly above all that we ask or think, according to the power that worketh in us."

Many people say today that tongues are the least gift of any that the Lord can give, and they do not need it, and ask what good is it to us? But by careful study of the Word, we see in the 14th chapter of Corinthians, Paul telling the church to "follow after charity and desire spiritual gifts." Charity means divine love without which we will never be able to enter heaven. Gifts all will fail, but divine love will last through all eternity. And right in the same verse he says, "Desire spiritual gifts, but rather that ye may prophecy," that is to say, preach in your own tongue, which will build up the saints and the church.

But he says in the next verse, "For he that speaketh in an unknown tongue, speaketh not unto men, but unto God, for no man understandeth him, howbeit in the Spirit, he speaketh mysteries, (R. V., 'hidden truth'). But he that prophesieth speaketh unto man to edification, exhortation and comfort." He that prophesies in his own tongue edifies the church: but he that speaks in unknown tongues edifies himself. His spirit is being edified, while the church is not edified, because they do not understand what he says unless the Lord gives somebody the interpretation of the tongues.

Here is where many stumble that have not this blessed gift to use in the Spirit. They say, "What good is it when you do not know what you are talking about?"

Praise God, every gift He gives is a good gift. It is very blessed, for when the Lord gets ready, He can speak in any language He chooses to speak. You ask, "Is not prophecy the best gift?" Prophecy is the best gift to the church, for it builds up the saints and edifies them and exalts them to higher things in the Lord Jesus. If a brother or sister is speaking in tongues and cannot speak any English, but preaches altogether in tongues and has no interpretation, they are less than he that prophesies, but if they interpret they are just as great.

May God help all of His precious people to read the 14th chapter of 1 Corinthians, and give them the real interpretation of the Word. May we all use our gift to the glory of God and not worship the gift. The Lord gives us power to use it to His own glory and honor.

Many times, when we were receiving this blessed Pentecost, we all used to break out in tongues; but we have learned to be quieter with the gift. Often when God sends a blessed wave upon us, we all may speak in tongues for awhile, but we will not keep it up while preaching service is going on, for we want to be obedient to the Word, that everything may be done decently and in order and without confusion. Amen.

January, 1907

SEYMOUR'S QUALIFICATIONS FOR THE BRIDEHOOD SAINTS

A major theme of the preaching and teaching at Azusa Street concerned the second coming of Christ and the qualifications to be ready for the soon expected rapture of the church. As usual, Seymour emphasized the necessity of being sanctified and living a holy life as well as being baptized in the Holy Spirit to be ready for the expected coming of Christ. Most of the messages in tongues and interpretations proclaimed the nearness of the rapture and called for the people to be prepared for the event. Azusa Street pilgrims preached on the theme so often that in England the Pentecostals were commonly called "the second comers."

In this article, Seymour depicts Rebecca as an Old Testament type of the bride of Christ, sanctified, purified and separated from the world. These people, like Rebecca were to be "holy and without blemish." To be qualified for the rapture they must have the Azusa Street testimony of being "saved, sanctified, and filled with the Holy Ghost." He ends by saying, "now we are living in the eventide of this dispensation, when the Holy Spirit is leading us, Christ's bride, to meet Him in the clouds." VS

REBECCA: TYPE OF THE BRIDE OF CHRIST

"I pray thee is there room in thy father's house for us to lodge in?" (Gen. 24). Those words were spoken by Eliezer, Abraham's eldest servant and steward of his house, to Rebecca when he had found her at the well in answer to his prayer. Eliezer (meaning "God's helper") is a type of the Holy Spirit, and Isaac is a type of Christ. Now as Eliezer was seeking a bride for Isaac, the son of Abraham, so the Holy Spirit today is seeking a bride for the Lord Jesus, God's only begotten Son.

Eliezer was sent to Abraham's country and to his kindred to take a wife for Isaac. So God our Father has sent the Holy Spirit from the glory land down into this world and He, the Spirit of Truth, is convicting the world of sin, righteousness and judgment, and is selecting out of the body of Christ His bride. He is seeking among His kindred, the sanctified, and Jesus is baptizing them with the Holy Ghost and fire, preparing them for the great marriage supper of the Lamb. Praise our God! Eliezer was under oath not to select the bride from the Canaanites, but from Abraham's kindred. So God is not selecting a bride for Christ among the sinners, for a sinner must first get saved and sanctified before he can be one with the Lord Jesus. Hebrews 2:11 says, "For both He that sanctifieth and they who are sanctified are all of one, for which cause He is not ashamed to call them brethren." So He is seeking a bride among His brethren, the sanctified.

"Christ so loved the church that He gave Himself for it; that He might sanctify and cleanse it with the washing of water by the Word; that He might present it unto Himself a glorious church, not having spot or wrinkle or any such thing: but that it should be holy and without blemish" (Eph. 5:25-27). So Jesus today is selecting a sanctified people, baptizing them with the Holy Ghost and fire to greet Him at His coming. Rebecca was a virgin, the type of a sanctified soul. So the Holy Ghost is standing at the heart of every pure virgin (sanctified soul) pleading, "I pray thee is there room in thy heart that I may come in and lodge?" O beloved, we see many of the sanctified people today rejecting the Holy Spirit, just as people rejected Christ when He was on earth here. It seems there is no room in their hearts for the baptism with the Holy Ghost and fire. May God help them to open their eyes and see that the time draweth nigh for His coming. O may Christ's waiting bride wake up and let the Holy Ghost come in.

Rebecca was a type of the wise virgins. When Eliezer met her at the well and asked her to let him drink a little water from her pitcher, O how sweet and ready she was. She answered and said, "Drink, my lord." And she hastened and let down her pitcher upon her hand and gave him drink, and it pleased him. The Spirit is a person. He can be pleased, He can be quenched and He can be insulted, as we find Ananias insulted Him. We please Him when we accept the words of Jesus. Then Jesus sends the Holy Spirit to witness in our hearts.

When Rebecca had done giving him drink, she said, "I will also draw water for thy camels." Christ's bride must do everything without murmuring. O how sweet it is when we have the mighty Spirit in our hearts; we are ready for service; we are ready for watering the whole entire world with the precious well of salvation in our heart. Beloved, when the Holy Ghost comes, He brings the well of salvation and rivers of living water.

"And it came to pass, as the camels had done drinking, that the man took a gold earring of half a shekel weight and two bracelets for her hands of ten shekels weight of gold." Praise God. This is what our beloved sanctified people receive when they receive the witness of the anointing of the Holy Ghost upon their hearts, as when Jesus breathed upon the disciples before Pentecost in the upper room, where He said, "Receive ye the Holy Ghost." The disciples had the witness in their hearts that very moment that "both He that sanctifieth and they who are sanctified are all of one." For He had opened the Scriptures to them, (Luke 24:32) and their understanding was opened, (Luke 24:45) and He had opened their eyes, "And their eyes were opened and they knew Him" (Luke 24:31). So with us, when we receive sanctification and the witness of the Spirit in our hearts to our sanctification, the Scriptures are opened to us, we understand them and our eyes are anointed. We see a picture of it in Rebecca. When she had received Eliezer and let him drink out of her pitcher which had watered the camels, he gave her the earrings and bracelets of gold. O beloved, may we let the Holy Ghost sup out of our heart pitcher, for the Lord says, "Behold I stand at the door and knock; if any man hear My voice and open the door, I will come in and sup with him and he with Me."

Rebecca wore her jewels. She did not put them aside, or into her pocket, for we read that Laban saw them on his sister's hands. When we have received the abiding anointing in our hearts, someone can always see it shining forth upon our faces. Praise God!

When Eliezer had fed the camels and come into the house, and when meat was set before him, he said, "I will not eat until I have told mine errand." O beloved, we should be so zealous about the bride of Christ that nothing will be able to turn us aside. We find the first overthrow in the human soul was through the appetite; and when the Holy Ghost sends us on His mission, may we not be satisfied until we have told it, and of His coming back to earth again.

Then he told his mission, how that Abraham had sent him to his kindred to take a wife for his son, and he said, "And now if ye will deal kindly and truly with my master, tell me, and if not, tell me." They said, "The thing proceedeth from the Lord" and gave Rebecca to be his master's wife. Where people are living under the guidance of God's Holy Spirit, it does not take them very long to hear the voice of God, and they are willing to obey. Praise God! Then Eliezer ate and tarried with them that night, because He had received the desire of his master's heart and his heart.

But on the morrow, her brother and mother said, "Let the damsel abide with us a few days, at least ten days." But he said, "Hinder me not." It is best, when we hear the words of God and the Spirit is upon us, to receive now the baptism with the

Holy Spirit, instead of waiting two or three days and meeting friends and meeting the devil, who will try to persuade us out of it. If Rebecca had remained, perhaps her friends might have talked her out of going with Eliezer over the plains away off to that distant land to her husband Isaac.

Eliezer said, "Hinder me not." O may we do nothing to hinder the entrance of the baptism with the Holy Ghost. We should see that everything is out of the way and nothing to stand between us and this glorious blessing. Then they called Rebecca and said to her, "Wilt thou go with this man?" And she said, "I will go." To receive the baptism with the Holy Ghost, we must forsake all and follow Jesus all the way. For the Lord Jesus says, "For this cause shall a man leave his father and mother, and cleave to his wife." So we that are Christ's bride must forsake all and cleave to Christ, as Rebecca left father and mother, brother and sister, and rode on the camel to meet Isaac.

"And Isaac went out to meditate in the fields at eventide; and he lifted up his eyes and saw, and behold the camels were coming. And Rebecca lifted up her eyes, and when she saw Isaac, she lighted off the camel" to meet him. Now we are living in the eventide of this dispensation, when the Holy Spirit is leading us, Christ's bride, to meet Him in the clouds.

Feb. – March, 1907

"GOD WILL THROW IN THE TONGUES"

Although Seymour seldom used Parham's phrase "Bible evidence" in reference to tongues, he clearly taught that tongues would accompany the Pentecostal baptism in the Holy Spirit. However, the experience of the Holy Spirit was always more important to Seymour than the tongues. As he said: "do not seek for tongues but for the promise of the Father, and pray for the baptism with the Holy Ghost, and God will throw in the tongues according to Acts 2:4." Also, probably more important to Seymour was the question of sanctification before the baptism in the Holy Spirit and speaking in tongues. As he often did, he warned the seekers "we are not seeking for tongues, but we are seeking the baptism with the Holy Ghost and fire." In other words, the experience of the Holy Spirit was more important than the evidence of tongues.

In this article, Seymour explains that tongues should not "puzzle" the speaker since he does not know what he is saying, but that the gift of interpretation would solve this problem. After receiving the baptism in the Holy Spirit, speaking in tongues "will come just as freely as the air we breathe." VS

THE BAPTISM WITH THE HOLY GHOST

Dear ones in Christ who are seeking the baptism with the Holy Ghost, do not seek for tongues but for the promise of the Father, and pray for the baptism with the Holy Ghost, and God will throw in the tongues according to Acts 2:4.

We read in Acts 1:4, 5, "And being assembled together with them, commanded them that they should not depart from Jerusalem, but wait for the promise of the Father, which, saith He, ye have heard of me. For John truly baptized with water; but ye shall be baptized with the Holy Ghost not many days hence."

This promise of the Father was preached unto the disciples by John the Baptist. And Jesus reminded the disciples about this baptism that John had preached to them in life. In England we find the same thing (Matt. 3:11). John, after warning the Jews and Pharisees against sin and hypocrisy, preached the doctrine of the baptism with the Holy Ghost. He said first,

"Bring forth therefore, fruits meet for repentance." God is sending out His precious ministers to preach repentance to the people and turn them from their sins and cause them to make restitution according to their ability, and to have faith in the Lord Jesus Christ and be saved. Glory to God!

And then they must get sanctified through the precious blood of Jesus Christ, for He says in John 17:14-19, "I pray not that Thou shouldest take them out of the world, but that Thou shouldest keep them from the evil. They are not of the world, even as I am not of the world, sanctify them through Thy truth: Thy Word is truth. As Thou hast sent Me into the world, even so have I also sent them into the world. And for their sakes I sanctify Myself, that they also might be sanctified through the truth." God wants His people to be sanctified, because He says again in Heb. 13:12, 13, "Wherefore Jesus also that He might sanctify the people with His own blood, suffered without the gate. Let us go forth therefore unto Him without the camp, bearing His reproach."

Then Jesus taught the disciples to tarry at Jerusalem. They obeyed Him and waited for the promise of the Father, "And when the day of Pentecost was fully come, they were all with one accord in one place. And suddenly there came a sound from heaven as of a rushing, mighty wind, and it filled all the house where they were sitting. And there appeared unto them cloven tongues like as of fire, and it sat upon each of them. And they were all filled with the Holy Ghost, and began to speak with other tongues, as the Spirit gave them utterance" (Acts 2:1-4).

Wind is always typical of the Spirit or of life. "And it filled all the house, where they were sitting." The rivers of salvation had come and had filled the whole place, and they all were immersed or baptized in the Holy Spirit. Praise God!

"And there appeared unto them cloven tongues like as of fire." Beloved, when we receive the baptism with the Holy

Ghost and fire, we surely will speak in tongues as the Spirit gives utterance. We are not seeking for tongues, but we are seeking the baptism with the Holy Ghost and fire. And when we receive it, we shall be so filled with the Holy Ghost, that He Himself will speak in the power of the Spirit.

"And they were all filled with the Holy Ghost, and began to speak with other tongues, as the Spirit gave them utterance." Now, beloved, do not be too concerned about your speaking in tongues, but let the Holy Ghost give you utterance, and it will come just as freely as the air we breathe. It is nothing worked up, but it comes from the heart. "With the heart man believeth unto righteousness; and with the mouth, confession is made unto salvation." So when the Holy Ghost life comes in, the mouth opens, through the power of the Spirit in the heart. Glory to God!

"There were, dwelling at Jerusalem, Jews, devout men, out of every nation under heaven. Now when this was noised abroad, the multitude came together, and were confounded, because that every man heard them speak in his own language. And they were all amazed and marveled, saying one to another, "Behold, are not all these which speak Galileans. And how hear we every man speak in our own tongue wherein, we were born?" (Acts 2:5-8).

Beloved, if you do not know the language that you speak, do not puzzle yourself about it, for the Lord did not promise us He would tell us what language we were speaking, but He promised us the interpretation of what we speak.

In seeking the baptism, first get a clear, definite witness in your soul that you have the abiding Christ within. Then there will be no trouble in receiving the Pentecostal baptism, through faith in our Lord and Savior, Jesus Christ, for it is a free gift that comes without repentance. Bless His holy name!

Feb. – March, 1907

SEYMOUR'S VIEW OF CHURCH GOVERNMENT

Seymour received from his mentor, Charles Fox Parham, a fear of autocratic church government. Parham taught that there should be no church organization, no hierarchy, and no offerings. In profound agreement with these views was Frank Bartleman the journalist who gave the world an eyewitness account of the Azusa Street revival in his 1925 book *How Pentecost Came to Los Angeles*. Yet, to have any ongoing ministry, a minimum of government was necessary to continue, regardless of ecclesiastical theories. Although Seymour was the legal pastor of the Azusa Street Mission and had a church board of Elders, he backed away from claiming leadership in the meetings. One man, William H. Durham, said that Seymour was "the meekest man I ever met." In a way, Seymour's humility led him to say that the Holy Spirit was the active head of the Azusa Street church.

In this article, Seymour proclaims a theocracy with the Holy Spirit as the "bishop of the church." In a way he was denying that Parham was the "Projector" or bishop of the movement as he acknowledged in the beginning of the Los Angeles meetings. Later in 1907, when Parham rejected Seymour's leadership and was put out of the church, total leadership devolved on Seymour who was now not only pastor of the local church, but the acknowledged leader of a new Pentecostal movement exploding worldwide without a formal organization.

In the ensuing years, Pentecostals proclaimed what Seymour was saying here, i.e that the Pentecostal Movement was a "movement without a man," saying that the Holy Ghost founded the movement. In other words, many Pentecostals did not wish to accord to either Parham or Seymour the honor of founding the movement with standing similar to that of a Luther, Calvin, or Wesley. Perhaps there was some racism in this claim since many new Pentecostals were uncomfortable acknowledging that a Black man was the founder of the movement. Also serious questions about Parham's lifestyle caused many to abandon his leadership.

In this article, Seymour also quotes a verse from the favorite hymn at Azusa Street, "The Comforter Has Come" which became a veritable international anthem for the new movement:

> Let every Christian tongue
> Proclaim the joyful sound,
> The Comforter has come!

VS

THE HOLY SPIRIT BISHOP OF THE CHURCH

It is the office work of the Holy Spirit to preside over the entire work of God on earth (John 10:3). Jesus was our Bishop while on earth, but now He has sent the Holy Ghost, amen, to take His place—not men (John 14:16; 15:26; 16:7-14). Praise His holy name!

The Holy Ghost is to infuse with divine power and to invest with heavenly authority. No religious assembly is legal without His presence and His transaction. We should recognize Him as the Teacher of Teachers.

The reason why there are so many of God's people without divine power today, without experimental salvation, wrought out in their hearts by the blood, by the power of the blessed Holy Spirit, is because they have not accepted Him as their Teacher, as their Leader, as their Comforter. Jesus said in His precious Word that if He went away He would send us another Comforter. The need of men and women today in their lives, is a Comforter. Praise our God! We have received this blessed Comforter, and it is heaven in our souls. We can wing with all our hearts:

"What matter where on earth we dwell
On mountain top, or in the dell,
In cottage or a mansion fair,
Where Jesus is, 'tis heaven there."

Bless His holy name! May God help every one of His blood bought children to receive this blessed Comforter. Glory to His name! Hallelujah! Hosanna to His omnipotent name! Oh, He is reigning in my soul! Hallelujah! I just feel like the song which says:

"Oh, spread the tidings round
Wherever man is found,
Wherever human hearts
And human woes abound,
Let every Christian tongue
Proclaim the joyful sound,
The Comforter has come!"

Many people today think we need new churches (that is to say church buildings), stone structures, brick structures, modern improvements, new choirs, trained singers right from the conservatories, paying from seven to fifteen hundred dollars a year for singing, fine pews, fine chandeliers, everything that could attract the human heart to win souls to the meeting house is used in this twentieth century. We find that they have reached the climax, but all of that has failed to bring divine power and salvation to precious souls. Sinners have gone to the meeting house, heard a nice, fine, eloquent oration on Jesus, or on some particular church, or on some noted man. The people have been made glad to go because they have seen great wealth, they have seen people in the very latest styles, in different costumes and loaded down with jewelry, decorated from head to foot with diamonds, gold and silver. The music in the church has been sweet, and it is found that a good many of the church people seem to be full of love, but there has always been a lack of power. We wonder why sinners are not being converted, and why it is that the church is always making improvements and failing to do the work that Christ called her to do. It is because men have taken the place of Christ and the Holy Spirit.

The church had the right idea that we need bishops and elders, but they must be given authority by our Lord and Savior Jesus Christ, and their qualifications for these offices must be the enduement of the power of the Holy Ghost. Jesus, after choosing His disciples, said in John 15:16, "You have not chosen me, but I have chosen you and ordained you that ye should go and bring forth fruit, and that your fruit should remain, that whatsoever ye shall ask of the Father, in my name, He may give it you." Praise our God! The Lord Jesus ordained His disciples with His own blessed hands, before going back to glory, but He put the credentials in their hearts on the day of Pentecost, when they were baptized with the Holy Ghost and fire. Hallelujah! This was the authority that made them His witnesses unto the uttermost parts of the earth, for without the blessed Holy Spirit, in all of His fullness we are not able to witness unto the uttermost parts of the earth. We must be coworkers with Him, Partakers of the Holy Ghost. Then, when He is in us, in all of His fullness, He will manifest Himself. Signs and miracles will follow. This is the office work of the Holy Spirit in the churches. Amen.

I pray God that all Christ's people and ministers everywhere will please stop by the headquarters, the Jerusalem before God, for their credentials. Then they are entitled to receive credentials from the visible church. But the main credential is to be baptized with the Holy Ghost. Instead of new preachers from the theological schools and academies, the same old preachers, baptized with the Holy Ghost and fire, the same old deacons, the same old plain church buildings will do. When the Holy Ghost comes in He will cleanse out dead forms and ceremonies, and will give life and power to His ministers and preachers, in the same old church buildings. But without the Holy Ghost they are simply tombstones.

We must always recognize that a meeting house is simply a place where Christ's people gather to worship, and not the church. The church is planted in our hearts, through the blood of Jesus Christ, for Christ said in Matthew 16:18, "Upon this rock will I build my church, and the gates of hell shall not prevail against it." We see, if these meeting houses and such buildings were really churches of Christ, the storms, cyclones and fire could not harm them; but we see them blown down by storms and burned down. But, through the precious blood of Christ, this church that He plants in our souls will stand throughout eternity.

The first thing in every assembly is to see that He, the Holy Ghost, is installed as the chairman. The reason why we have so many dried up missions and churches today, is because they have not the Holy Ghost as the chairman. They have some man in His place. Man is all right in his place, that is when he is filled with the power of the Holy Ghost, for it is not man that does the work, but the Holy Ghost from the glory land, sent by Jesus to work through this tabernacle of clay. Wherever you find the Holy Ghost as the chairman in any assembly, you will find a fruitful assembly, you will find children being born unto God.

Just as it takes a father and a mother to bring forth children of this natural life, so it takes the Word and the Spirit to bring forth children of the spiritual birth. There must be a father and there must be a mother. God chooses human instruments to preach the Word unto the people and the Holy Ghost gives birth to everyone who receives the Word of Christ, which means the new birth. Praise our God, the Lord will bring forth sons and daughters unto his administration.

Jesus Christ is the archbishop of these assemblies, and He must be recognized. Also we must recognize the Holy Spirit in all of His office work. He takes the members into the church, which is the body of Christ. Through repentance to God and faith in Jesus, they become the members of the church of Christ. And they remain members as long as they live free from sin. When they commence sinning, the Holy Ghost, the chairman and bishop, the presiding elder, turns them out, and they know when they are turned out of this church. They don't have to go and ask their pastor or their preacher, for they feel within their own soul that the glory has left them—the joy, the peace, the rest and comfort. Then when they feel the lack in their souls, if they will confess their sins God, the Holy Ghost, will accept them back into the church.

Oh, thank God for this holy way. I am so glad that sham battles are over. Men and women must live straight, holy, pure lives, free from sin, or else they have no part with Christ Jesus. When men and women are filled with the Holy Ghost, everywhere they go living waters will flow. The Lord promised that out of our being living rivers of water should flow. This is the Holy Ghost. Amen! The mighty Pison, the Gihon, the Hiddekel, the Euphrates of our soul will flow, representing the rivers of salvation. Amen.

September, 1907

"MARRIAGE IS FOR LIFE"

As a child of the Holiness Movement, Seymour adhered to the strictest views on divorce and remarriage. The common view of the time was that divorce was permitted if one spouse committed fornication, but remarriage was out of the question, even for the innocent party. The reasoning was that if a man divorced his wife and remarried another, he then had two living wives. The only way a divorced person could remarry was if the former wife died. Then he was free to remarry since he would then have only one living wife. Although the view applied to everyone, ministers were under special scrutiny in view of their high calling. This strict view was widely accepted in Victorian America at a time when divorce was practically unthinkable, especially for a sanctified Christian.

The result of this teaching played out in the lives of several leading Pentecostal pioneers. A well known case was that of Bishop Joseph H. King, a founder of the Pentecostal Holiness Church. After a few months of marriage his wife divorced him since she no longer wanted to be married "to a Holiness preacher," although King was still an ordained Methodist minister. He was 20 years old at the time. Accepting the principles stated by Seymour, King lived for the next 30 years as a celibate single man until he got news that his former wife had died. Then, at 50 years of age, he remarried and raised a family of four children. The story of Charles Mason, founder of the Church of God in Christ, was similar to that of King. After his wife divorced him, Mason refused to remarry until he knew that his wife had passed away. He also remarried and raised a family after living and ministering for many years as a single man.

Other Pentecostal leaders had even stricter views than those of Seymour. His assistant at Azusa Street, Florence Crawford, taught that one could not remarry even when the former spouse had died. This eventually led to a serious split in her church in Portland, Oregon. As one can imagine, the vexing problem of divorce and remarriage was destined to plague the Pentecostal churches for decades until most churches allowed the innocent party to remarry. VS

THE MARRIAGE TIE

Marriage is a divine institution which God Himself has instituted. "And the Lord God said, It is not good that man should be alone, I will make him an help meet for him. Therefore shall a man leave his father and his mother and shall cleave unto his wife; and they twain shall be one flesh" (Gen 2:18, 24). "Neither was the man created for the woman, but the woman for the man" (1 Cor. 11:9).

God commended it. "Whoso findeth a wife findeth a good thing, and obtaineth favour of the Lord" (Prov. 18:22; also see Gen. 2:18).

God is in it. "And He answered and said unto them, Have ye not read that He which made them at the beginning made them male and female. Wherefore they are no more twain but one flesh. What therefore God hath joined together, let not man put asunder" (Matt. 19:4, 6).

It is honorable in all. "Marriage is honorable in all and the bed undefiled, but whoremongers and adulterers God will judge" (Heb. 13:4).

Christ attended a wedding in Canaan. He went to adorn it, to beautify it with His presence. "And the third day there was a marriage in Cana of Galilee, and the mother of Jesus was there. And both Jesus was called and His disciples to the marriage" (John 2:1, 2).

The forbidding to marry is the doctrine of devil. "Now the Spirit speaketh expressly, that in the latter times some shall depart from the faith, giving heed to seducing spirits, and doctrines of devils; ... forbidding to marry" (1 Tim. 4:1, 3).

Marriage Binding for Life

God has approved of but one wife and one husband. "Therefore shall a man leave his father and his mother, and shall cleave unto his wife; and they twain shall be one flesh" (Gen. 2:24). "The Pharisees also came unto Him, tempting Him, and saying unto Him, Is it lawful for a man to put away his wife for every cause? And He answered and said unto them, Have ye not read, that He which made them at the beginning made them male and female, and said, For this cause shall a man leave father and mother, and shall cleave to his wife; and they twain shalt be one flesh? Wherefore they are no more twain but one flesh. What therefore God hath joined together, let not man put asunder" (Matt. 19:3-6).

The husband and wife are bound together for life. "For the woman which hath an husband is bound by the law to her husband so long as he liveth: but if the husband be dead, she is loosed from the law of her husband (Rom. 7:2). The wife is bound by the law as long as her husband liveth; but if her husband be dead, she is at liberty to be married to whom she will; only in the Lord" (1 Cor. 7:39).

No court of man should sever the marriage tie. "Wherefore they are no more twain, but one flesh. What therefore God hath joined together, let not man put asunder" (Matt. 19:6). Death alone severs the marriage tie (Heb. 13:4).

Moses' Law of Divorce

Under Moses' law, he suffered men to divorce their wives and marry again, because of the hardness of their hearts. "They say unto Him, Why did Moses then command to give a writing of divorcement, and to put her away? He saith unto them, Moses, because of the hardness of your hearts suffered you to put away your wives; but from the beginning it was not so" (Matt. 19:7, 8). Under Moses' law they had been accustomed, for any uncleanness, adultery, fornication or some cause not as much as that, to put away the wife by giving her a bill of divorcement, and she could go and be another man's wife. But under the New Testament law, the law of Christ, she is bound by the law to her husband til death.

The Edenic Standard of Matrimony

Jesus did away with the divorce law, and restored matrimony back to the Edenic standard. Under Moses' law, the sacredness of matrimony was lost through the hardness of hearts. But under the law of grace, it is restored back as in the beginning of grace. Praise God. God's promises are true and sure. Hallelujah! Amen.

Under the New Testament law, the law of Christ, there is but one reason why a man may put away his wife, but no right to marry again. This cause is fornication or adultery. "It hath been said, Whosoever shall put away his wife, let him give her a writing of divorcement; but I say unto you, That whosoever shall put away his wife, saving for the cause of fornication, causeth her to commit adultery; and whosoever shall marry her that is divorced committeth adultery" (Matt. 5:31, 32). "And I say unto you, Whosoever shall put away his wife, except it be for fornication, and shall marry another committeth adultery; and whosoever marrieth her which is put away doth commit adultery" (Matt. 19:9). These two scriptures are just the same in meaning. Matt. 5:31, 32 is the key to the whole subject. It settles the question.

Forbidden to Marry Again

After a man has lawfully put away his wife, or a wife has lawfully put away her husband, they are positively forbidden to marry again, under the New Testament law, until the former companion is dead. "And He saith unto them, whosoever shall put away his wife, and marry another, committeth adultery against her. And if a woman shall put away her husband, and be married to another, she committeth adultery" (Mark 10:11,

12). "Whosoever putteth away his wife and marrieth another, committeth adultery; and whosoever marrieth her that is put away from her husband committeth adultery" (Luke 16:18). "For the woman which hath an husband is bound by the law to her husband so long as he liveth; but if the husband be dead, she is loosed from the law of her husband. So then if, while her husband liveth, she be married to another man, she shall be called an adulteress; but if her husband be dead, she is free from that law; so that she is no adulteress, though she be married to another man" (Rom. 7:2, 3).

Adultery and Fornication

The act of adultery is between a married person and another who is not the lawful companion. Both parties may be married or only one. When only one is married, the act is called fornication. Jesus said, "Whosoever shall put away his wife, saving for the cause of fornication causeth her to commit adultery" (Matt. 19:9; 5:32). These sins are just the same, only one is committed while living with a husband and the other is when one has separated and married again.

No man can enter the kingdom of heaven without confessing and forsaking adultery and fornication. "Now the works of the flesh are manifest, which are these, adultery, fornication, uncleanness, lasciviousness, envyings, murders, drunkenness, revellings, and such like; of the which I tell you before, as I have also told you in time past, that they which do such things shall not inherit the kingdom of God" (Gal. 5:19, 21). "Let the wicked forsake his way, and the unrighteous man his thoughts; and let him return unto the Lord, and He will have mercy upon him; and to our God, for He will abundantly pardon" (Isa. 55:7).

The Innocent Party

If Jesus had intended that the innocent party should marry, He would have said so, and would not have said, Moses suffered it because of the hardness of your hearts. Jesus makes it very plain. If the innocent party marries, they are living in adultery. Jesus is showing the sacredness of matrimony. Dear beloved, let us obey God in spite of everything. There is one Scripture where many people are tied up. It is Matt. 19:9, where Jesus said, "But I say unto you that whosoever shall put away his wife, except for the cause of fornication, and shall marry another committeth adultery, and whosoever marrieth her that is put away committeth adultery." Now dear loved ones, let us stop and pray over this. "Except it be for fornication and marrieth another." Some think that this party would be entitled to marry again, but let us stop and see what Jesus is teaching here. If he puts away his wife except for the cause of fornication, he committeth a sin, because he will cause her to commit adultery. Therefore he is bound by the law as long as she lives, bound right to the Edenic standard. Amen.

Dear loved ones, if Jesus had instituted that the innocent party could get another wife, He would be instituting the same thing that was permitted by Moses, and would have the church filled with that today.

Now the reason Jesus gave him permission to put away his wife for the cause of fornication was that she is already adulterous, so her adultery gave him a lawful right to separate. While it gives him that right yet it does not give him the right to get another wife, while she lives.

Paul in 1 Tim. 3:2 says, "A bishop then must be blameless, the husband of one wife. He also says, "Let not a widow be taken into the number under three score years old, having been the wife of one man" (1 Tim. 5:9). This shows plainly that they recognized in the church that a man was to have one wife and a woman one husband.

After Light Has Come

Rom. 7:2, 3 and 1 Cor. 7:39 give us very clear light. O may God help us to accept Bible salvation, instead of having our opinion and losing our souls. Dear beloved, you that have two wives or two husbands, before you had light on it, you lived that way and had no condemnation. God did not condemn you until you received the light upon His Word on this subject; but now God holds you responsible for the light. If you continue in the old life after light has come upon you, then you will be in the sight of God an adulterer or an adulteress, and you are bound to lose your experience or substitute something in the place of what God hath wrought. "If we walk in the light, as He is in the light, we have fellowship one with another, and the blood of Jesus Christ His Son cleanseth us from all sin." Let us obey God's Word if it takes our right eye or right hand.

So we find under the New Testament there is no putting away the first wife and getting another. Death is the only thing that severs the marriage tie (Rom. 7:2 and 1 Cor. 7:39).

September, 1907

"GLORY TO HIS HOLY NAME"

It was common for early Pentecostals to punctuate their spoken sermons and testimonies with spontaneous phrases of praise. Often such praises were given as a shout. Just as Seymour might shout out praises in his sermons such as "hallelujah," "amen," "Praise God," or "glory," he often did the same in his written testimonies. In this short article, one can almost hear him shout out the phrases "Glory to His name!" and "Glory to His Holy name!" as he wrote the article. VS

TESTIMONY AND PRAISE TO GOD

O, I feel the coming of our Lord and Saviour Jesus Christ drawing nigh. Hallelujah! Glory to His name! I am so glad that the Lord is holding the winds until the angel has sealed all the saints of the living God in their foreheads, the baptism of the Holy Ghost. The Midnight cry will soon be made, when the morning and the night shall come. It will be morning in our souls, to those that are waiting for His coming; but the awful black night of Egypt will come upon all the world. May God help all of His precious waiting bride to be watching, waiting until our Lord shall come.

Oh, I am so thankful that I can work for my Christ and my God. The time is short when our blessed Jesus shall return to this earth, and snatch away His waiting bride. After six thousand years of toil and labor, we are going to have one thousand years of rest with our Lord and Saviour Jesus Christ. Glory to His holy name.

June to September, 1907

"TARRY UNTIL"

This article is one of the clearest statements of Seymour's Pentecostal theology. With thousands of people from all over the world flocking to Azusa Street to receive their personal Pentecostal experience with the expected evidence of speaking in tongues, Seymour was constantly explaining how to receive the experience. Here he begins with several favorite Scriptures to convince the seeker of the scriptural basis for his theology. As we have seen before, he teaches a three step process. First is justification by faith, the second, sanctification, and the third the baptism in the Holy Spirit with the accompaniment of tongues.

Here he also explains the early Pentecostal practice of "tarrying" for the Holy Ghost. The large upstairs prayer room was the place reserved for tarrying after one had proved downstairs that he was justified and sanctified. Only then could he go to the "upper room" to pray for the Holy Spirit, usually surrounded by altar workers who helped him "pray through" to the Pentecostal blessing. VS

TO ONE SEEKING THE HOLY GHOST

Dear Beloved in Christ Jesus:

The Lord Jesus has said in His precious Word, "Blessed are they which do hunger and thirst after righteousness, for they shall be filled" (Matthew 5:6). God's promises are true and sure. We can rest upon His promises. He says, "Blessed are the pure in heart, for they shall see God" (Matthew 5:8). "Blessed are the poor in spirit, for theirs is the kingdom of heaven" (Matthew 5:3).

The Lord Jesus is always ready to fill the hungry, thirsty soul, for He said in His precious Word, "He that believeth on Me, as the scripture hath said, out of his innermost being shall flow rivers of living water (but this spake He of the Spirit, which they that believe on Him should receive: for the Holy Ghost was not yet given; because that Jesus was not yet glorified)" (John 7:38, 39). But, Praise God, He is given to us today.

All we have to do is to obey the first chapter of Acts, and wait for the promise of the Father upon our souls. The Lord Jesus said in His precious Word, "Behold I send the promise of My Father upon you; but tarry ye in the city of Jerusalem, until ye be endued with power from on high" (Luke 24:45). "For John truly baptized with water; but ye shall be baptized with the Holy Ghost not many days hence... Ye shall receive power after that the Holy Ghost is come upon you; and ye shall be witnesses unto Me both in Jerusalem, and in all Judea, and in Samaria, and unto the uttermost part of the earth" (Acts 1:5,8). They tarried until they received the almighty power of the baptism with the Holy Spirit upon their souls. Then God put the credentials in their hearts, and put the ring of authority on their finger, and sealed them in the forehead with the Father's name, and wrote on their heart the name of the New Jerusalem, and put in their hand the stone with the name written that no man knoweth save he that receiveth it. Praise the Lord, for His mercy endureth forever. Let us stand upon His promises. They are sure, they will not break.

The Lord Jesus says, "Behold I give you power to tread on serpents and scorpions; and over all the power of the enemy; and nothing shall by any means hurt you" (Luke 10:19). Dear loved one, the Lord Jesus when He rose from the dead, said, "All power is given unto Me in heaven and earth. Go ye therefore, and teach all nations, baptizing them in the name of the Father, and of the Son and of the Holy Ghost" (Matthew 28:18, 19). "He that believeth and is baptized shall be saved; but he that believeth not shall be damned. And these signs shall follow them that believe; in My name shall they cast out devils; they shall speak with new tongues; they shall take up serpents; and if they drink any deadly thing, it shall not hurt them; they shall lay hands on the sick and they shall recover" (Mark 16:16-18). And they went forth and preached everywhere, the Lord working with them, and confirming the Word with signs following. Praise His dear name, for He is just the same today.

The first thing in order to receive this precious and wonderful baptism with the Holy Spirit, we want to have a clear knowledge of justification by faith according to the Bible. Romans 5:1, "Therefore being justified by faith, we have peace with God through our Lord Jesus Christ," faith that all our actual sins may be washed away. Actual sin means committed sin.

And then the second step is to have a real knowledge of sanctification, which frees us from original sin—the sin that we were born with, which we inherited from our father Adam. We were not responsible for that sin until we received light, for we could not repent of a sin that we did not commit. When we came to the Lord as a sinner, we repented to God of our actual sins, and God for Christ's sake pardoned us and washed our sin and pollution away, and planted eternal life in our souls. Afterwards we saw in the Word of God, "This is the will of God, even your sanctification" (1 Thessalonians 4:3, also John 17:15-19). We consecrated ourselves to God, and the Lord Jesus sanctified our souls, and made us every whit clean.

Then after we were clearly sanctified, we prayed to God for the baptism with the Holy Spirit. So He sent the Holy Spirit to our hearts and filled us with His blessed Spirit, and He gave us the Bible evidence, according to the 2nd chapter of Acts verses 1 to 4, speaking with other tongues as the Spirit gives utterance.

Praise our God, He is the same yesterday, today and forever, Receive Him just now and He will fill you. Amen. Don't be discouraged but pray until you are filled, for the Lord says, "Men ought always to pray and not to faint." Don't stop because you do not receive the baptism with the Holy Ghost at the first, but continue until you are filled. The Lord Jesus told His disciples to tarry until they were endued with power from on high. Many people today are willing to tarry just so long, and then they give up and fail to receive their personal Pentecost that would measure with the Bible. The Lord Jesus says, "Ye shall be filled." He says to the person that hungers and thirsts after righteousness, and He says they are blessed.

So if there is a hunger and thirst in our souls for righteousness, we are blest of Him. Praise His dear Name!

September, 1907.

A SINCERE PASTORAL LETTER

This article seems to come straight from the Pastor's heart to his flock, the Azusa Street congregation. Although the Holy Spirit was highly emphasized at Azusa Street, the meetings constantly centered on Jesus. Unlike most Protestants who usually referred to Jesus as "Christ," Seymour and most Pentecostals to this day prefer to use the more personal word "Jesus." In fact, in later years Pentecostals were sometimes called the "Jesus Movement." Again he repeats the classic Azusa Street testimony, "a live minister represents one that is saved, sanctified and filled with the Holy Spirit."

As did most Pentecostals, Seymour looks at the seven churches of Asia Minor and locates the Twentieth Century church with the Laodicean Church "when the church has become as formal as the Laodiceans." Here he warns against impure doctrine and the sins of fornication and adultery as well as "backbiting, whispering, tattling or prejudice and partiality." This is a great example of Seymour's pastor's heart warning against losing the pristine Pentecostal "fire and Power" that fired the movement from the beginning. VS

CHRIST'S MESSAGES TO THE CHURCH

The last message given to the church was by the Holy Ghost, from our Lord and Saviour Jesus Christ through Brother John on the Isle of Patmos. Dear beloved, we read these words in Revelation 1:5-7, "Unto Him that loved us and washed us from our sins in His own blood." Hallelujah to His name. "And hath made us kings and priests unto God and His Father: to Him be glory and dominion for ever and ever. Amen. Behold, He cometh with clouds; and every eye shall see Him, and they also which pierced Him; and all kindreds of the earth shall wail because of Him. Even so. Amen."

This is the beginning of this wonderful and blessed message given to our beloved Apostle John while he was suffering for the Word of God and for the testimony of Jesus Christ. Jesus knew all about His servant, though He had been living in heaven more than half a century after His ascension. And He came and visited that beloved apostle, the disciple who loved Jesus and leaned on His bosom. He now was old but had been faithful to the trust that Jesus had given him. He had passed through awful trials and tribulations for this precious gospel, even being boiled in a caldron of oil, tradition tells us; but, blessed be God they were not able to kill him. And when they got tired of this precious Holy Ghost gospel messenger, preaching to them the faith of Jesus, they banished him to the Isle of Patmos. And while he was in the Spirit on the Lord's day, our blessed Jesus Christ, the Son of the living God, our great Redeemer, came and gave him this wonderful revelation, and introduced Himself to John as, "I am Alpha and Omega, the beginning and the ending, said the Lord, which is, and which was, and which is to come, the Almighty." Hallelujah.

O beloved, the Lord Jesus knows all about our trials and tribulations, because He was a man of sorrows and acquainted with grief. His whole life was a life of suffering. We read in Heb. 5:8, 9. "Though He were a Son, yet learned He obedience by the things which He suffered. And being made perfect, He became the author of eternal salvation unto all them that obey." O bless our God. Just to think that Jesus was God's Son, and all things were made by Him and for Him; yet He was foreordained before the foundation of the world that He should die. He was slain before the foundation of the world. So the Word of God became flesh and dwelt among men and was handled by men and lived in this world. And at the age of 33 years, He paid the debt on Calvary's cross. O beloved, if we expect to reign with Him, we must suffer with Him—not that people must be sick or unhealthy or go with a long face, but we must bear all things and keep the faith of Jesus in our hearts. Our lives now are with the suffering Christ; and "it doth not yet appear what we shall be, but we know that when He shall appear, we shall be like Him; for we shall see Him as He is." Glory to Jesus.

After Jesus introduced Himself, He gave John these blessed messages to the church, John was permitted to see from the beginning of the church age on down to the white throne judgment, the final winding up of the world. He was permitted to see the overcomers. He was permitted to see the millennial reign with Jesus in triumph over the kingdoms of Satan; to see this old world pass away, to see the new heavens and new earth, and the New Jerusalem coming down from God out of heaven. John saw things past, things present and in the future. He had witnessed the glory and power of the apostolic church, saw the falling away of the church, and God sent him to the church with this blessed message: that she should come back to her first love.

The Vision of Jesus in His Church

The most striking passage of Scripture in the first chapter is where John was permitted to see Jesus walking among the golden candlesticks, which represent the church. Christ is in His church today to fill men and women, to heal their bodies, save and sanctify their souls, and to put His finger upon every wrong and mean thing in the church. His rebuke is against it, for He hates sin today as much as He ever did when He walked on the Sea of Galilee. Glory to His name. Jesus hates impure doctrine just as much as when He rebuked the Pharisees for their impure doctrine.

John beheld Jesus in His glorified body. What a holy scene it was: the Son of God clothed with a garment down to the foot and girt about the paps with a golden girdle. "His head and His hairs were white like wool, as white as snow." Hallelujah. There is nothing but purity and holiness in our Saviour. And "His eyes were as a flame of fire." Glory to Jesus. "And His feet like to fine brass, as if they burned in a furnace. And His voice as the sound of many waters" which represents many people. Bless God.

"And He had in His right hand seven stars." This represents His Holy Ghost ministers. Jesus has them in His hand, that is to say that He gave them the authority to preach the gospel and power over devils. All of our authority and power comes from Jesus. It is so sweet when we know that we have authority from Jesus. Bless His holy name. O beloved, when we know Jesus Christ has His minister in His hand, we know that minister is a live preacher. Glory to Jesus. Hallelujah. A live minister represents one that is saved, sanctified and filled with the Holy Spirit. Then the same life, the same authority that Jesus promised we will find in his life.

"And out of His mouth went a sharp two-edged sword, and His countenance was as the sun shineth in his strength," the glory of God shining through the blessed Christ. "And when I saw Him, I fell at His feet as one dead. And He laid His right hand upon me, saying unto me, Fear not; I am the first and the last." Praise God, Jesus is alive and because He lives everyone that gets Christ is alive in the blessed Holy Spirit. The blood of Jesus Christ does give life, power and fire, joy, peace, happiness and faith. Hallelujah to His name.

"I am He that liveth and was dead, and behold, I am alive

for evermore." Bless His holy name. He wanted John to know that He was the same one that hung and bled and died and shed His precious blood on Calvary's cross, went down into the grave, and rose again. This ought to make the whole body of Christ's people everywhere happy to know that Jesus is alive for evermore. Hallelujah to His name.

Then He said, "And have the keys of hell and of death." Bless God. No wonder Brother David said, "Though I walk through the valley of the shadow of death, I will fear no evil, for Thou art with me." When we get Jesus Christ in our hearts, we can use the Word and it is a comfort to us to know that we have passed from death to life.

Then He told John particularly, "Write these things which thou hast seen, and the things which are and the things which shall be hereafter."

The Message to the Church of Ephesus

Then He gave him the messages to the seven churches. "And to the angel of the church at Ephesus write, These things saith He that holdeth the seven stars in His right hand who walketh in the midst of the seven golden candlesticks." Hallelujah to His name. Ephesus was a city of Asia, quite a commercial city, a city of wealth, refinement, culture and great learning. It was where John preached and where Paul had labored. Many people there had been saved and baptized with the Spirit. Paul had witnessed a great scene in Ephesus where He had preached the gospel of the Son of God and of the doctrine of the baptism with the Holy Spirit, and 12 men after hearing of this blessed doctrine, received water baptism, and when Paul laid his hands on them, they received the baptism with the Holy Ghost and spake with tongues and prophesied (Acts 19:6). So Ephesus was a favored place, but the message was sent to it and to all the churches of Asia. This is a true picture of the Lord Jesus; eyes upon the church ever since its beginning, and will be unto the end. We are living near the close of the Gentile age down in the Laodicean period, when the church has become as formal as the Laodiceans. This message was first to the church of Ephesus.

I Know Thy Works

The Lord Jesus said, "I know thy works." God knows our works, He knows our hearts. "And thy labor and thy patience, and how thou canst not bear them which are evil; and thou has tried them which say they are apostles, and are not, and hast found them liars; and hast borne and hast patience, and for My name's sake hast labored and hast not fainted." Bless our God. That is more than many churches today could receive from the Master. Jesus commended them for what they had done. He commended them for their faithfulness. He is not like men. He knows our hearts, our trials, our conditions. But bless God, He does not make any allowance for sin. He hates sin today as much as He ever did. Yet He does not come to destroy us or condemn us, but to seek and to save us.

"Nevertheless I have somewhat against thee, because thou hast left thy first love." The Lord does not want anything to get between us and Him. I pray every precious child in these times that are getting the Holy Spirit not go into apostasy, but may they be a burning and a shining light for God, just as we were when we first received the baptism with the Holy Spirit. God wants us to keep the same anointing that we received and let nothing separate us from Christ.

Repentance

We find Jesus still preaches the same doctrine of repentance that He preached while on earth. In order to get right with God, He says, "Remember from whence thou art fallen and repent and do the first works, or else I will come unto thee quickly, and will remove thy candlestick out of his place, except thou repent." Dear beloved, if there is anything wrong in your life and Jesus has His finger upon it, O may you give it up, for Jesus is truly in His church today. This is the Holy Ghost dispensation and He does convince men of sin, righteousness and the judgment, and if we will be honest, God will bless us.

To the Church Today

When a church or mission finds that the power of God begins to leave, they should come as a whole and confess, and let all get down before God and repent and pray to God until the old time fire and power and love come back again. Many times the Holy Spirit will leave an assembly, mission or church because the pastor grieves Him and sometimes not only the pastor but the whole body commences backbiting, whispering, tattling or prejudice and partiality creep in, until the whole becomes corrupted and Jesus is just ready to spew them out of His mouth. But O beloved, let us then come to the 2nd chapter of Revelation and see what Jesus says to the assembly. He expects to find the church, when He comes back to earth again, just as full of fire and power and the signs following, as it was when He organized it on the day of Pentecost. Bless His holy name. May God help all His precious praying children to get back to the old Pentecostal power and fire and love. The church at that time was as terrible as an army with banners. She conquered every power of evil. Hypocrites were not able to remain in it any more than Ananias and Sapphira. God gave such wonderful love to His people.

Then He gave messages to every church, showing that Jesus' eyes are upon every church. His finger this day is upon every heart that does not measure to the fullness of holiness. God wants a holy church and all wrong cleansed away—

fornication and adultery, two wives, two husbands, not paying grocery bills, water bill, furniture bills, coal bills, gas bills and all honest bills. God wants His people to be true and holy and He will work. Nothing can hinder. Bless His holy name.

I thank God for this wonderful message to the church, a message from heaven, given by Jesus to show that He is in the church, that He does walk among the golden candlesticks. He is in heaven, but through the power of the Holy Spirit, He walks in the church today. Nothing can be hidden from His pure eyes. He wants people to live the highest and deepest consecration to Him. He does not want their love for Him divided. Their first love is to Him.

Impure Doctrine

We find many of Christ's people tangled up in these days, committing spiritual fornication as well as physical fornication and adultery. They say, "Let us all come together; if we are not one in doctrine, we can be one in spirit." But, dear ones, we cannot all be one, except through the Word of God. He says, "But this thou hast, that thou hatest the deeds of the Nicolaitans, which I also hate." I suppose that the apostolic church at Ephesus allowed people that were not teaching straight doctrine, not solid in the Word of God, to remain in fellowship with them; and Jesus saw that a little leaven would leaven the whole, and His finger was right upon that impure doctrine. It had to be removed out of the church or He would remove the light and break the church up. When we find things wrong, contrary to Scripture, I care not how dear it is, it must be removed. We cannot bring Agag among the children of Israel, for God says He must die. Saul saved Agag, which represented saving himself, and the carnal nature or old man; but Samuel said Agag must die, and he drew his sword and slew him. Christ's precious Word, which is the sword of

Samuel, puts all carnality and sin to death. It means perfect obedience to walk with the Lord. There are many people in these last days that are not going to live a Bible salvation, they are going to take chances. But may God help everyone, if their right hand or right eye offend them to cast it from them. It is better to enter into life maimed, than for soul and body to be cast into hell fire.

The Lord says, "He that hath an ear let him hear what the Spirit saith unto the churches; To him that overcometh will I give to eat of the tree of life which is in the midst of the paradise of God." O beloved, if we expect to reign with the Lord and Saviour Jesus Christ, we must overcome the world, the flesh, and the devil. There will be many that will be saved but will not be full overcomers to reign on this earth with our Lord. He will give us power to overcome if we are willing. Bless His holy name.

October to January, 1908

"I HAVE BEEN ASKED SO MUCH ON THIS QUESTION"

Seymour wrote this article in response to many questions his members asked about marriage in the light of the soon expected second coming of Christ. In this case, Seymour writes out of painful experience. In the early days of the revival, the pastor was attracted to a young African American lady by the name of Jenny Moore. At the same time, there were rumors that a white woman who worked at the mission, Clara Lum, wanted to marry Seymour, which was practically unthinkable at the time. It is said that Seymour sought the counsel of C.H. Mason, founder of the Church of God in Christ, about the advisability of the marriage. When Mason strongly discouraged it, Seymour turned back to Jenny Moore and proposed marriage to her. This greatly upset some of the other leaders of the mission, including Florence Crawford, a very strong proponent of the sanctification experience. Their advice to Seymour was that time was so short before the return of Jesus that he had no time to marry. Despite this flurry of opposition, Seymour and Moore married and lived very happily thereafter.

Seymour preached this sermon, on which this article was based, a few of months before his marriage to Jennie Evans Moore on May 13, 1908. The marriage was considered controversial by some who left the Los Angeles mission after the marriage took place.

This article in part justifies the Seymour and Jenny Moore marriage on biblical grounds against some of the more legalistic holiness views of the time. One of the strictest teachings was called "marital purity" which forbade sex in marriage except for procreation, with regular checkups by church authorities to enforce the rule. Seymour, who hated divorce and remarriage, nevertheless had a healthy view of sex in marriage. VS

To the Married:
1 Corinthians 7

In these days, so many deceptive spirits are in the world, that we have felt impressed by the blessed Holy Spirit to write a letter on the seventh chapter of First Corinthians, that blessed letter which Paul has sent to the church.

The Corinthian church was one of Paul's most gifted churches, and just as it is today, where a church is very gifted, the only safeguard from deceptive spirits is by rightly dividing the Word of God, to keep out fanaticism. We may let down on some lines and rise on others, but God wants everything to be balanced by the Word of God. Paul writing to Timothy says, "Hold fast the form of sound words, which thou hast heard of me, in faith and love which is in Christ Jesus. That good thing which was committed unto thee keep by the Holy Ghost which dwelleth in us" (2 Tim. 1:13, 14). And again He says, "But continue thou in the things which thou hast learned and hast been assured of, knowing of whom thou hast learned them; and that from a child thou hast known the holy Scriptures, which are able to make thee wise unto salvation through faith which is in Christ Jesus. All Scripture is given by inspiration of God, and is profitable for doctrine, for reproof, for correction, for instruction in righteousness: that the man of God may be perfect, thoroughly furnished unto all good works" (2 Tim. 3:15-17). So the Lord God wants us to search and compare Scriptures with Scriptures.

This Corinthian church had run into free loveism [sic], and a good many isms. Great division had arisen in it; it had split into several parts, and Paul had to settle them down into the Word of God. He writes this letter to them, for they had got into awful trouble.

Paul tells them in the first verse of this chapter to avoid immorality. He says, "Now concerning the things whereof ye wrote unto me, it is good for a man not to touch a woman" (He does not mean a married man here, he means a man that is single, as verses 8 and 26 show). He says in the 7th verse, "Every man hath his proper gift of God." And to those that can receive this gift, Paul writes in verse 8, "I say therefore to the unmarried and widows, it is good for them if they abide even as I." That is to say, by living a single life, they would have more power in the Spirit. He writes this to the church, to any who are saved, sanctified and filled with the Holy Spirit. Paul thought it was best, but he showed that everyone had his proper gift of God. So he did not put any bondage upon the people of Christ, because he had no Scripture for it.

He says in the second and third verses, "Nevertheless, to

avoid fornication, let every man have his own wife, and every woman have her own husband. Let the husband renc unto the wife due benevolence: and likewise also the w unto the husband." This of course means conjugal intercou between man and wife. "The wife hath not power of her o body, but the husband: and likewise also the husband h not power of his own body, but the wife." That is to say, t the husband has no authority to live separated, without consent of his wife; and the wife has no authority to her to live separated without the husband. Then he says in the verse, "Defraud ye not one another, except it be with con for a time, that ye may give yourselves to fasting and pra and come together again, that Satan tempt you not for y incontinency." That is to say that every wife and husb should abstain from impurity, and give themselves to fas for a time. It should be by mutual agreement between two to fast for power and blessing, and many times to a impurity. But he advised them to come again, "that S tempt you not for your incontinency." Paul here does make this a law, but as one that had the Holy Spirit, he them this advice. He adds in the 6th verse, "But I speak th permission and not of commandment." In Romans 1:2(Paul shows there is a natural use for a wife, which is not Speaking of the ungodly, he says, "For this cause God them up unto vile affections: for even their women did ch the natural use into that which is against nature." May help us to be clear teachers of His Word.

"I would that all men were even as I myself. But man has his proper gift of God, one after this manne another after that. Paul is referring here to Matthew where Jesus told the Pharisees that there were some me were born eunuchs from their mother's womb (that is t unable to have wives), some have been made eunuchs o (for other advantages in life) and there were some eunuc

the kingdom of heaven's sake. Men had prayed to God for this gift or blessing, just as Paul who said he wished all men were like him: he became no doubt a eunuch for the kingdom of heaven's sake. Jesus Himself said, "All men cannot receive this saying, save they to whom it is given" (Matt. 19:11). So Jesus did not put any bondage on men and women, but a man today that has received the power to become a eunuch for the kingdom of heaven's sake can live a single life with all holiness and purity. Praise our God!

We must rightly divide the Scriptures and compare Scripture with Scripture so that there be no confusion and no deceptive spirit or wrong teaching may creep in. Paul says in verses 29 to 31, "But this I say brethren, the time is short: it remaineth that both they that have wives be as though they had none; and they that weep as though they wept not; and they that rejoice as though they rejoiced not; and they that buy as though they possessed not; and they that use the world as not abusing it: for the fashion of this world passeth away." Bless the Lord! Now Paul in speaking this, did not put any bondage on mothers to fear that they would not be able to meet Jesus in His coming, because they were bringing forth children. Mothers and fathers that are saved and sanctified to whom the Lord has given this gift of bringing forth children can live a pure and holy life before God and be of the bride of Christ, just as the bishop that teaches this holy gospel can be the husband of one wife and raise his children in the fear of God.

Married couples who are mutually agreed, having received from the Lord power over both body, soul and spirit, God does not ask them to desire, but may they live as God has called them. Many times God gives this power to the husband before to the wife. Many times the wife has it; but in order to save the husband she has to submit to the husband. For God is not the author of confusion. This brings us back to the

third verse of this same chapter. Also in Ephesians 5th chapter and 22nd verse, we read, "Wives, submit yourselves unto your own husbands, as unto the Lord." Please read on down to the 33rd verse. God does not make the husband the tyrant or cruel sovereign over the wife, neither does He make the wife to exercise tyranny over the husband, but He makes both one. God knows our hearts and our lives.

Someone may ask what Jesus meant in Matt. 24:19, "And woe unto them that are with child, and to them that give suck in those days." Well, beloved, here Jesus' heart was upon the people that would suffer in the awful tribulation that was coming to Jerusalem forty years after His ascension. He says to them, "But pray ye that your flight be not in the winter, neither on the Sabbath day." Jesus was the Son of God but He was a man of prayer. He asked His disciples to pray with Him in the Garden of Gethsemane. He knew that in the destruction of Jerusalem, if they prayed to God, the Father would not permit it to come to pass in the winter, neither on the Sabbath day. He knew if it was on the Sabbath day, the Jews would be keeping the old Mosaic law, "Of new moons and of Sabbath days, which are a shadow of things to come, but the body is of Christ" (Col. 2:16) (The greatest thing that people need in this day is Christ, and then all the days will come in their order and in their place). Jesus knew if their flight occurred on the Sabbath day, all the gates of Jerusalem would be shut and the Christians could not get out, and the mothers could not escape; so His heart went out for the precious women. The Lord Jesus Christ knows all about our struggles. He knows all about our sufferings and our trials. He is touched with every infirmity and He remembers us. Bless His holy name.

May God help everyone that is getting saved to stay within the lids of God's Word and wait on God, and He will make all things right. Now we can give up anything that we see is really of self-gratification. The Lord wants us to be temperate in all things. Bless His holy name. People that are desiring to get the victory over spirit, soul and body, can have it if they will trust God.

I have been asked so much on this question, and I can only give what God has revealed to me through His precious Word. Bless His holy name!

January, 1908

"HOLINESS OR HELL"

There was never any doubt that Seymour was totally Wesleyan in his doctrine of Sanctification. Here he uses a phrase that was popular with many Holiness preachers of the day, "holiness or hell." By the beginning of the Azusa Street revival in 1906, there were two emerging views on second blessing sanctification, one the radical view of "eradication" of the sin nature and the other the "suppression" of the sin nature. Eradicationists used the phrase "crucifixion of the old man" to say that the sin nature was removed "root and branch" at sanctification. This became the view of the most radical Holiness teachers at the turn of the century. As a member of the "Evening Light Saints," this was the view that Seymour held for life.

The other view was that sin was controlled and suppressed but not completely removed, these more moderate Holiness advocates came to be known as "suppressionists." In time, this became the basic view of the Keswick "Higher Life" movement after 1875. In time the Pentecostal Movement divided over this question, but for Seymour and his Azusa Street Mission, it was "holiness or hell." VS

SANCTIFIED ON THE CROSS

"I pray not that Thou shouldest take them out of the world, but that Thou shouldest keep them from the evil. They are not of the world even as I am not of the world. Sanctify they through Thy truth, Thy word is truth." Jesus is still praying this prayer today for every believer to come and be sanctified. Glory to God! Sanctification makes us one with the Lord Jesus (Heb. 2:11). Sanctification makes us holy as Jesus is. Then the prayer of Jesus is answered, and we become one with Him, even as He is one with the Father. Bless His holy name.

He says again in 1 Thess. 4:3, "For this is the will of God even your sanctification." So it is His will for every soul to be saved from all sin, actual and original. We get our actual sins cleansed away through the blood of Jesus Christ at the cross, but our original sin we got cleansed on the cross. It must be a real death to the old man. Romans 6:6, 7, "Knowing this that our old man is crucified with Him, that the body of sin might be destroyed, that henceforth we should not serve sin: for he that is dead is freed from sin." So it takes the death of the old man in order that Christ might be sanctified in us. It is not sufficient to have the old man stunned or knocked down, for he will rise again.

God is calling His people to true holiness in these days. We thank God for the blessed light that He is giving us. He says in 2 Tim. 2:21, "If a man therefore purge himself from these, he shall be a vessel unto honor, sanctified and meet for the Master's use." He means for us to be purged from uncleanness and all kinds of sin. Then we shall be a vessel unto honor, sanctified and meet for the Master's use, and prepared unto every good work. Sanctification makes us holy and destroys the breed of sin, the love of sin and carnality. It makes us pure and whiter than snow. Bless His holy name!

The Lord Jesus says, "Blessed are the pure in heart."

Sanctification makes us pure in heart. Any man that is saved and sanctified can feel the fire burning in his heart, when he calls on the name of Jesus. O may God help men and women everywhere to lead a holy life, free from sin, for the Holy Spirit seeks to lead you out of sin into the marvelous light of the Son of God.

The Word says, "Follow peace with all men and holiness without which no man shall see the Lord." So, beloved, when we get Jesus Christ our King of Peace in our hearts, we have the almighty Christ, the everlasting Father, the Prince of Peace. "Thou wilt keep him in perfect peace whose mind is stayed on Thee, because He trusteth in Thee." We shall have wisdom, righteousness and power for God is righteous in all His ways and holy in all His acts. This holiness means perfect love in our hearts, perfect love that casteth out fear.

Brother Paul says in order to become holy and live a holy life, we should abstain from all appearance of evil. Then the apostle adds, "And the very God of peace sanctify you wholly, and I pray God your whole spirit and soul and body be preserved blameless unto the coming of our Lord Jesus Christ" (1 Thess. 5:23). "To the end He may establish your hearts unblameable in holiness before God, even our father, at the coming of our Lord Jesus Christ with all His saints" (1Thess. 3:13). Bless His holy name. O beloved, after you have received the light, it is holiness or hell. God is calling for men and women in these days that will live a holy life free from sin. We should remain before God until His all cleansing blood makes us holy—body, soul and spirit.

May, 1908

"GOD CAN TAKE A WORM AND THRESH A MOUNTAIN"

Without question, the central attraction at Azusa Street was the baptism in the Holy Spirit with evidence of speaking in tongues. But other major doctrines were also emphasized, such as justification by faith, entire sanctification, divine healing, and the second coming of Jesus. There was also an implicit understanding of the Trinity as seen in this article when he stated "He needed the Third Person of the Trinity to do His work."

In this article, Seymour uses several phrases that were very popular in his theology. These include "the latter Rain," "the sanctified life," and "the Comforter has come." The latter one was the title of the favorite hymn at Azusa Street, "O spread the tidings around wherever man is found, the Comforter has come." With this kind of Spirit-filled people, Seymour declared that "God can take a worm and thresh a mountain."

Indeed. God and his little flock at Azusa Street were becoming a tremendous force in world Christianity. Those who the world considered "worms" were now "threshing the mountain" in the worldwide outpouring of the Holy Spirit that came forth from Azusa Street. VS

THE BAPTISM OF THE HOLY GHOST

The Azusa standard of the baptism with the Holy Ghost is according to the Bible in Acts 1:5, 8; Acts 2:4 and Luke 24:49. Bless His holy name. Hallelujah to the Lamb for the baptism of the Holy Ghost and fire and speaking in tongues as the Spirit gives utterance.

Jesus gave the church at Pentecost the greatest lesson of how to carry on a revival, and it would be well for every church to follow Jesus' standard of the baptism of the Holy Ghost and fire.

"And when the day of Pentecost was fully come, they were all with one accord, in one place." O beloved, there is where the secret is: one accord, one place, one heart, one soul, one mind, one prayer. If God can get a people anywhere in one accord and in one place, of one heart mind and soul, believing for this great power, it will fall and Pentecostal results will follow. Glory to God!

Apostolic Faith doctrine means one accord, one soul, one heart. May God help every child of His to live in Jesus' prayer, "That they all may be one, as Thou, Father, art in Me and I in Thee; that all may be one in us; that the world may believe that Thou hast sent Me." Praise God. O how my heart cries out to God in these days that He would make every child of His see the necessity of living in the 17th chapter of John, that we may be one in the body of Christ, as Jesus has prayed.

When we are sanctified through the truth, then we are one in Christ, and we can get into one accord for the gift or power of the Holy Ghost, and God will come in like a rushing mighty wind and fill every heart with the power of the Holy Spirit. Glory to His holy name. Bless God! O how I praise Him for this wonderful salvation that is spreading over this great earth. The baptism of the Holy Ghost brings the glory of God to our hearts.

The Holy Ghost Is Power

There is a great difference between a sanctified person and one that is baptized with the Holy Ghost and fire. A sanctified person is cleansed and filled with divine love, but the one that is baptized with the Holy Ghost has the power of God on his soul and has power with God and men, power over all the kingdoms of Satan and over all his emissaries. God can take a worm and thresh a mountain. Glory to God. Hallelujah!

In all Jesus' great revivals and miracles, the work was wrought by the power of the Holy Ghost flowing through His sanctified humanity. When the Holy Ghost comes and takes us as His instruments, this is the power that convicts men and women and causes them to see that there is a reality in serving Jesus Christ. O beloved, we ought to thank God that He has made us the tabernacles of the Holy Ghost. When you have the Holy Ghost, you have an empire, a power within yourself. Elijah was a power in himself through the Holy Ghost. He brought down fire from heaven. So when we get the power of the Holy Ghost, we will see the heavens open and the Holy Ghost power falling on earth, power over sickness, diseases and death.

The Lord never revoked the commission He gave, to His disciples, "Heal the sick, cleanse the lepers, raise the dead," and He is going to perform these things if He can get a people in unity. The Holy Spirit is power with God and man. You have power with God as Elijah had. God put man over all His works; but we know that when Adam sinned, he lost a great deal of his power; but now through the blood of Jesus, He says, "Behold, I give you power to tread on serpents and scorpions, and over all the powers of the enemy." The Lord Jesus wants a church when He comes back to praise Him for this wonderful salvation that is spreading over this great earth. The baptism of the Holy Ghost brings the glory of God to our hearts.

Tarry in One Accord

O may every child of God seek his real personal Pentecost, stop quibbling and come to the standard that Jesus laid down for us in Acts 2, "And suddenly there came a sound from heaven as a rushing mighty wind, and it filled all the house where they were sitting." Glory to God! O beloved, if you wait on God for this baptism of the Holy Ghost just now, and can get two or three people together that are sanctified through the blood of Christ, and all get into one accord, God will send the baptism of the Holy Ghost upon your souls as the rain falls from heaven. You may not have a preacher to come to you and preach the doctrine of the Holy Ghost and fire, but you can obey Jesus' saying in the passage, "Where two or three are gathered together in My name, there am I in the midst of them." This is Jesus' baptism; and if two or three are gathered together in His name and pray for the baptism of the Holy Ghost, they can have it this day or this night, because it is the promise of the Father. Glory to God!

This was the Spirit that filled the house as a rushing mighty wind. The Holy Ghost is typified by wind, air, breath, life, fire. "And there appeared unto them cloven tongues like as of fire, and it sat upon each of them and they were all filled with the Holy Ghost and began to speak with other tongues as the Spirit gave them utterance." So, beloved, when you get your personal Pentecost, the signs will follow in speaking with tongues as the Spirit gives utterance. This is true. Wait on God and you will find it a truth in your own life. God's promises are true and sure.

The Baptism Falls on a Clean Heart

Jesus is our example. "And Jesus being full of the Holy Ghost, returned from Jordan, and was led by the Spirit." We find in reading the Bible that the baptism with the Holy Ghost and fire falls on a clean sanctified life, for we see according to the Scriptures that Jesus was "holy, harmless, undefiled," and filled with wisdom and favor with God and man, before God anointed Him with the Holy Ghost and power. For in Luke 2:40, we read, "Jesus waxed strong in spirit, filled with wisdom, and the grace of God was upon Him;" and in Luke 2:52, "And Jesus increased in wisdom and stature, and in favor with God and man."

After Jesus was empowered with the Holy Ghost at Jordan, He returned in the power of the Spirit into Galilee, and there went out a fame of Him through all the region round about. Glory to God! He was not any more holy or any more meek, but had greater authority. "He taught in their synagogues, being glorified of all."

Beloved, if Jesus who was God Himself, needed the Holy Ghost to empower Him for His ministry and His miracles, how much more do we children need the Holy Ghost baptism today? O that men and women would tarry for the baptism with the Holy Ghost and fire upon their souls, that the glory may be seen upon them just as it was upon the disciples of the day of Pentecost in the fiery emblem of tongues. The tongues of fire represented the great Shekinah glory. So today the Shekinah glory rests day and night upon those who are baptized with the Holy Ghost, while He abides in their souls. For His presence is with us. Glory to His name. I thank Him for this wonderful salvation. Let us sing His praises through all the world that all men may know that the Comforter has come. Bless His dear name!

Jesus' First Sermon After His Baptism

"And He came to Nazareth where He was brought up; and as His custom was, He went into the synagogue on the Sabbath day and stood up for to read. And there was delivered unto Him the book of the prophet Esias. And when He had opened the book, He found the place where it is written," The Spirit of the Lord is upon Me because He hath anointed Me to preach the gospel to the poor; He hath sent Me to heal the brokenhearted, to preach deliverance to the captives, and recovering of sight to the blind, to set at liberty them that are bruised, to preach the acceptable year of the Lord" (Luke 4:18, 19). Hallelujah. Glory to God! This is Jesus' sermon after His baptism with the Holy Ghost, preaching in the synagogue. He acknowledged that the Spirit of God was upon Him.

Jesus was the Son of God and born of the Holy Ghost and filled with the Holy Ghost from His mother's womb; but the baptism of the Holy Ghost came upon His sanctified humanity at the Jordan. In His humanity, He needed the Third Person of the Trinity to do His work. And He could truly say that His fingers became instruments of the Holy Ghost to cast out devils.

The Holy Ghost Flows Through Pure Channels

If men and women today will consecrate themselves to God, and get their hands and feet and eyes and affections, body and soul, all sanctified, how the Holy Ghost will use such people. He will find pure channels to flow through, sanctified avenues for His power. People will be saved, sanctified, healed and baptized with the Holy Ghost and fire.

The baptism of the Holy Ghost comes through our Lord and Savior Jesus Christ by faith in His Word. In order to receive it, we must first be sanctified. Then we can become His witnesses unto the uttermost parts of the earth. You will never have an experience to measure with Acts 2:4 and 16, 17, until you get your personal Pentecost or the baptism with the Holy Ghost and fire (Matt. 3:11).

This is the latter rain that God is pouring out upon His humble children in the last days. We are preaching a gospel that measures with the great commission that Jesus gave His disciples on the day when He arose from the dead. "Go ye therefore and teach all nations, baptizing them in the name of the Father, and of the Son, and of the Holy Ghost: teaching them to observe all things whatsoever I have commanded you: and lo, I am with you always, even unto the end of the world. Amen! (Matt. 28:19, 20). They received the power to measure with this commission on the day of Pentecost (Acts 2:4). Bless the Lord. O how I bless God to see His mighty power manifested in these last days. God wants His people to receive the baptism with the Holy Ghost and fire.

May, 1908

"THEY HAVE THE SPIRIT OF PENTECOST"

Early Pentecostals were fired by the belief that Jesus might come and rapture the church at any moment. The most important thing for them was to be filled with the Spirit and get as many people saved before the end. Many, including Seymour, believed that the baptism in the Holy Spirit with tongues was the "seal" of the bridehood saints. In other words, only those who spoke in tongues would be prepared to go up in the rapture. "Every man and woman that receives the baptism of the Holy Ghost is the bride of Christ" according to Seymour.

Of course, Seymour makes the point that that bride must also be sanctified, "pure and spotless." These pure and Spirit filled ones will have "a missionary spirit for saving souls." Indeed, the Pentecostal power that emanated from Azusa Street sparked one of the most powerful missionary movements in history of the Church as Azusa "pilgrims" went all over the world shouting the message that "the Comforter has come" to snatch away a holy and spotless Bride for Christ. VS

THE HOLY GHOST AND THE BRIDE

We read in Revelation 22:17, "The Spirit and the bride say come." O how sweet it is for us to have this blessed privilege of being a coworker with the Holy Ghost. He inspires us with faith in God's Word and endues us with power for service for the Master. Bless His dear name!

Every man and woman that receives the baptism of the Holy Ghost is the bride of Christ. They have a missionary spirit for saving souls. They have the spirit of Pentecost. Glory to God!

"And let him that heareth say, come; and let him that is athirst, come, and whosoever will, let him take the water of life freely." O what a blessed text. The bride of Christ is calling the thirsty to come to Jesus, because this is the work of the Holy Ghost in the believer. He intercedes for the lost; He groans for them.

The Spirit also calls the believer to come to Jesus and get sanctified. He points the sanctified to Jesus for his baptism with the Holy Ghost. When you are baptized with the Holy Ghost, you will have power to call sinners to Jesus, and they will be saved, and sanctified, and baptized with the Holy Ghost and fire. Amen!

Christ's bride is pure and spotless. "Thou art all fair, my love," clean, free from sin and all impurity. He gave Himself for her, that He might sanctify and cleanse the church with the washing of water by the Word. That He might present it to Himself a glorious church, not having spot or wrinkle or any such thing, but that it should be holy and without blemish (Eph. 5:25,27).

Christ's bride has but one husband (2 Cor. 11:2). She is subject to Him (Eph. 5:25). The Bridegroom is the Son of God (2 Cor. 11:2).

We are married to Christ now in the Spirit (Rom. 7:2, 4).

Not only when He comes are we married to Christ but right now, if you are sanctified and baptized with the Holy Ghost and fire, you are married to Him already. God has a people to measure up to the Bible standard in this great salvation. Bless His holy name. Amen!

May, 1908

SECTION TWO

PART B

SEYMOUR'S

Doctrines and Discipline

by

Vinson Synan

Seymour's *Doctrines and Discipline*

After the glory days of Azusa Street from 1906 to 1909, the Azusa Street Mission fell on hard times as scores of Pentecostal congregations were formed in the Los Angeles area and all over the nation and the world. After 1909, Seymour and the mission lost touch with their followers and supporters because of the loss of the *Apostolic Faith* mailing list to Florence Crawford and Clara Lum, who moved the paper to Portland, Oregon. In addition to this, more than one preacher, mostly white ministers, came and tried to take over the mission from Seymour because of the vast and storied revival that had taken place there. One of these, William H. Durham from Chicago, held a mighty revival in the mission in 1911 that once again filled the mission with excited worshippers. Although he spoke in tongues at Azusa in 1907, Durham came with his new "finished work" theology, which denied the second blessing of sanctification. Since he was so committed to the holiness experience, Seymour returned to Azusa Street and locked Durham out.

Although the Mission continued to be world famous, fewer people came to attend the regular services. In time, the mission was reduced to the original Black members who had followed Seymour from the Bonnie Brae meetings in 1906. It became essentially a small Black independent Pentecostal congregation led by Pastor Seymour and his wife, Jenny, who served as his assistant. When he died in 1922, she became the pastor and served until the mission was closed after her death; it was later demolished in 1938 after foreclosure due to unpaid taxes.

Even though Seymour was ignored by most Pentecostals after 1909, he continued to travel and preach around the nation. On these trips, especially in Virginia and Ohio, he organized congregations that wanted to join his organization. Although they were few in number, Seymour saw the need of publishing a book containing the doctrines, bylaws, forms, and ceremonies for his new denomination. In 1915, he published the guide book, which he named *The Doctrines and Discipline of the Apostolic Faith Mission of Los Angeles, California.* He added the city and state at the end of the name to distinguish it from Charles Parham's Apostolic Faith Movement headquartered in Baxter Springs, Kansas, and Florence Crawford's Apostolic Faith movement in Portland, Oregon. Seymour published many signed sermons in the *Apostolic Faith* magazine, but this was the only book he ever published.

Although major parts of the *Doctrines and Discipline* were copied from a *Discipline* of the African Methodist Episcopal Church, many parts were written by Seymour to establish the doctrines, identity, and constitution of his own church. The preface is Seymour's apologetic for publishing the book and explains that people who chose speaking in tongues alone as the evidence of the baptism in the Holy Ghost were sadly mistaken. In fact he called "initial evidence" teaching, "an open door for witches and spiritualists and free loveism [sic]." Although he recognized the validity of tongues as one of the evidences of the baptism in the Holy Spirit, he saw holiness and the sanctified life as the greatest evidences of having received the Pentecostal experience.

The Apostolic Address

In the opening section of his book, Seymour gives a short history and explanation of why he was organizing a new denomination. Though he always opened his heart and church to people of all races and ethnicities, he was troubled by many white preachers who brought division, confusion, and at times "wildfire and fanaticism" to his flock. Two prominent whites who attempted to take over the leadership from Seymour were no less than Charles Parham, his former mentor, and William H. Durham, his most outstanding follower. With apologies, he explained that whites could not be "directors" of the corporation and the racial separation that became necessary was only "for peace," and not because of racism. Henceforth only "people of color" would be qualified to head the church.

Here he also names things that he considered contrary to "sound doctrine." They included "artificial dancing," "soul sleep," the "Jesus only" doctrine, the seventh day Sabbath, and the "holy kiss." He sternly opposed the "annihilation of the wicked" doctrine (also known as "soul sleep" that was so dear to the heart of his former mentor Charles Parham.

Minutes of Incorporation

These are the necessary minutes of the meeting of the trustees on May 19, 1914, who drew up the legal documents to incorporate the Apostolic Faith Mission of Los Angeles, California, as a non-profit corporation.

The Constitution of the Apostolic Faith Mission

The constitution was adopted in order to fulfill the laws of California for a non-profit organization. It was meant to serve as a legal umbrella or covering for any churches that joined Seymour's organization. Items of interest are that Seymour and his wife were the sole trustees "for life" with power to "expel or suspend any member for any misconduct or violation of the scriptures." The presiding officer was the

Bishop (Seymour) and his successors who "shall be a colored person thoroughly converted and sanctified." There was no requirement that the bishop had spoken in tongues as was true with most Pentecostal denominations at the time. Other trustees and officers were also listed.

By requiring that the leaders be people of color, Seymour joined in the movement of racial segregation that was becoming standard among Pentecostals despite the statement of Frank Bartleman that at Azusa Street "the 'color line' was washed away in the Blood." It is remarkable that Seymour wrote his Constitution only one month after the organization of the Assemblies of God, which occurred in April of 1914 in Hot Springs, Arkansas. The organization of the Assemblies of God partly represented a racial separation when about 300 White ministers that had received credentials from the Church of God in Christ, a predominately Black church led by Charles Harrison Mason, joined in forming the new church. Indeed, racial separations continued to occur so much so that by 1924, almost the entire American denominational Pentecostal churches were segregated along racial lines.

Doctrinal Statement

The doctrinal statement begins as a copy of the statement of faith that appeared in each issue of *The Apostolic Faith* published by Seymour at Azusa Street from 1906 to 1909. In the *Doctrines and Discipline*, Seymour expands the prior statement by vastly expanding the section on entire sanctification and adding a section on "Amended Articles of the Doctrines." Most of the "Articles of Faith" are taken whole cloth from the classic 25 articles of faith that John Wesley published for his Methodist societies in 1784. These were revised from the 39 Articles of the Church of England that were adopted in

1563 after the Anglicans separated from the Roman Catholic Church.

After the "Articles of Faith" section, Seymour added several pages of 25 questions and answers on doctrinal issues, including speaking in tongues. In summary, Seymour rejected the idea that tongues was the only "Bible evidence" of the Baptism in the Holy Spirit, but he continued to see it as a valid "sign" of receiving the Pentecostal experience. To him, if one did not exhibit the fruit of the Spirit in living a sanctified and holy life, tongues would then become a "sounding brass and a tinkling cymbal." His total view on tongues can be summarized in his often published statement in the *Apostolic Faith*: "The Baptism with the Holy Ghost is a gift of power upon the sanctified life; so when we get it we have the same evidence as the Disciples received on the Day of Pentecost (Acts 2:3, 4), in speaking in new tongues."

The *Doctrinal Statement* shows that Seymour remained a Trinitarian, that he accepted three "ordinances", i.e. water baptism, the Lord's supper, and feet washing. He rejected infant baptism, antinomianism, and Calvinism, as well as the annihilation of the wicked. In effect, he continued to be a Wesleyan-Arminian perfectionist with the added dimension of Pentecostalism.

Marriage and the Family

This rather large section shows the high priority that Seymour placed on a Christian home, family life, and the sacredness of the marriage vows. Throughout his life he opposed marriage after divorce. One could only remarry after the death of the first spouse.

Forms and Church Ceremonies

The last major part of the *Doctrines and Discipline* contains forms and ceremonies that could be used by his ministers. These include ceremonies for weddings, funerals, ordination, and feet washing. With the exception of feet washing, most of these were standard forms used by the Methodists and other churches at the time.

Summary

In reading the *Doctrines and Discipline,* modern scholars are puzzled by two things. Seymour's later views on tongues rejecting "initial evidence" and his rule that only people of color could lead the church in the future. Perhaps his denial of tongues as evidence was influenced by the many cases of moral failure where one might claim tongues as a continuing evidence of being Spirit-filled despite a life that indicated the opposite. It seems that he saw evidential value of tongues at the time of the baptism in the Holy Spirit, but not as evidence of continuing to be filled. After all, speaking in tongues was the great attraction at Azusa Street. One can see the way many of those who spoke in tongues disappointed Seymour over the years.

The fact that Seymour stipulated that only people of color could head his newly organized denomination seems to contradict his openness to all peoples and races during the glory days at Azusa Street. Perhaps this was caused by the several attempts by white ministers to wrest control of the mission in the years after 1909. The fact that Florence Crawford, Clara Lum, and William H. Durham were white may have been a major influence in his thinking. Also other white ministers tried unsuccessfully to take over the mission in later years. This might have added to Seymour's fear of a white takeover of the mission.

In his last years, Seymour was increasingly ignored by the new Pentecostal leaders, most of whom founded their own denominations, both Black and White. Many Blacks joined the Church of God in Christ under Bishop C.H. Mason, an Azusa Street recipient. Others joined the Church of God in Cleveland, Tennessee, under the leadership of A.J. Tomlinson and the Pentecostal Holiness Church under J.H. King. Later, multitudes joined the Assemblies of God after 1914, and others joined the Oneness churches, the Pentecostal Assemblies of the World, and the United Pentecostal Church. The *Doctrines and Discipline*, therefore, was used by the very few churches that Seymour organized in his travels after 1909. These congregations were located mostly in California, Virginia, and Ohio.

But the influence of Seymour and Azusa Street had already become legendary in the religious world. Although Pentecostal theology was established by Seymour's mentor, Charles Fox Parham, in Topeka, Kansas, in 1901, the Azusa Street revival established the Pentecostal movement as a worldwide phenomenon with over 600 million followers by 2006, a century after the revival began in Los Angeles.

Today, Seymour is recognized worldwide, not only as the founder of a small Black Holiness-Pentecostal church, but as the father of global Pentecostalism. Yet the *Doctrines and Discipline* gives future generations a glimpse of his mature theology as well as his views on church government.

A Note for Researchers

The book *Doctrines and Discipline* has been reproduced exactly as the very rare original 1915 edition. It has been a labor of love for my wife Carol and me to keep the same pagination, fonts, and page divisions as in the original.

There were so many typographical errors that we decided not to add the Latin word *sic* after each one as is usually done, they would have greatly distracted from the material. For historical accuracy we wanted the writing to be just as it appeared in the original.

The pagination at the top of each page is the same as in the original edition so that researcher's footnotes will match the original page numbers for the purpose of citations.

The following is the entire *Doctrines and Discipline of the Azusa Street Apostolic Faith Mission* exactly as it was published by William J. Seymour in 1915.

Vinson Synan
December, 2011

THE DOCTRINES
AND
DISCIPLINE

OF THE

AZUSA STREET APOSTOLIC FAITH MISSION

Of Los Angeles, Cal.

1915

WITH SCRIPTURE READINGS

BY

W. J. SEYMOUR

ITS FOUNDER AND GENERAL OVERSEER

Corrected Index

May none of us be like Ahab, to rob our brother of their vineyard. I King 21:14-20.

Be sure your sin will find you out. Numbers 32:23.

Judas's sin found him. Cain's sin found him.

PREFACE

Thy testimonies are very sure: holiness becometh thy house, Lord, forever. Psa. 93:5. God's church is Holy. Holiness is her only ornament Isa. 23:18. And her merchandise and her hire shall be Holiness to the Lord: it shall not be treasured nor laid up: for her merchandise shall be for them that dwell before the Lord to eat sufficiently and have durable clothing. Bless his name, salvation lies in the Blood of Jesus. He says, "Abide in me and I in you. The same will bring forth much fruits. If you love me, keep my commandments" Jn. 15. That is, abide in his word and if we abide in his word we are under the Blood and it cleanses us from all sin. Bless God forever. Amen! Sanctification means holiness. Holiness means purity. To be pure means to be sanctified. There is no life sweeter than Holiness unto the Lord, for he is holy and therefore commands us to be holy. We must keep holy unto the Lord. This work must stand for everything that is in the word of God. The power of the Holy Ghost (Acts 2:1-4; Acts 10:44-48; Acts 19:1-6.). Ye shall know the truth and the truth shall make you free. St. John 8:31-32.

We take members in our church on probation, but not unconverted persons. They must know God and have a desire to go on to perfection. Heb. 6:1-4.

Wherever the doctrine of the Baptism in the Holy Spirit will only being known as the evidence of speaking in tongues, that work will be an open door for witches and spiritualists, and free loveism. That work will suffer, because all kinds of spirits can come in. The word of God is given to Holy men and women, not to devils. God's word will stand forever. 1 Pet. 1:22-23.

When we leave the word of God and begin to go by signs and voices we will wind up in Spiritualism. God's word is God's law. The Holy Spirit came to give us power to stand on the infallible word and overcome these false spirits.

I know since God has given me strength to write these rules we will understand each other better, trusting so by the good Lord.

After much work, God has enabled me to put forth this book with the rule and Doctrine of our church. Many things put in this little book have done me good by studying them. I hope in the name of the Lord it may do all the readers of our work good.

W.J. SEYMOUR

CHAPTER 1.

Propositions and Statements.

Prop. 1. The Bible is a Divine Revelation given of God to men, and is a complete and infallible guide and standard of authority in all matters of religion and morals; whatever it teaches is to be believed, and whatever it commands is to be obeyed; whatever it commends is to be accepted as both right and useful; whatever it condemns is to be avoided as both wrong and hurtful; but what it neither commands nor teaches is not to be imposed on the conscience as of religious obligation.

Prop. 2. The New Testament is the constitution of Christianity, the charter of the Christian Church, the only authoritative code of ecclesiastical law, and the warrant and justification of all Christian institutions. In it alone is life and immortality brought to light, the way of escape from wrath revealed, and all things necessary to salvation made plain; while its messages are a gospel of peace on earth and of hope to a lost world.

We must take the Bible as the infallible word of God. Luke 24:25-31; Luke 24:44-45; John 5:39.

Prop. 3. None but regenerated persons ought to be, or properly can be, members of a Christian Church, which is a spiritual body separate from the world and distinct from the state, and to be composed of spiritual members only.

Prop. 4. Christ is the only Head over, and Lawgiver to, His church. Consequently the church cannot make laws, but only execute those which He has given. Nor can any man, or body of men, legislate for the church. The New Testament alone is their statute book, by which, without change, the body of Christ is to govern itself.

THE NEW BIRTH.

St. John 3:5-6. Rom. 8:7, 8; Tit. 3:5; Salvation comes through the blood of Jesus Christ. When we get it, we will know it, and if we lose it we will know it. There is only one way to get it: It is by repenting and believing the gospel. St. Mark 1:15.

Salvation is not feeling; it is a real knowledge by the Holy Spirit, bearing witness with our spirit. Rom. 8:14-16. Jesus said to Pontius Pilate, when Pilate asked him if he then was a King. Since Jesus had told him that he had a Kingdom, but His kingdom was not of this world, so Pilate believed if he was a King then he had a Kingdom.

Jesus told him his Kingdom was not of this world. He said, "if my Kingdom was of this world then would my servants fight, that I should not be delivered to the Jews; but now is my Kingdom not from hence." Pilate asked Him about His Kingdom and Kingship, so he confessed he was a King over his people in the Holy Spirit, for he said: "To this end was I born, and that I should bear witness unto the truth." So when we get the Salvation of God into our hearts we will bear witness to the truth; not lies, but like the disciples on their wal to Emmaus when Jesus met them and spoke about the truth, their hearts bared witness to the truth, Luke 24:13-32.

Some people to-day cannot believe they have the Holy Ghost without some outward signs; that is Heathenism. The witness of the Holy Spirit inward is the greatest knowledge of knowing God, for he is invisible. St. John 14:17. It is all right to have the signs following, but not to pin our faith to outward manifestations. We are to go by the word of God. Our thought must be in harmony with the Bible or else we will have a strange religion. We must not teach any more than the Apostles. 1 Cor. 12:1-34; 1 Cor. 13:1-13; 1 Cor. 14:1-40.

1. The Character of the Church.—A church constitutes a kind of spiritual kingdom in the world, but not of the world; whose king is Christ; whose law is his word; whose institutions are his ordinances; whose duty is his service; whose reward is his blessing.

In all matters of faith and conscience, as well as in all matters of internal order and government, a church is "under law to Christ;"(1 Cor. ix. 21) but as men and citizens, its members must "submit themselves to governors," (1 Peter ii.14) like other men, so far as shall not interfere with, or contravene, the claims of the divine law and authority upon them—they must "render unto Cesar the things that are Cesar's, and unto God the things that are God's," (Matt. 22:21) remembering that God's claims are supreme, and annihilate all claims that contradict or oppose them

2. The Design of Church.—The evident design of our Saviour in founding and preserving the church in the world, was, that it should be a monument in the midst of guilty men, bearing perpetual witness against the wickedness of the world, and to the goodness of God. But especially that she should be living testimonies to the work of redemption, "the light of the world," and "the salt of the earth." Matt. 5:13, 14.

The Church constitute the effective instrumentality by which the will of God and the knowledge of salvation through Christ are made known to men; at the same time she form homes for the saints on earth; sheep-folds for the safety of the flock, and schools for the instruction and training of the children of the covenant; while she encourages the penitent and warn the careless. The church should well understand her "high calling," and seek to accomplish it, "according to the will of God." Gal. 1:4.

3. The Authority of the Church.—The authority of a church is limited to its own memmbers, and applies to all matters of Christian character, and whatever involves the welfare of religion. It is designed to secure in all its members a conduct and conversation "becoming godliness."

This authority is derived directly from God; not from states, nor princes, nor people; not from its own officers, nor its members, nor from any other source of ecclesiastical or civil power or right. But Christ "is head over all things to the church," (Eph. 1:22) and also as of right, "the church is subject to Christ (Eph. 5:24).

CHURCH MEMBERSHIP

The character of a building depends very much on the materials of which it is constructed. Christian disciples "are builded together for a habitation of God, through the Spirit." Eph. 2:21-22; 1 Peter 2:1-15.

Some times the material of the church is in such a shape until it limit God in his great salvation. In order for a church to prosper, she must obey Jesus' teaching in all things. Jesus can not put his approval on a church that won't obey his teachings. In the Book of Revelation, the church had backslided so far from Jesus' teaching until we find him knocking at the door for admittance, so when a church has backsliden so far from God it can not demand anything from God until it repent of its sin Rev. 2:1-8.

The proper material for the character of the church, is men and women saved from sin and hate sin, and living free from fornication and adultery. Acts 15:29. And all uncleanness and having faith in God's word, believing for the Faith that was once delivered to the Saints. Jude 1-3.

The church would have to believe in Healing the Sick, Casting out Demons and believe in all the signs following the church, as Christ said would follow. Acts 4:29-31; Acts 2:1-4.

Our colored brethren must love our white brethren and respect them in the truth so that the word of God can have its free course, and our white brethren must love their colored brethren and respect them in the truth so that the Holy Spirit won't be greaved. I hope we won't have any more trouble and division spirit.

W.J. SEYMOUR

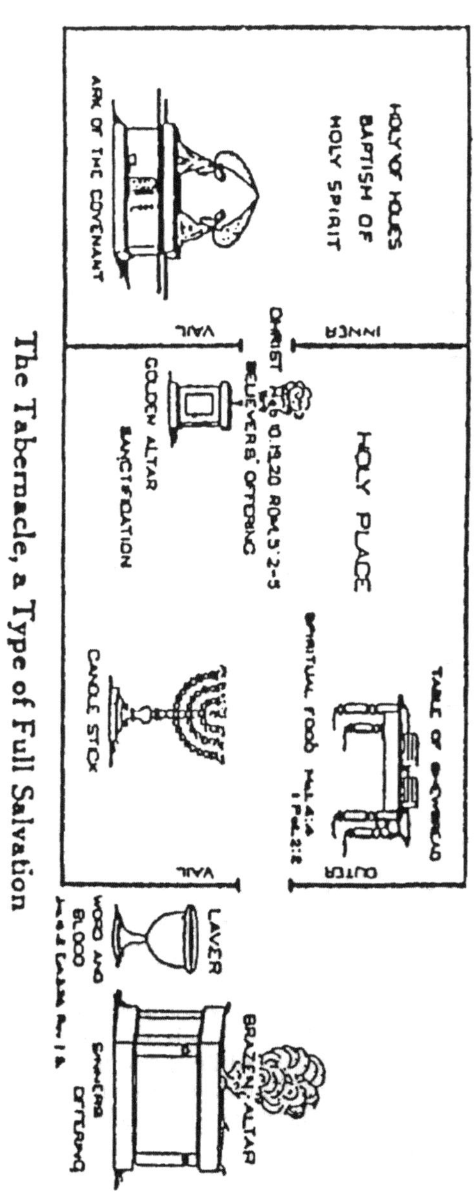

The Tabernacle, a Type of Full Salvation

APOSTOLIC ADDRESS

To the Members of the Apostolic Faith Church.

Dearly Beloved Brethren; We esteem it our privilege and duty most earnestly to recommend to you this volume, which contains the Doctrines and Disciplines of our Church, both of which, as we believe, are agreeable to the word of God, the only and the sufficient rule of faith and practice. Yet the Church, using the liberty given to it by its Lord, and taught by the experience of a long series of years and by observations made on ancient and modern Churches, has from time to time modified its Discipline so as better to secure the end for which it was cofounded.

We believe that God's design in raising up the Apostolic Faith Church in America was to evangelize over these lands. As a proof hereof we have seen since 1906 that time of an extraordinary work of God extending throughout all the United States and Territories and throughout the whole world.

In 1906, the colored people of the City of Los Angeles felt they were led by the Holy Spirit that they decided to have Elder W. J. Seymour, of Houston, Texas, to come to Los Angeles, Cal., and give them some Bible teaching. He came Feb. 22nd, and started Feb. 24th 1906. From his teaching one of the greatest revivals was held in the city of Los Angeles. People of all nations came and got their cup full. Some came from Africa, some came from India, China, Japan, and England.

Very soon division arose through some of our brethren, and the Holy Spirit was grieved. We want all of our white brethren and white sisters to feel free in our churches and missions, in spite of all the trouble we have had with some of our white brethren in causing diversion, and spreading wild fire and fanaticism. Some of our colored brethren caught the disease of this spirit of division also. We find according to God's word to be one in the Holy Spirit, not in the flesh; but in the Holy Spirit, for we are one body. 1 Cor. 12:12-14. If some of our white brethren have prejudices and discrimination (Gal. 2:11-20), we can't do it, because God calls us to follow the Bible. Matt. 17:8; Matt. 23. We must love all men as Christ commands. (Heb. 12:14). Now because we don't take them for directors it is not for discrimination, but for peace. To keep down race war in the Churches and friction, so they can have greater liberty and freedom in the Holy Spirit. We are sorry for this, but it is the best now and in later years for the work. We hope every one that reads these lines may realize it is for the best; not for the worse. Some of our white brethren and sisters have never left us in all the division; they have stuck to us. We love our white brethrens and sisters and welcome them. Jesus Christ takes in all people in his Salvation. Christ is all and for all. He is neither black nor white man, nor Chinaman, nor Hindoo, nor Japanese, but God. God is Spirit because without his spirit we cannot be saved. St. John 3:3-5; Rom. 8:9.

We don't believe in the doctrine of the artificial dancing that lots of people are calling the Holy Ghost dancing. David danced before the Lord. He danced with all his might. The Ark was a type of the Presence of Christ. David, laying aside his royal majesty, girdled himself with a linen ephod; this represent that he had come in the immediate Presence of God as a sinner to Humble himself; it represented that he was naked before the Lord, in his heart. He felt he could not be to be humbled, because God had been merciful to them in returning His Presence on the Ark which meant His Glory, so David danced before the Lord, not before the people, for a show or form, but before the Lord; the people saw him, and his wife, but it was in God's Presence, so everything we do must be to the Glory of God.

We believe in rejoicing in the Holy Spirit. We believe in shouting and leaping as the New Testament endorses.

SOUND DOCTRINE

We must have sound doctrines in our work. We don't believe that the soul sleeps in the grave until the resurrection morning. The next we don't believe in being baptized in the name of Jesus only. We believe in baptizing in the name of the Father, and the Son, and the Holy Ghost, as Jesus taught His disciples (Matt. 28:19-20). We do not believe in keeping Saturday as the Christian Sabbath, we do not believe in dipping a person three times in order that he may be properly baptized. We believe in burying the candidate once in the name of the Father, and in the Son, and in the Holy Ghost. Amen. We don't believe in the Fleshy Doctrine of the male and female kissing and calling it the Holy Kiss. It hurts the cause of Christ, and caused our good to be evily spoken of. We believe in the Holy Brethren greeting the Brethren, and the Holy Sisters greeting the Holy Sisters with a kiss.

RULES FOR THE MINISTRY

Discipline

The Discipline of the Azusa St. Apostolic Faith Mission is the New Testament which is the perfect law of government

1. We must have government in all things.
2 Tim. 3:17:
Psa. 119:142
John 1:17
Gal. 6:2:

2. The Bible teaches the qualification of the ministry.
Luke 24:49.
Act 1:5, 8.
Acts 2:4.
Titus 1:9, 11.
Cor. 3: 6.

3. It teaches the character of a true minister.
1 Tim. 3:1-7
1 Tim. 412.
Titus 2: 7:8.

4. It teaches the duties of a true minister.
Acts 20:28
John 21:15

5. It gives the circuit for the ministry.
Matt. 28:19.
Mark 16:15, 16.

6. It gives instructions us to their ordination.
Acts 13:2, 4.
Titus 1:4, 9.

7. It gives instructions how to proceed in case a ministry goes astray.
Gal. 6:1, 2.
2 Thes. 3:15.
2 Tim. 2:24, 26.
1 Tim. 5:19, 20.
2 Thes. 3:16.

8. It teaches how to deal with the members. It teaches their duty to each other.
James 4:11.
Col. 3: 16.
1 Peter 1:22,
1 Thes. 5:11,14,15,
Matt. 14:15.
Heb. 13: 1.
Heb. 13’1.
Rom. 13:1
Rom. 13:10

9. It teaches them how to proceed in case of trespass.
Luke 18:3, 5.
Matt. 18:15 18.
Col. 3:12,14,
Eph. 4:31, 32

10. A disciple that contains more than the New Testamment is faulty, and it contains too much; if less than the New Testament it is faulty; it contains too little.
Deut. 4:2.
Prov. 30. 5,6
Rev. 22:18.

Chirst govern his church which he purshesed with his own blood, through his word by the operation of the spirit.

HOW SACRED IS THE MARRIAGE TIE

No remarriage while the first part of the first covenant are living.

And the third day there was a marriage in Cana of Galilee; and the mother of Jesus was there: and both Jesus was called, and his disciples, to the marriage.

And when they wanted wine, the mother of Jesus saith unto him, They have no wine. Jesus saith untod her, Woman, what have I to do with thee? mine hour is not yet come.

His mother saith unto the servants, Whatsoever he saith unto you do it.

And there were set there six waterpots of stone, after the manner of the purifying of the Jews, containing two or three firkins apiece. Jesus saith unto them, Fill the waterpots with water. And they filled them up to the brim. And he saith unto them, Draw out now, and bear unto the governor of the feast. And they bare it.

When the ruler of the feast had tasted the water that was made wine, and knew not whence it was: (but the servants which drew the water knew;) the governor of the feast called the bridegroom, and saith unto him, Every man at the beginning doth set forth good wine; and when men have well drunk, then that which is worse, but thou hast kept the good wine until now. Jesus has the best wine, His Spirit.

This beginnig of miracels did Jesus in Cana of Galilee, and manifested forth his glory; and his disciples believed on him.

And after this he went down to Capernaum, he, and his mother, and his brethren, and his disciples: and they continued there not many days.

And the Lord God said, It is not good that the man should be alone; I will make him a help-meet for him.

And out of the ground the Lord God formed every beast of the field, and every fowl of the air; and brought them unto Adam to see what he would call them: and whatsoever Adam called every living creatre, that was the name thereof.

And Adam gave names to all cattle, and to the fowl of the air, and to every beast of the field; but for Adam there was not found an help meet for him.

And the Lord God caused a deep sleep to fall upon Adam, and he slept: and he took one of his ribs, and closed up the flesh instead thereof; and the rib, which the Lord God had taken from man, made he a woman, and brought her unto the man. And Adam said, This is now bone of my bones, and flesh of my flesh: she shall be called Woman, because she was taken out of Man.

Therefore, shall a man leave his father and his mother, and shall cleave unto his wife: and they shall be one flesh.

Matt. 19:

The Pharisees also came unto him, tempting him, and saying utno him. Is it lawful for a man to put away his wife for every cause?

And he answered and said unto them, Have ye not read,

that he which made them at the beginning made them male and female, and said, For this cause shall a man leave father and mother, and shall cleave to his wife: and they twain shall be one flesh?

Wherefore they are no more twain, but one flesh. What therefore God hath joined together, let not man put asunder. They say unto him, Why did Moses then command to give a writing of divorcement, and to put her away?

He saith unto them, Moses because of the hardness of your hearts suffered you to put away your wives: but from the beginning it was not so.

And Jesus answered and said unto them, For the hardness of your heart he wrote you this precept.

But from the beginning of the creation God made them male and female.

For this cause shall man leave his father and mother, and cleave to his wife; and they twain shall be one flesh: so then they are no more twain, but one flesh.

What therefore God hath joined together, let not man put asunder.

And in the house his disciples asked him again of the same matter.

And he saith unto them, Whosoever shall put away his wife, and marry another, commiteth adultry against her.

If a woman shall put away her husband, and be married to another, she committeth adultry.

Wives, submit yourselves unto your own husbands, as unto the Lord; for the husband is the head of the wife, even as Christ is the head of the church: and he is the saviour of the body.

Terefore as the church is subject unto Christ, so let the wives be to their own husbands in everything. Husbands, love your wives, even as Christ also loved the church, and gave himself for it; that he might sanctify and cleanse it with the washing of water by the word, that he might present it to himself a glorious church, not having spot, or wrinkle, or any such thing; but that it should be holy and without blemish.

So ought men to love their wives as their own bodies. He that loveth his wife loveth himself, for no man ever yet hated his own flesh; but nourisheth and cherisheth it, even as the Lord the church: for we are members of his body, of his flesh, and of his bones.

For this cause shall a man leave his father and mother, and shall be joined unto his wife, and they two shall be one flesh.

This is a great mystery; but I speak concerning Christ and the church.

Nevertheless, let every one of you in particular so love his wife even as himself; and the wife see that she reverence her husband.

Wives, submit yourselves unto your own husband, as it is fit in the Lord. Husbands, love your wives, and be not bitter against them.

SEPARATION.

Mat. 19:6.

I. Concerning Divorcement.

1. There were no divorces in the beginning.
   Mat. 19:3-8.
2. Moses allowed men to put away their wives for any cause. If she found no favor in her husband's eyes, if he saw any unbecoming thing in her he could give her a bill of divorcement, send her away, and she might become another man's wife.
   Deut. 24:1-4, 1.XX.
   Mat. 19:7,8.
3. Moses suffered men to divorce their wives and marry again because of the hardness of their hearts.
   Mat. 19:7,8.
4. Jesus did away with the divorce law, and restored matrimony back to the Edenic standard.
   Mat. 19:3,8.
5. Under the New Testament no court on earth should dissolve the marriage relation.
   Mark 10:2-9.
   Mat. 19:5,6.
6. Under the New Testament Husband and wife are bound together for life, death alone severs

ADULTERY.

Heb. 18:4.

I. Under the New Testament, Adultery Implies.

1. An act of Adultery.
   John 8:4.
2. A hidden lust of the heart.
   Mat. 5:28.
3. A state.
   Mat. 19:9.

II. The Act of Adultery is

1. Coition between a marmied person and the opposite sex who is not the lawful companion. Both parties may be married, or only one.
2. This act is also called fornication.
   1 Cor. 5:1-13.
   Mat. 19:9.
   Mat. 5:32.

III. Secret Adultery is as follows:

1. Looking on a woman to lust after her.
   Mat. 5:28.
   2 Pet. 2:14.
2. The secret lust and thought of the heart.
   Gen. 6:5.
   Mark 7:21-23.

IV. The state of adultery is as follows:

1. After putting a companion away, if the husband or wife marries another, while the first one lives,

the marriage tie.
Rom. 7:2, 3.
1. Cor. 7:39.

7. Under the New Testament there is but one cause for which a man can put away his wife.
8. After a man has lawfully put away his wife, or a wife has lawfully put away her husband, they are positively forbidden to marry again until the former companion is dead.
Mark 10:11,12.
Luke 6:18.
Rom. 7:2,3.

II. Concerning Departing.

1. Let the wife not depart from her husband.
1 Cor. 7:10.

they are guilty of adultery.
Mark 10:11,12.
Luke 16:18.
1 Cor. 7:39.
Rom. 7:2,3.

2. Whosoever marries a man or women who has been put away is guilty of adultery.
Mat. 5:32.
Luke 16:18.

V. No man in adultery can enter Christ's Kingdom without confessing and forsaking his sin.
Gal. 5:19-21.
Isa. 55:7.

UNSCRIPTURAL MARIAGES.

I. To marry a second companion while a former lives is adultery—sin—and is forbidden.
Mark 10:11,12.
7:2,3.

II. To marry a person who has a living companion is adultery—sin—and is forbidden.
Mat. 5:23.
Luke 16:18.
1 John 3:4.

1. The above is the law of Christ, and sin is the transgression of the law.
1 John 3:4.
2. To transgress God's law man must have a knowledge of that law.
(a) Where no law is,

III. Men who have a knowledge of the teachings of Christ's law regarding marriage, and then with that knowledge marry a second living companion, or a divorced wife or husband while their former companion lives, wilfully transgress the law, 1 John 3:4, are guilty before God of sin—adultery—and must forsake their sin, 1 John 1:9. If we confess our sins He will pardon us. All such unscriptural marriages must be dissolved to get clear from the sinful state of adultry.
Prov. 28:13.
Isa. 1:16,17.
Gal. 5:19-21.

there is no transgression.
Rom. 4:15.

(b) Sin is not imputed where there is no law.
Rom. 5:13.

(c) When men have no knowledge of God's law, they have no sin.
John 13: 22-24.
John 9: 39-41.

(d) Light brings condemnation. but where no light is there is no condemnation.
John 3:14.

3. From the foregoingscripture we learn that sin is a wilful transgression of God's law. To commit sin men must have a knowledge of God's law. and transgress it knowingly—either the written law of the law of their conscience.
Rom. 2:14-16.
I Cor. 6: 9-10

IV. If men entered the unscriptural marriages, even though ignorant of the written law, yet, condemned by the law of their conscience, such are not clear before God.
Rom. 2:12, 14-16.

V. People who have entered unscriptural marriages in total ignorance of the teachings of Christ, and whose conscience did not condemn them because of the general low plane of teaching on this subject throughout the world, such individuals committed no sin—until the light came and they fail to walk in the light. St. John 3:19.

The Bible says: "He that covereth his sin shall not prosper; but whosoever confesseth and forsaketh them shall have mercy. Prov. 28:13, 1 John 1:9.

MELCHIZEDEK.

I. He was a man—A priest.
Gen. 14:18.

II. He was a type of Christ.
Heb. 5:6.

III. Neither Melchizedek nor Christ were united to the Jewish priesthood.
Psa. 110:4.
Heb. 7:21.
Zech. 6:13.

1. He was ordained direct from heaven.
Gen. 14: 18.
and death, acording to The Jewish custom.
Heb. 7:3.

IV. The Lord had a people on Earth before he called Abraham from or of the Chaldeans.
Gen. 12:1.
Gen. 15:7.
Gen. 5:22.

V. The calling of Abraham was for a special purpose.
Gen. 17:6.
Gen. 12:1,2.

2. Christ our high priest came into office the same way.
   John 8:54.
   Heb. 5:5.
   Acts 3:13.
3. Melchizedek's descent was not counted from Levi and Aaron.
   Neh. 7:6.
4. Neither was Jesus Christ's.
   Heb. 7:11, 19.
   Gal. 2:21.
   Heb. 8:7.
5. Christ was not of the tribe of Levi, nor of the family of Aaron, but of Judah.
   Heb. 7:10-14.
6. There was no record kept of Melchizedek's or Christ's birth, parentage.
   Gen. 22:18.
   Gen. 26:4.
   Gal. 3:8.

VI. There was no Mosaical law when God called Abraham.
   Heb. 11:9.
   Gal. 3:17.
   Rom. 5:13,14.
   Deut. 5:2,3.

VII. The plan of Salvation did not come through the Sinaiatic code.
   Gen. 17:4.
   Rom. 4:13.
   Gal. 3:27.

VIII. The law of Grace is separate from the law of Moses.
   Rom. 4:14-18.
   John 15:22.
   John 1:17.

ARTICLES OF RELIGION

I. Of Faith in the Holy Trinity.

1. There is but one living and true God, everlasting, without body or parts, of infinite power, wisdom, and goodness; the maker and preserver of all things, visible and invisible. And in unity of this Godhead there are three persons, of one substance, power, and eternity—the Father, the Son, and the Holy Ghost. Matt. 28:19-20; 1 John 5:6-9.

II. Of the Word, or Son of God, who was made very Man.

2. The Son, who is the Word of the Father, the very and eternal God, of one substance with the Father, took man's nature in the womb of the blessed Virgin; so that two whole and perfect natures, that is to say, the Godhead and Manhood, were joined together in one person, never to be divided: whereof is one Christ, very God and very Man, who truly suffered, was crucified, dead, and buried, to reconcile his Father to us, and to be a sacrifice, not only for original guilt, but also for the actual sins of men.

II. Of the Resurrection of Christ.

3. Christ did truly rise again from the dead, and took again his body, with all things appertaining to the perfection of man's nature, wherewith he ascended into heaven, and there sitteth until he return to judge all men at the last day.

IV. Of the Holy Ghost.

4. The Holy Ghost, proceeding from the Father and the Son, is of one substance, majesty, and glory with the Father and the Son, very and eternal God.

V. The Sufficiency of the Holy Scripture for Salvation.

5. The Holy Scriptures contain all things necessary to salvation; so that whatsoever is not read therein, nor may be proved thereby, is not to be required of any man that it should be believed as an article of faith, or be thought requisite or necessary to salvation. In the name of the Holy Scriptures we do understand those canonical books of the Old and New Testament of whose authority was never any doubt in the Church. The names of the canonical books are:

Genesis, Exodus, Leviticus, Numbers, Deuteronomy, Joshua, Judges, Ruth, The First Book of Samuel, The Second Book of Samuel, The First Book of Kings, The Second Book of Kings, The First Book of Chronicles, The Second Book of Chronicles, The Book of Ezra, The Book of Nehemiah, The Book of Esther, The Book of Job, the Psalms, The Proverbs, Ecclesiastes or the Preacher, Cantica or Song of Solomon, Four Prophets the greater, Twelve Prophets the less.

All the books of the New Testament, as they are commonly received, we do receive and account canonical.

VI. Of the Old Testament.

6. The Old Testament is not contrary to the New; for both in the Old and New Testament everlasting life is offered to mankind by Christ, who is the only Mediator between God and man, being both God and Man. Wherefore they are not to be heard who feign that the old fathers did look only for transitory promises. Although the law given from God by Moses as touching ceremonies and rites doth not bind Christians, nor ought the civil precepts thereof of necessity be received in any commonwealth; yet, notwithstanding, no Christian whatsoever is free from the obedience of the commandments which are called moral.

VII. Of Original or Birth Sin.

7. Original sin standeth not in the following of Adam (as the Pelagians do vainly talk), but it is the corruption of the nature of every man, that naturally is engendered of the offspring of Adam, whereby man is very far gone from original righteousness, and of his own nature inclined to evil, and that continually.

VIII. Of Free Will.

8. The condition of man after the fall of Adam is such that he cannot turn and prepare himself, by his own natural strength and works, to faith, and calling upon God; wherefore we have no power to do good works, pleasant and acceptable to God, without the grace of God by Christ preventing us, that we may have a good will, and working with us, when we have that good will.

IX. Of the Justification of Man.

9. We are accounted righteous before God only for the merit of our Lord and Saviour Jesus Christ, by faith, and not for our own works or deservings. Wherefore, that we are justified by faith only is a most wholesome doctrine, and very full of comfort.

X. Of Good Works.

10. Although good works which are the fruits of faith, and follow after justification, cannot put away our sins, and endure the severity of God's judgments; yet are they pleasing and acceptable to God in Christ, and spring out of a true and lively faith, insomuch that by them a living faith may be as evidently known as a tree is discerned by its fruit.

XI. Of Works of Supererogation.

11. Voluntary works—besides, over, and above God's commandments—which are called works of supererogation, cannot be taught without arrogancy and impiety. For by them men do declare that they do not only render unto God as much as they are bound to do, but that they do more for his sake than of bounden duty is required; whereas Christ saith plainly. When ye have done all that is commanded of you, say, We are unprofitable servants.

XII. Of Sin after Justification.

12. Not every sin willingly committed after justification is the sin against the Holy Ghost, and unpardonable. Wherefore, the grant of repentance is not to be denied to such as fall into sin after justification: After we have received the Holy Ghost, we may depart from grace given, and fall into sin, and by the grace of God, rise again and amend our lives. And therefore they are to be condemned who say they can no more sin as long as they live here; or deny the place of forgiveness to such as truly repent.

XIII. Of the Church.

13. The visible Church of Christ is a congregation of faithful men in which the pure word of God is preached, and the Sacraments duly administered according to Christ's ordinance, in all those things that of necessity are requisite to the same.

XIV. Of Purgatory.

14. The Romish doctrine concerning purgatory, pardon, worshiping and adoration, as well as images as of relics, and also invocation of saints, is a fond thing, vainly invented, and grounded upon no warrant of Scripture, but repugnant to the word of God.

XV. Os Speaking in the Congregation in such a Tongue as the People understand.

15. It is a thing plainly repugnant to the word of God, and the custom of the primitive Church, to have public prayer in the Church, or to administer the Sacraments, in a tongue not understood by the people. 1 Cor. 14:1-33.

XVI. Of the Sacraments.

16. Sacraments ordained of Christ are not only badges or tokens of Christian men's profession, but rather they are certain signs of grace, and God's good will toward us, by the which he doth work invisibly in us, and doth not only quicken, but also strengthen and confirm, our faith in him.

There are three Sacraments ordained of Christ our Lord in the Gospel; that is to say, Baptism and the Lord's Supper, and Feet Washing.

The Sacraments were not ordained of Christ to be gazed upon, or to be carried about; but that we should duly use them. And in such only as worthily receive the same they have a wholesome effect or operation: but they that receive them unworthily, purchase to themselves condemnation, as St Paul saith, 1 Cor. xi, 29.

XVII. Of Baptism.

17. Baptism is not only a sign of profession and mark of difference whereby Christians are distinguished from others that are not baptized; but it is also a sign of regeneration or the new birth.

XVIII. Of the Lord's Supper.

18. The Supper of the Lord is not only a sign of the love that Christians ought to have among themselves one to another, but rather is a Sacrament of our redemeption by Christ's death; insomuch that, to such as rightly, worthily, and with faith receive the same, the bread which we break is a partaking of the body of Christ; and likewise the cup of blessing is a partaking of the blood of Christ.

Transubstantiation, or the change of the substance of bread and wine in the Supper of our Lord, cannot be proved by Holy Writ, but is repugnant to the plain words of Scripture, overthroweth the nature of a Sacrament, and hath given occasion to many superstitions.

The body of Christ is given, taken, and eaten in the Supper, only after a heavenly and spiritual manner. And the means whereby the body of Christ is received and eaten in the Supper is faith.

The Sacrament of the Lord's Supper was not by Christ's ordinance reserved, carried about, lifted up, or worshiped.

XIX. Of both Kinds.

19. The Cup of the Lord is not to be denied to the Lay

People; for both the parts of the Lord's Supper, by Christ's ordinance and commandment, ought to be administered to all Christians alike.

XX. Of the one Oblation of Christ, finished upon the Cross.

20. The offering of Christ, once made, is that perfect redemption, propitiation, and satisfaction for all the sins of the whole world, both original and actual; and there s none other satisfaction for sin but that alone. Wherefore the sacrifice of masses, in the which it is commonly said that the priest doth offer Christ for the quick and the dead, to have remission of pain or guilt, is a blasphemous fable and dangerous deceit.

XXI. Of the Marriage of Ministers.

21. The Ministers of Christ are not commanded by God's law either to vow the estate of single life, or to abstain from marriage; therefore it is lawful for them, as for all other Christians, to marry at their own discretion, as they shall judge the same to serve best to godliness. 1 Tim. 4:1-7.

XXII. Of the Rites and Ceremonies of Churches.

Whosoever, through his private judgment, willingly and purposely doth openly break the rites and ceremonies of the Church to which he belongs, which are not repugnant to the word of God, ought to be rebuked openly (that others may fear to do the like), as one that offendeth against the common order of the Church, and woundeth the consciences of weak brethren.

XXIII. Of Christian Men's Goods.

23. The riches and goods of Christians are not common, as touching the right, title, and possession of the same, as some do falsely boast. Notwithstanding, every man ought, of such things as he possesseth, liberally to give alms to the poor, according to his ability.

XXIV. Of a Christian Man's Oath.

24. As we confess that vain and rash swearing is forbidden Christian men by your Lord Jesus Christ and James his Apostle; so we judge that the Christian religion doth not prohibit, but that a man may swear when the magistrate requireth, in a cause of faith and charity, so it be done according to the Prophet's teaching, in justice, judgment, and truth.

ARTICLES OF RELIGION

I. Of Faith in the Holy Trinity.

There is but one living and true God, everlasting, without body or parts, of infinite power, wisdom and goodness: the Maker and Preserver of all things, visible and invisible. And in unity of this Godhead, there are three persons, of one substance, power and eternity: the Father, the Son, the Holy Ghost.

II. Of the Word or Son of God, who was made very man.

The Son, who is the Word of the Father, the very and eternal God, of one substance with the Father, took man's nature in the womb of the blessed Virgin; so that two whole and perfect natures, that is to say, the Godhead and manhood, were joined together in one person, never to be divided; whereof is one Christ, very God and very man, who truly suffered, was crucified, dead and buried, to reconcile his Father to us, and to be a sacrifice, not only for original guilt, but also for the actual sins of men. 1 John 2:1:2.

III. Of the Resurrection of Christ.

Christ did truly rise again from the dead, and took again his body with all things appertaining to the perfection of man's nature, wherewith he ascended into heaven, and there sitteth until he return to judge all men at the last day.

IV. Of the Holy Ghost.

The Holy Ghost, proceeding from the Father and the Son, is of one substance, majesty, and glory, with the Father and the Son, very and eternal God.

V. The Sufficiency of the Holy Scriptures for Salvation.

The Holy Scriptures contain all things necessary to salvation; so that whatsoever is not read therein, nor may be proved thereby, is not to be required of any man that it should be believed as an article of faith, or be thought requisite or necessary to salvation. In the name of the Holy Scriptures, we do understand those canonical books of the Old and New Testament, of whose authority was never any doubt in the church.

CHAPTER III

CATECHISM ON FAITH

I. Question 1. What is it to be justified?

Answer. To be pardoned and received into God's favor, into such a state, that if we continue therein, we shall be finally saved.

Ques. 2. ls faith the condition of justification?

Ans. Yes, for every one that believeth not, is condemned; and every one who believes, is justified. Rom. 5:1-3.

Ques. 3. But must not repentance and works meet for repentance, go before this faith?

Ans. Without doubt; if by repentance you mean conviction of sin, and by works met from repentance, obeying God, forgiving our brother, leaving off from evil, doing good, and using his ordinances according to the power we have received.

Ques. 4. What is faith?

Ans. Faith in general is a divine, supernatural evidence, or conviction of things not seen—not discoverable by our bodily senses, as being either past, future or spiritual. Justifying faith implies not only a divine evidence or conviction, that God was in Christ, reconciling the world to himself, but a sure trust and confidence that Christ died for my sins, that he loved me and gave himself for me. And the moment a penitent sinner believes this, God pardons and absolves him.

Ques. 5. Have all Christians this faith? May not a man be justified and not know it?

Ans. That all true Christians have such faith as implies assurance of God's love, appears from Rom. viii.15; 2 Cor. xiii.5; Eph. iv. 32; Heb. viii. 10; 1 John iv. 10; v. 19. And that no man can be justified and not know it St. John 3:11; first John 5:10. It appears further from then ature of the thing; for faith after repentance, is ease after pain, rest after toil, light after darkness. It appears also from the immediate, as well as the distant fruits thereof.

Ques. 6. But may not a man go to heaven without it?

Ans. It does not appear from Holy Writ that a man who has heard the gospel can; Mark xvi. 16 whatever a heathen may do, Rom. ii. 14, 15, 16.

Ques. 7. What are the immediate fruits of justifying faith?

Ans. Peace, joy, love, power over all outward sin, and power to keep down inward sin.

Ques. 8. Does anyone believe who has not the witness in himself, or any longer than he sees, loves and obeys God?

Ans. We apprehend not,seeing God being the very essence

of faith; love and obedience being the inseparable properties of it.

Ques. 9. What sins are consistent with justifying faith?

Ans. No wilful sin. If a believer wilfully sins, he casts away his faith. Neither is it possible he should have justifying faith again without previously repenting. Heb. 6:1, 4.

Ques. 10. Must every believer come into a state of doubt or fear, or darkness? Will he do so unless by ignorance or unfaithfulness? Does God other wise withdraw himself.

Ans. It is certain a believer need never come again into condemnation. It seems he need not come into a state of doubt or fear, or darkness, and that (ordinarily at least) he will not unless by ignorance or unfaithfulness. Yet it is true, that the first joy seldom lasts long; that it is followed by doubts and fears; and that God frequently permits great heaviness before any large manifestation of himself.

Ques. 11. Are works necessary to the continuance of faith?

Ans. Without doubt; for many forfeit the free gift of God, either by sins of omission or commission.

Ques. 12. Can faith be lost for want of works?

Ans. The more we exert our faith, the more it is increased. To him that hath shall be given Matt. 25:29.

Ques. 14. St. Paul says, Abraham was not justified by works; St. James, he was justified by works. Do they not contradict each other?

Ans.. No; 1st, Because they do not speak of the same justification. St. Paul speaks of that justification which was when Abraham was seventy-five years old, about twenty-five years before Isaac was born. St. James of that justification, which was when he offered up Isaac on the altar. 2nd, Because they do not speak of the same works:

St. Paul speaking of works that precede faith; St. James, of works that spring from it.

Ques. 15. In what sense is Adam's sin imputed to all mankind?

Ans. In Adam all die, i.e., Rom. 5:12. 1st, Our bodies then become mortal; 2nd, Our souls died, i.e., were disunited from God. And hence, 3d, We are all born with a sinful, devilish nature, by reason whereof; 4th, We are children of wrath, liable to death eternal. Rom. v. 18; Eph. ii. 3.

Ques. 16. In what sense is the righteousness of Christ imputed to all mankind, or to believers?

Ans. We do not find it expressly affirmed in Scripture, that God imputes the righteous of Christ to any; although we do find that faith is imputed to us for righteousness. The text, "As by one man's disobedience, many were made sinners, so by the obedience of one, many were made righteous," we conceive, means, by the merits of Christ all men are cleared from the guilt of Adam's actual transgression. We conceive further. Through the obedience and death of Christ, 1st., The bodies of all men become immortal after the resurrection; 2nd, Their souls receive a capacity of spiritual life; and 3d, An actual spark or seed thereof; 4th, All believers become children of grace reconciled to God, and 5th, made partakers of the divine nature.

Ques. 17. Have we, then, unawares, leaned too much towards Calvinism?

Ans. We are afraid we have.

Ques. 18. Have we not also leaned too much towards Antinomianism?

Ans. We are afraid we have.

Ques. 19. What is Antinomianism?

Ans. The doctrines which make void the law through faith the Doctrine of Antinomianism is so close to the perfect law of grace until we have to look closely to know the difference it says all Jesus.

therefore Christians are not obliged to observed it; 3d, That

Ques. 20. What are the main pillars thereof?

Ans. 1st. That Christ abolished the moral law; 2d. That one branch of Christian liberty is liberty from obeying the commandments of God; 4th, That it is bondage to do a thing because it is commanded, or forbear because it is forbidden; 5th, That a believer is not obliged to use the ordinances of God to do good works 6th. That a preacher ought not to exhort to good works; not unbelievers, because it is hurtful; not believers, because it is needless.

Ques. 21. What was the occasion of St. Paul's writing his epistle to the Galatians?

Ans. The coming of certain men amongst the Galatians, who taught, "Except ye be circumcised and keep the law of Moses, ye cannot be saved."

Ques. 22. What is the main design herein?

Ans. To prove, 1st, That no man can be saved, or justified by the works of the law, either moral or ritual; 2d. That every believer in Christ is justified by faith without the works of the law.

Ques. 23. What does he mean by the works of the law? Gal. ii. 16, etc.

Ans. All works which do not spring from faith in Christ.

Ques. . What by being under the law? Gal. iii. 23.

Ans.. Under the Mosaic dispensation.

Ques. 25. What law has Christ abolished?

Ans. The Ritual law of Moses; not the moral law, for every believer keeps this moral law in his heart.

Ques. 26. What is meant by liberty? Gal v. 1.

Ans. Liberty, 1st, from the law, 2d, from sin.

II Ques. 1. How comes what is written on justification to be so intricate and obscure? Is this obscurity from the nature of the thing itself, or from the fault or weakness of those who generally treated about it?

Ans. We apprehend this obscurity does not arise from the nature of the subject; but partly from the extreme warmth of most writers who have treated it.

Ques. 2. We affirm that faith in Christ is the sole condition of justification. But does not repentance go before that faith? Yea, and, supposing that there be opportunity for them, fruits or works meet for repentance?

Ans. Without doubt they do.

Ques. 3. How then can we deny them to be conditions of justification? Is not this a mere strif of words?

Ans. It seems not, though it has been grievously abused. But so the abuse cease, let the use remain.

Ques. 4. Shall we read over together Mr. Baxter's aphorisms concerning justification?

Ans.. By all means.

Ques. 5. Is an assurance of God's pardoning love absolutely necessary to our being in his favor? Or may there possibly be some exempt cases?

Ans. Yes.

Ans. We dare not possibly say there are not.

Ques. 6. Is such an assurance absolutely necessary to inward and outward holiness?

Ans. Yes.

Ques. 7. Is it indispensably necessary to final salvation?

Ans. Love hopeth all things. We know not how far any man may fall under the case of invincible ignorance.

Ques. 9. Does a man believe any longer than he feels reconciled to God?

Ans. We conceive not. But we allow there may be infinite degrees of seeing God; even as many as there are between him that sees the sun, when it shines on his eyelids closed, and him who stands with his eyes wide open in the full blaze of his beams.

Ques. 10. Does a man believe any longer than he loves God?

Ans. In no wise. For neither circumcision nor uncircumcision avails, without faith working by love.

Ques. 11. Have we duly considered the case of Cornelius?

Was he not in the favor of God when his prayer and alms came up for a memorial before God, i.e. before he believed in Christ?

Ans. It does seem that he was in some degree. But we speak not of those who have heard the Gospel.

Ques. 12. But were those works of his splendid sins?

Ans. No; nor were they done without the grace of Christ.

Ques. 16. Can faith be lost through disobedience?

Ans. It can. A believer first inwardly disobeys, inclines to sin with his heart; then his intercourse with God is cut off i.e., his faith is lost. And after this he may fall into outward sin, being now weak and like another man.

Ques. 17. How can such a one recover faith?

Ans. By repenting and doing the first works. Rev. ii. 5; Hebrews 6:1-3.

Ques. 18. Whence is it that so great a majority of those who believe, fall more or less in doubt or fear?

Ans. Chiefly from their own ignorance or unfaithfulness; often from their own not watching unto prayer; perhaps from some defect or want of the power of God in the preaching they hear.

Ques.19. Is there not a defect in us? Do we preach as we did at first? have we not changed our doctrines? I am afraid we have preached too much on tongues being the evidence of the gift of the Holy Spirit instead as one of the signs following the believer. Mark 16:16-18.

Ans. 1st. At first we preached almost wholly to unbelievers. To those, therefore, we spake almost continually of remission of sin through the death of Christ and the nature of faith in his blood. And so we do still among those who need to be taught the first elements of the Gospel of Christ..

2d. But those in whom the foundation is already laid, we exhort to go on to perfection. Heb. 6:1-6; Heb. 10:26-27.

3d. Yet we now preach, and that continually, faith in Christ as our prophet, priest, and king; as least as clearly, as strongly and as fully, as we did several years ago.

Ques. 20. Do not some of our preachers preach too much of the wrath, and too little of the love of God?

Ans. We fear that they have leaned to that extreme, and hence some of their hearers have lost the joy of faith.

Ques. 21. Need we ever preach the terrors of the Lord to those who know they are accepted of him?

Ans. No; it is folly so to do, for love is to them the strongest of all motives.

Ques. 22. Do we ordinarily represent a justified state so great and happy as it is?

Ans. Perhaps not; a believer walking in the light is inexpressibly great and happy.

Ques. 23. Should we not have a care of depreciating justification, in order to exalt the state of Holy sanctification?

Ans. Undoubtedly we should be aware of this, for one may insensibly slide into it.

Ques. 24 How should we avoid it.

Ans. When we are going to speak of entire sanctification, let us first describe the bless of a justified state, as strongly as possible.

Ques. 25. Does not the truth of the Gospel lie very near both Calvinism and Antinomianism?

Ans. Indeed it does, as it were within a hair's breadth; so that it is altogether foolish and sinful, because we do not altogether agree with one or the other, to run from them as far as we can.

Ques. 26. Wherein may we come to the very verge of Calvinism?

Ans. 1st. In ascribing all good to the free grace of God. 2d. In denying all natural free-will, and all power antecedent to grace; and, 3d. In excluding all merit from man even for what he has or does by the grace of God.

Ques. 27. Wherein may we come to the edge of Antinomianism? Antinomianism was a sect originated by John Abricola of Germany about the year 1535.

Ans. 1st. In exalting the merits and love of Christ. 2nd. In rejoicing evermore.

Ques. 28. Does faith supersede (set aside the necessity of) holiness or good works?

Ans. In nowise. So far from it that it implies both as a cause does its effects.

III. **Ques**. **1.** Can an unbeliever (whatever he be in other respects) challenge anything of God's justice?

Ans... He cannot, nothing but hell; and this is a point on which we cannot insist too much.

Ques. 2. Do we exempt men of their own righteousness, as we did at first? Do we sufficiently labor, when they begin to be convinced of sin, to take away all they lean upon? Should we not then endeavor, with all our might, to overturn their false foundation? Yes.

Ans. This was at first one of our principal points; and it ought to be so still; for till all other foundations are overturned, they cannot build on Christ. 1 Cor. 3: 1 –16.

Ques. **3.** Did we not then purposely throw them into convictions; into strong sorrow and fear? Nay, did we not strive to make them inconsolable, refusing to be comforted?

Ans. We did. And so should we do still; for the stronger the conviction the speedier is the deliverance. And none so soon receive the peace of God, as those who steadily refuse all other comfort.

Ques. 4. What is sincerity?

Ans. Willingness to know and do the whole will of God. The lowest species thereof seems to be faithfulness in that which is little.

Ques. 5. Has God any regard for man's sincerity?

Ans. So far, that no man in any state can possibly please God without it; neither in any moment wherein he is not sincere.

Ques. 6. But can it be conceived that God has any regard to the sincerity of an unbeliever?

Ans. Yes, so much that if he perseveres therein God will infallibly give him faith.

Ques. 7. What regard may we conceive him to have to the sincerity of a believer?

Ans. So much that in every sincere believer he fulfill all the great and precious promises.

Ques. 8. Whom do you term a sincere believer.

Ans. One that walks in the light, as God is in the light.

Ques. 9. Is sincerity the same with a single eye?

Ans. Not altogether: the latter refers to our intentions, the former to our will or desires.

Ques. 10. Is it not all in all?

Ans. All will follow persevering sincerity. God gives everything with it; nothing without it.

Ques. 11. Are not then sincerity and faith equivalent terms?

Ans. By no means. It is at least as nearly related to works as it is to faith. For example; who is sincere before he believes? He that then does all he can; he that,according to the power he has received, brings forth fruits meet for repentance. Who is sincere after he believes? He that from a sense of God's love, is zealous of all good works.

Ques. 12. Is not sincerity what St. Paul terms a willing mind? 1 Cor. viii. 12. Yes, if the word were taken in a general sense; for it is a constant disposition to use all the grace given.

Ques. 13. But do we not then set sincerity on a level with faith?

Ans. No: for we allow a man may be sincere and not be justified, as he may be penitent and not be justified (not as yet) but he cannot have faith and not be justified. The very moment he believes he is justified. Rom. 5: 1: 12.

Ques. 14. But do we not give up faith and put sincerity in its place as the condition of our acceptance with God.

Ans. We believe it is one condition of our acceptance, as repentance likewise is. And we believe it is a condition of our continuing in a state of acceptance with God. Yet we do not put it in the place of faith. It is by faith the merits of Christ are applied to my soul. But if I am not sincere they are not applied.

Ques. 15. Is not this that going about to establish your own righteousness, whereof St. Paul speaks?

Ans. St. Paul there manifestly speaks of unbelievers who sought to be accepted for the sake of their own righteousness. We do not seek to be accepted for the sake of our sincerity; but through the merits of Christ alone. In deed, so long as any man believes he cannot go about (in St. Paul's sense) to establish his own righteousness.

Ques. 16. But do you consider that we are under the covenant of grace; and that the covenant of works is now abolished?

Ans. All mankind are under the covenant of grace, from the very hour that the original was made. If by the covenant of works you mean that of unsinning obediance made with Adam before the fall; no man but Adam was ever under that covernant, for it was abolished before Cain was born. Yet it is not so abolished, but that it will stand, in a measure, even to the end of the world: that is if we do this, we shall live; if not, we shall die eternally; if we do well we shall live with God in glory; if evil, we shall die the 2nd., death. For every man shall be judged in that, and rewarded according to his works.

Ques. 17. What means then; to him that believeth, his faith is counted for righteousness?

Ans. That God forgives him that is unrighteousness as soon as he believes, accepting his faith instead of perfect righteousness. But then observe Universal Righteousness follows though it did not precede faith?

Ques. 18. But is faith thus counted to us for righteousness, at whatever time we believe?

Ans. Yes. In whatsoever moment we believe all our past sins vanish away. They are as though they never had been, and we stand clear in the sight of God.

Ques. 19. Are not the assurance of faith, the inspiration of the Holy Ghost, and the revelation of Christ in us, terms of nearly the same import?

Ans. He that denies one of them, must deny all; they are so closely connected.

Ques. 20. Are they ordinarily, where the pure gospel is preached, essential to our acceptance?

Ans: Undoubtedly they are, and as such to be insisted on in the strongest terms.

Ques. 21. Is not the whole dispute of salvation by faith, or by works, a mere strife of words?

Ans. In asserting salvation by faith we mean this: 1st, That pardon (salvation begun) is received by faith, producing works. 2d. That holiness (salvation continued) is faith working by love. 3d. That Heaven, (salvation finished) is the reward of this faith.

If you assert salvation by works, or by faith and works, mean the same thing, (understanding by faith, the revelation of Christ in us, by salvation, pardon, holiness, glory) we will not strive with you at all. If you do not, this is not a strife of words, but the very vitals, the essence of Christianity is the thing in question.

Ques. 22. Wherein does our doctrine now differ from that preached by Mr. Wesley at Oxford?

Ans. Chiefly in these two points: 1st, He then knew nothing of that righteousness of faith in justification; nor 2d, Of that nature of faith itself, as implying consciousness of pardon.

Ques. 23. May not some degree of the love of God go before a distinct sense of justification?

Ans. We believe it may.

Ques. 24. Can any degree of holiness or sanctification?

Ans. Many degrees of outward holiness may; yea, and some degrees of meekness, and several other tempers which would be **branches of Christian holiness,** but that they do not spring from Christian principles. For the abiding love of God cannot spring but from a **faith in a pardoning God.** And no true Christian holiness can exist without that love of God for its foundation.

Ques. 25. Is every man as soon as he believes a new creature, sanctified, pure in heart? Has he then a new heart? Does Christ dwell therein? And is he a temple of the Holy Ghost?

Ans. All these things may be affirmed of every believer in a true sense. Let us not, therefore, contradict those who maintain it. Why should we contend about words?

RECEPTION OF MEMBERS

Form for receiving Persons onto the Church as Probationers.

Those who are received into the church as probationers

shall be called forward by name, and the minister, addressing the congregation shall say:

Dearly Beloved Brethren: That none may be admitted hastily into the church, we receive all persons seeking fellowship with us on profssion of faith into a preparatory membership on trial; in which proof may be made, both to themselves and to the church of the sincerity and depth of their convictions and of the strength of their purpose to lead a new life in Christ.

The persons here present desire to be so admitted. You will hear their answers to the questions put to them, and if you make no objections they will be received. Acts 6:4.

It is needful, however, that you be reminded of your responsibility, as having previously entered this holy fellowship, and as now representing the church into which they seek admission. Remembering ther inexperence and how much they must learn in order to become good soldiers of Jesus Christ, see to it that they find in you holy examples of life and loving help in the true serving of their Lord and ours. I beseech you so to order your own lives that these new disciples may take no detriment from you, but that it may ever be cause for thanksgiving to God that they were led into this fellowship.

Then, addressing the persons seeking admission on probation, the minister shall say:

Dearly beloved, you have, by the grace of God, made your decision to follow Christ and to serve him. Your confidence in so doing is not to be based on any notion of fitness or worthiness in yourselves, but solely on the merits of our Lord Jesus Christ, and on his death and intercession for us.

That the church may know your purpose, you will answer the questions I am now to ask you.

Have you an earnest desire to be saved from all your sins? Do you desire to be Holy and wholly sanctified to God? Do you desire to be filled with the Holy Spirit?

Ans. I do.

Will you guard yourselves against all things contrary to the teaching of God's word, and endeavor to lead a Holy Life, following the commandments of God?

Ans. I will endeavor so to do by His grace.

Are you purposed to give reverent attendance upon the apointed means of grace in the ministry of the word, and in public and private worship of God?

Ans. I am so determined, with the help of God

No objection being offered, the Minister shall then announce that the candidates are admitted as probationers and shall assign them to the watch care of the Church. Then shall the

Minister offer extemporary prayer for the people that are coming into the church. As the Holy Spirit move on Him to pray.

FORM FOR RECEIVING PERSONS INTO THE CHURCH AFTER PROBATION

On the day appointed, all that are to be received into the church shall be called forward and the Minister addressing the congregation shall say:

Dearly Beloved Brethren: The Scriptures teach us that the Church is the household of God, the body of which Christ is head; and that it is the design of the Gospel to bring together in one all who are in Christ. The fellowship of the church is the communion that its members enjoy one with another. The ends of this fellowship are, the maintenance of sound doctrine and of the ordinances of Christian worship, and the exercise of that power of godly admonition and discipline which Christ has committed to his church for the promotion of holiness. It is the duty of all men to unite in this fellowship, for it is only those that "be planted in the house of the Lord" that "shall flourish in the courts of our God." Its more particular duties are, to promote peace and unity; to bear one another's burdens; to prevent each other's stumbling; to seek the intimacy of friendly society among themselves; to continue steadfast in the faith and worship of the gospel; and to pray and sympathize with each other. Among its privileges are, peculiar incitements to holiness from the hearing of God's word and the sharing in God's ordinances; the being placed under the watchful care of pastors; and the enjoyment of the blessings which are promised only to those who are of the Household of Faith. Into this holy fellowship the persons before you who have already received the Sacrament of the Lord's Supper and of Baptism and the ordinance of footwashing, and have been born of the Spirit and have been under the care of proper leaders for six months on trial, come seeking admission. We now purpose in the fear of God to question them as to their faith and purposes, that you may know that they are proper persons to be admitted into the church. Acts 20:28-32.

Then addressing the applicants for admission the Minister shall say:

Dearly beloved, you are come hither seeking the great privilege of union with the church our Saviour has purchased with his own blood. We rejoice in the grace of God vouchsafed unto you in that he has called you to be his followers, and that thus far you have run well. You have heard how blessed are the privileges, and how solemn are the duties of membership in Christ's Church; and before you are fully admitted thereto, it is proper that you do here publicly renew your vows, confess your faith, and declare your purpose, by answering the following questions:

Do you here, in the presence of God and of this Congregation, renew the solemn promise contained in the Baptismal Covenant, ratifying and confirming the same, and acknowledging yourselves bound faithfully to observe and keep that Covenant?

Ans. I do.

Have you saving faith in the Lord Jesus Christ?

Ans. I know I have in his blood.

Do you believe in the doctrines of the Holy Scriptures as set forth in the Articles of Religion of the Apostolic Faith Church?

Ans. I do.

Will you cheerfully be governed by the rules of the Apostolic Faith Church? Hold sacred the Ordinances of God, and endeavor, as much as in you lies, to promote the welfare of your brethren and the advancement of the Redeemer's Kingdom?

Ans. I will by his grace.

Will you contribute of your earthly substance, according to your ability, to the support of the Gospel and the various benevolent enterprises of the church?

Ans. I will.

Then the Minister addressing the Church shall say:

Brethren, these persons have given satisfactory responses to our inquiries, have any of you reason to allege why they should not be received into full membership in the church?

No objections being alleged, the Minister shall say to the candidates:

We welcome you to the communion of the church of God; and, in testimony of our Christian affection and the cordiality with which we receive you, I hereby extend to you the right hand of fellowship; and may God grant that you may be a faithful and useful member of the church militant until you are called to the fellowship of the church triumphant, which is without fault before the throne of God.

Then shall the Minister offer extemporary prayer, for the members received into the church and have members to shake their hands.

MEMBERSHIP

Chapter 1.

Reception on Probation

No one to be taken on probation except he is born of God or on watch care, except he or she knows the Lord.

In order to prevent improper persons from gaining admission into the church of Jesus Christ, and in order to the exercise of the power of godly admonition and discipline Matthew.16:13-18; Acts 5:1-11; Acts 8:18-24.

1. Let great care be taken in receiving persons on probation and let no one be enrolled as a watch care member unless he give satisfactory evidence of an earnest desire to be saved from all sin and enjoy the fellowship of God's people. Let the pastor and the deacon and elders see that all persons on probation be early made acquainted with the doctrine, and rules and regulations of the Apostolic Faith Church.

2. Probationers are expected to conform carefully to all the rules and usages of the church. They are entitled to all its spiritual privileges and aids; but they may not be members in full until they have proven themselves to be true in every way.

Admission into Full Membership

1. Let no one be admitted into Full Membership in the Church until he has been at least six months on probation, has been recommended by the leaders and elders meeting or, where no such meeting is held, by his leader. If he has been born of the Spirit and baptized, and on examination by the pastor before the church, has given satisfactory assurances both of the correctness of his faith and of his willingness to observe and keep the rules of the church.

2. Nevertheless, a member in good standing in an Orthodox Evangelical Church desiring to unite with us may, on giving satisfactory answers to the unusual inquiries, be received at once into full membership, if they have been born of the spirit and believe our doctrine.

3. Let the pastor and the committee on church records be careful to see that the names of all persons received into the church are duly recorded, and the pastor shall report at each monthly meeting all changes that have occurred in the membership during the monthly meeting.

Qualification and Work.

No one in our church shall be known as a preacher because

he or she speaks in tongues: no one in our work shall be known as receiving the Holy Ghost simply because he or she speaks in tongues alone. 1 Corinthian 13.

CHAPTER I.

The Call to Preach

In order that we may try those persons who profess to be moved by the Holy Ghost to preach, let the following questions be asked, namely:

1. Do they know God as a pardoning God? Have they the love of God abiding in them? Do they desire nothing but God? Are they holy in all manner of conversation? Have they been sanctified wholly unto God? John 17:15-17; 1 Thess. 4 and 3, 5, 22-24; Acts 2-4; Acts 19:6.

2. Have they gifts, as well as grace, for the work? Have they, in some tolerable degree, a clear, sound understanding; a right judgment in the things of God; a just conception of salvation by faith? Has God given them any degree of utterance? Do they speak justly, readily, clearly? Have they been anointed by the Holy Ghost? Have any been truly convinced of sin and converted to God under their preaching? Have any been sanctified and healed and baptized in the Holy Ghost through their preaching? And are believers edified by their preaching?

3. As long as these marks concur in anyone we believe he is called by God to preach. These we receive as sufficient proof that he is moved by the Holy Ghost.

Rules For a Preacher's Conduct

Rule 1. Be diligent. Never me unemployed. Never be triflingly employed. Never trifle away time. Neither spend any more time at any place than is strictly necessary.

Rule 2. Be serious. Let your motto be "Holiness to the Lord." Avoid all lightness, jesting and foolish talking.

Rule 3. Converse sparingly, and conduct yourself prudently with women. 1 Tim. 5:2.

Rule 4. Believe evil of no one without good evidence; unless you see it done take need how you credit it. Put the best construction on everything. You know the judge is always supposed to be on the prisoner's side.

Rule 5. Speak evil of no one, because your word especially, would eat as doth a canker. Keep your thoughts within your own breast till you come to the person concerned.

Rule 6. Tell every one under your care what you think

wrong in his conduct and temper, and that lovingly and plainly, as soon as may be; else it will fester in your heart. Make all haste to cast the fire out of your bosom.

Rule 7. Avoid all affectation. A preacher of the gospel is the servant of all.

Rule 8. Be ashamed of nothing but sin.

Rule 9. Be punctual. Do everything exactly at the time. And, do not mend our rules, but keep them; not for wrath but for conscience' sake.

Rule 10. You have nothing to do but to save souls; therefore sppend and be spent in this work; and go always not only to those that want you, but those that want you most.

Observe! It is not your business only to preach so many times and to take care of this or that Mission but to save as many as you can; to bring as many sinners as

you can to repentance, and with all your power to build them up in that holiness without which they cannot see the Lord. And remember 1 an Apostolic Faith Preacher is to mind every point, great and small, in the Discipline. Therefore, you will need to exercise all the wisdom and grace you have.

Rule 11. Act in all things not according to your own will, but as a Son in the Gospel. As such, it is your duty to employ your time in the manner in which we direct; in preaching and visiting from house to house; in reading, meditation and prayer. Above all, if you labor with us in the Lord's vineyard, it is needful you should do that part of the work which we advise, at those times and places which we judge most for his glory.

Smaller advices which might be of use to us are perhaps these: First, Be sure never to disappoint a congregation. Second, Begin at the time appointed. Third, Let your whole deportment be serious, weighty and solemn.

SPIRITUAL QUALIFICATION

The duty of a preacher is: First, To preach. Second, To meet the members of the church. Third, To visit the sick.

A preacher should be qualified for his charge by walking closely with God and having his work greatly at heart and by understanding and loving discipline, ours in particular.

We do not sufficiently watch over each other. Should we not frequently ask each other: Do you walk closely with God? Have you now fellowship with the Father and the Son? Do you spend the day in the manner with which the Lord would be pleased? Do you converse seriously, usefully and closely?

To be made particular: Do you use all the means of grace yourself and enforce the use of them on all other persons?

The means of grace are either instituted or prudential.

Instituted are:

Prayer: private, family and public, consisting of deprecation, pretition, intercession and thanksgiving. Do you use each of these? Do you forcast daily, wherever you are, to secure time for private devotion? Do you practice it everywhere? Do you ask everywhere: Have you family prayer? Do you ask individuals: Do you use private prayer every morning and evening in particular?

Searching the Scriptures. First: Reading; constantly some part of every day; regularly, all the Bible in order; carefully, with prayer; seriously, with prayer before and after; fruitfully, immediately practicing what you learn there. Second: Meditating; at set times; by rule. Third: Hearing, at every opportunity, with prayer before, at, after. Have you a Bible always about you? Footwashing. Do you use this ordinance at every opportunity?

The Lord's Supper. Do you use this at every opportunity? With solemn prayer before? With earnest and deliberate self-devotion?

Fasting. Do you use as much abstinence and fasting every week as your health, strength, and labor will permit?

Christian Conference. Are you convinced how important and how difficult it is to order your conversation aright? Is it always in grace? Seasoned with salt? Meet to minister grace to the hearers? Do you not converse too long at a time? Is not an hour commonly enough? Would it not be well always to have a determined end in view? And to pray before and after it?

PRUDENTIAL means we may use either as Christians as Apostolics or as preachers.

As Christians: What particular rules have you in order to grow in grace? What arts of holy living?

As Apostolic: Do you ever miss your prayer meeting?

As Apostolics: Have you thoroughly considered your duty- And do you make a conscience of executing every part of it? Do you meet every meeting and the leaders?

These means may be used without fruit. But there are some means which cannot,

namely: watching, denying ourselves, taking up our cross, exercise of the presence of God.

1. Do you steadily watch against the world? Yourself? Your besettinf sin? Heb. 12:1-2.

And we are not more knowing because we are idle. We forget our first rule. "Be diligent." Never be unemployed.

Never be triflingly employed. Neither spend any more time at any place than is strictly necessary. We fear there is altogether a fault in this mater, and that few of us are clear. Which of us spend as many hours a day in God's work as we did formerly in man's work. We talk—talk—or read what comes next to hand. We must, absolutely must cure this evil, or betray the cause of God. But how? First: Read the most useful books and that regularly and constantly.

THE NECESSITY OF UNION AMONG OURSELVES

Let us be deeply sensible (from what we have known) of the evil of a division in principle, spirit or practice, and the dreadful consequences to ourselves and others. If we are united, what can stand before us? If we divide, we shall destroy ourselves (Gal. 5:15-17), and the work of God, and the souls of our people.

In order to a closer union with each other. First: Let us be deeply convinced of the absolute necessity of it. Second: Pray earnestly for, and speak freely to each other. Third: When we meet let us never part without prayer. Fourth: Take great care not to despise each other's gifts. Fifth: Never speak lightly of each other. Sixth: Let us defend each other's character in everything so far as in consistent with truth. Seventh: Labor in honor each to prefer the other before himself. We recommend a serious perusal of The Causes, Evils and Cures of Heart and Church Divisions.

DEPORTMENT AT THE CONFERENCE OR CONVENTION

It is desired that all things be considered on these occasions as in the immediate presence of God. That every per-

son speak freely whatever is in his heart.

In order, therefore, that we may best improve our time at the Convention. First: While we are conversing let us have an especial care to set God always before us. Second: In the intermendiate hours let us redeem all the time we can for privat exercise. Third: There let us give ourselves to prayer for one another, and for a blessing on our labor.

WHERE AND HOW TO PREACH

It is by no means advisable for us to preach in as many places as we can without forming any mission. We have made the trial in various places, and that for a considerable time. But all that seed has fallen by the wayside. There is scarcely any fruit remaining.

We should endeavor to preach most. First: Where there is the greatest number of quiet and willing hearers. Second: Where there is most fruit. Let us walk so close to God that his spirit will direct us. Acts 8:26, 39.

We ought diligently to observe in what places God is pleased at any time to pour out his Spirit more abundantly, and at that time to send more laborers than usual into that part of the harvest.

The best general method of preaching is: First, To convince. Second: To offer Christ. Third: To invite. Fourth: To build up. And to do this in some measure in every sermon.

The most effectual way of preaching Christ is to preach him in all his offices, and to declare his law, as well as his Gospel, both to believers and unbelievers. Let us strongly and closely insist upon inward and outward holiness in all its branches.

THE TRIAL OF AN ACCUSED MEMBER

I. Immoral Conduct

A member of the church accused of immorality shall be brought to trial before a Committee of not less than five members of the church who are in good standing. They shall be chosen by the preacher in charge, and, if he judge it to be necessary, he may select them and the parties may challenge for cause. The preacher, in charge shall preside in the trial, and shall cause a correct record of the proceedings and evidence to be made.

If the accused person be found guilty by the decision of a majority of the committee and the crime be such as is expressly forbidden in the word of God, sufficient to exclude a person from the kingdom of grace and glory, let the preacher in charge expel him.

But if in view of mitigating circumstances and of humble and penitent confession the committee find that a lower penalty is proper, it may either impose censure on the offender, or suspend him from all Church privileges fo ra definite time, at its discretion.

IMPRUDENT AND UNCHRISTIAN CONDUCT

In cases of neglect of duties of any kind, imprudent conduct, indulging sinful tempers or words, the buying, selling or using intoxicating liquors as a beverage, signing petitions in favor of granting lcense for the sale of intoxicanting liquors, becoming bondsmen for persons engaged in such traffic, renting property as a place in or on which to manufacture or sell intoxicating liquors, dancing, playing at games of chance, attending theatres, horse races, circuses, dancing parties, or patronizing dancing schools, or taking such other amusements as are obviously of misleading or questionable moral tendency, or disobedience to the order and Discipline of the Church—first, let private reproof be given by the pastor or leader, and if there be an acknowledgement of the fault, and proper humiliation, the person may be borne with. On the second offense the pastor or leader may take one or two discreet members of the church. On a third offense let him be brought to trial, and if found guilty, and there be no sign of real humiliation, he shall be expelled.

NEGLECT OF THE MEANS OF GRACE

When a member of our church habitually neglects the means of grace, such as the public worship of God, the Supper of the Lord, family and private prayer, searching the Scriptures, praise meetings and prayer meeting:—

1. Let the preacher in charge, whenever it is practicable, visit him and explain to him the consequence if he continue to neglect.

2. If he do not amend, let the preacher in charge bring his case before a committee of not less than five who are members in good standing before which he shall be cited to appear. And if he be found guilty of wilful neglect by the decision of a majority of the members before whom the case is brought, let him be excluded.

Disobedient members have ruled the preacher in this church before. Tit. 1:5-14; 1 Thes. 5:12-23.

CAUSING DISSENSION

If a member of our church shall be accused of endeavoring to sow dissension in any of our churches by inveighing against either our Doctrines or Discipline, the person so offending shall first be reproved by the preacher in charge; and if he persist in such pernicious practice, he shall be brought to trial, and, if found guilty, shall be expelled.

DISAGREEMENT IN BUSINESS; ARBITRATION

On any disagreement between two or more members of our church concerning business transactions which cannot be settled by the parties, the preacher in charge shall inquire into the circumstances of the case, and shall recommend to the parties a reference, consisting of two arbiters chosen by one party, and two chosen by the other party, which four arbiters so chosen shall choose a fifth; the five arbiters being members of our church. The preacher in charge shall preside, and the disciplinary forms of trial shall be observed.

If either party refuse to abide by the judgment of the arbiters, he shall be brought to trial, and if he fail to show sufficient cause for such refusal, he shall be expelled.

If, in the case of debt or dispute, one of the parties is a minister, one of the duties laid on the preacher in charge in the foregoing paragraph shall be performed by the presiding elder of the minister concerned. If both are ministers, the presiding elder of either may act in the case.

INSOLVENCY

The preachers in charge are required to execute all our rules fully and strenuously against all frauds and particularly against dishonest insolvencies, suffering none to remain in our church on any account who are found guilty of any fraud.

To prevent scandal, when any member of the church fails in business, or contracts debts which he is not able to pay, let two or three judicious members of the church inspect the accounts, contracts and circumstances of the supposed delinquent; and if they judge that he has behaved dishonestly or borrowed money withoua a probability of paying, let him be brought to trial, and, if found guilty, expelled.

GENERAL DIRECTIONS CONCERNING TRIALS

In all cases of trial of members let all witnesses for the church be duly notified by the preacher in charge.

The order concerning absent witnesses and witnesses from without shall be the same as that observed in the trial of ministers. The accused shall have the right to call to his assistance as counsel any member or minister in good and regular standing in the Apostolic Faith Church.

AMENDED ARTICLES OF INCORPORATION OF THE APOSTOLIC FAITH MISSION

WHEREAS, at a meting of the members of the Apostolic Faith Mission, a corporation, regularly and legally called and held at the office of said Corporation at 312 Azusa Street, City of Los Angeles, County of Los Angeles, State of California, on the 19th day of May, 1914, at the hour of 7:30 P.M. all of the members of said Apostolic Faith Mission in good standing being present and voting, it was determined by resolution passed and adopted by unanimous vote, duly recorded, to amend the Articles of Incorporation of said corporation which were heretofore, to-wit: on the 24th day of April, 1907, duly filed in the office of the County Clerk of Los Angeles County, State of California; that said Amended Articles and the Constitution which is a part of these Articles of Incorporation, as hereinafter set forth were read, duly considered and adopted by the members of said Apostolic Faith Mission; that at said time and place the said Board of Trustees of said Apostolic Faith Mission, at its meeting duly and regularly called, unanimously adopt said hereinafter ammendments including said Constitution which are a part of these amended articles of incorporation.

NOW, THEREFORE, these Amended Articles of Incorporation and Constitution, Witnesseth:

I.

That the name of this corporation shall be the APOSTOLIC FAITH MISSION and shall be carried on in the interests of and for the benefit of the colored people of the State of California, but the people of all countries, climes, and nations shall be welcome.

II.

That the purposes for which this corporation is formed are to do evangelistic work, conduct, maintain, control, carry on, supervise and found missions and also Revivals, Campmeetings, street and prison work in the State of California and elsewhere, by its members, and those who become members by compliance with the Constitution and By-Laws and the tenets and beleifs of the Apostolic Faith Missions; to establish Sunday Schools, supervise and carry on Apostolic Endeavors. It shall have the power to acquire such real and personal property as may be necessary for its use in carrying out its purposes and objects, and dispose of the same when no longer necessary for its use. It shall have the power to encumber all property, both real and personal, owned by it, when deemed advisable so to do; and generally to perform all acts requisite and necessary to more fully carry out its purposes aforesaid.

III.

That the place where the principal business of the corporation is to be transacted is the City of Los Angeles, County of Los Angeles, State of California.

IV.

That the term for which this incorporation is to exist is fifty (50) years from and after the date of the original incorporation.

V.

The number of its Trustees shall be three or five, and the names and addresses of the undersigned, who are hereby named as trustees of the corporation for the first year after the filing of these articles are:

Spencer James, 1632 West 35th Place, Los Angeles, Cal.

James Ross, 312 Azusa St., Los Angeles, Cal.

And the name and residence of the one appointed for the first two years is:

Richard Asbery, 312 Azusa St., Los Angeles, Cal.

And the names and residences of the ones appointed for the first three years are:

Rev. W. J. Seymour, 312 Azusa St., Los Angeles, Cal.

Jennie E. M. Seymour, 312 Azusa St., Los Angeles, Cal.

That the said Trustees are to be selected in the manner provided for in the Constitution and By-laws of the Apostolic Faith Church.

VI.

That on the 19th day of May, 1914, in the City of Los Angeles, County of Los Angeles, State of California, an election was held for Trustees; that said election was held in accordance with a resolution at the last regular prior meeting of the said Apostolic Faith Mission, held on the 12th day of June in the office of said Corporation at the City of Los Angeles, County of Los Angeles, State of California; that notice of such meeting for the election of directors or trustees was given to the members of said Apostolic Faith Mission; that a majority of the members of said corporation who were present voted at such election, and that the result thereof was that the trustees hereinbefore named were duly elected for the respective terms.

VII.

That this Corporation has no capital stock and is not formed for profit.

CONSTITUTION OF THE APOSTOLIC FAITH MISSION

ARTICLE A.

Section 1. The name of this corporation shall be the "APOSTOLIC FAITH MISSION"

Sec. 2. The objects of this corporation are set in "II," of the Amended Articles as above set forth.

Sec. 3. There shall be no political discussions or any other discussions contrary to the Law of God. The Bishop shall decide what discussions shall take place in the Mission.

ARTICLE B.

This Mision shall have jurisdiction over all Subordinate Missions that may hereafter be formed or come under the supervision of this Mission. It shall have the right and power of granting charters to subordinate missions hereafter formed, or of suspending or annulling or revoking the same for proper cause.

ARTICLE C.

This Mission shall be composed of one bishop, one Vice Bishop, one Secretary, one Treasurer, five Trustees, three Deacons, two Deaconesses, two Elders, one Superintendent of Sunday Schools, one Superintendent of Apostolic Endeavor. The Bishop, Vice- Bishop and Trustees must be people of Color.

SECTION D.

The Mission shall hold its annual meeting on the first Monday in April at 7:30 P.M. of each and every year. There shall be such other meetings as the Bishop may elect.

ARTICLE E.

The elective officers shall be the Board of Trustees who are elected as follows: Two for one year, one for two years and two for three years. All to be elected by ballot or the yea or no. That said Trustees have been elected as hereinbefore set forth.

After the first year there shall be three trustees only.

The Bishop and wife shall be Trustees for life.

ARTICLE F.

The Founder and Organizer of the Mission shall be the

Bishop. He shall be a colored person, thoroughly converted and sanctified.

ARTICLE G.

The other officers, Trustees and Bishop, shall be appointed by the Bishop and hold office during such time as the Bishop may direct and be subject to removal by the Bishop.

The Bishop shall approve all members taken into this Mission, grant charters, revoke charters, establish rules and discipline for the guidance of the Mission. Preside and lead at all meetings. Appoint all officers except the Trustees. Remove all officers except Trustees and perform any and such other and further duties that may devolve upon him from time to time. The Bishop and wife shall be Trustees for life time. The Bishop and wife shall be Head Trustees of the church. The Bishop shall remove trustees only for failing to obey the laws and doctrines of the church.

The Vice Bishop shall be appointed by the Bishop and he shall be a colored man who has served the Mission faithfully and well. His duties are as follows: Upon the death, removal, resignation or disqualification of the Bishop, the Vice Bishop shall succeed the Bishop. The Vice Bishop shall assist the Bishop as he may direct. Help the Bishop ordain preachers of the Gospel as well as Missionaries.

The duties of the other officers shall be as the Bishop may provide.

ARTICLE H.

There shall be such other committees as the Bishop may provide and from time to time select, all to serve under the direction of the Bishop and in the interests of the Mission.

ARTICLE I.

There may be such other subordinate Missions as may from time to time be established.

That upon the written request of not less than Twenty-Fve persons who are converted, a Mission may be founded and established. There must be passed a resolution by said twenty-five persons to the effect that they desire to found an Apostolic Faith Mission. The resolution expressing their desire must be forwarded to this Mission. If the Bishop is satisfied with the resolution he may then proceed to grant a charter to said Mission, which is all times under the control and supervision of this Mission. When the said charter is granted, the said Mission becomes a part of this Mission.

ARTICLE J.

The Bishop shall have power to hear all matters pertaining to the expulsion of any member of said Mission and of any Subordinate Mission.

The Bishop shall have power to expell or suspend any member for any misconduct or for any violations of the Scriptures. Every member against whom any charge is filed shall have a hearing before the Bishop and two other members or officers chosen by the Bishop. If after hearing the evidence the said member may be expelled or suspended from the Mission if the Bishop and one member so order. But no one shall be expelled or suspended from the membership without the Bishop's consent.

ARTICLE K.

This Constitution may be amended in the manner provided by the consent of the Bishop or by law.

THE SUPPORT OF THE MINISTRY

Our ministers that labor in the work of the Lord and give all their time to the Gospel should be supported by the Gospel. 1 Tim. 5:17-18. Those that labor in Doctrine and giving the word should be nicely carried, for they are worthy of it. 1 Cor. 9:7-11. We must support the Gospel or the Gospel will die on our hands and the enemy will get in and destroy the flock of God. How would a man know that he was born of the Spirit, if he did not have the inward witness? He would have to look for some outward sign. But God's word says he that believeth on the son of God, hath the witness in himself. 1 John 5:10. How do we take the gift of tongues? We believe that all God's children that have Faith in God can pray to God for an out pouring of the Holy Spirit upon the Holy sanctified life and receive a great filling of the Holy Spirit and speak in new tongues, as the spirit gives utterance. But we don't base our Faith on it as essential to our salvation. Some one will ask: How do you know when you will get the Holy Ghost? He, the spirit of truth, will guide you into all truth. St. John 16:13. The gift of the Holy Ghost is more than speaking in the tongues. He is wisdom, power, truth, holiness. He is a person that teaches us the truth.

How does our doctrine differ with the other Pentecostal brethren? First, they claime that a man or woman has not the Holy Spirit, except they speak in tongues. So that is contrary to the teaching of Christ. Matt. 7:21-23. If we would base our faith on tongues being the evidence of the gift of the Holy

Ghost, it would knock out our faith in the blood of Christ, and the inward witness of the Holy Spirit bearing witness with our spirit. Rom. 8:14-16.

ANNIHILATE

To reduce to nothing or non-existence; to destroy the existence of; to cause to cease to be.

We don't believe in the doctrine of the Annihiation of the wicked. That is the reason why we could not stand for tongues being the evidence of the Baptism in the Holy Ghost and fire. If tongues was the evidence of the gift of the Holy Spirit, then men and women that have received the gift of tongues could not believed contrary to the teachings of the Holy Spirit. Since tongues is not the evidence of the Baptism in the Holy Spirit, men and women can receive it and yet be destitute of the truth. It's one of the signs, not the evidence Mark 16:16-18. The Holy Spirit came from heaven to guide us in to all truth. So Annihilation of the soul is not the Holy Spirit, nor Jesus' teaching, for both the Holy Spirit and Jesus' teaching are all the same. Annihilation of the wicked, or the Annihilation of a soul is contrary to Scripture. Matt. 10:28. Jesus said in Matt. 10:28: "And fear not them which kill the body, but not able to kill the soul." Jesus showed that our soul or inner spirit is immortal Matt. 10:28; Rev. 6:9-11; 1 Pet. 3:3-4. Annihilation means to reduce to nothing or non-existence; to destroy the existence of; to cause to cease to be. If man's soul was not immortal, he would be no higher than the beast or the apes and monkeys, but not so. Our body's are the only thing that are mortal

The Doctrine of Materialism was advocated by The Ancient Sect of the Sadducees. Acts 23:8.

The Sadducees was a sect that did not believe in the doctrine of the resurrection of the dead; they did not believe in Angel or Spirit. But the Pharisees confessed both Acts. 23:8. Now, many people of to-day that deny the Immortality of the soul is nothing but modern Sadducees, saying man's soul is just his breath. Man has a spirit. God only hath Immortality. 1 Tim. 6:15-16.

Materialism is the doctrine that denies the Immortality of the soul. They maintain that the soul of man is not a spirit substance distinct from matter:

1. God only hath immortality.
   1 Tim. 6:15, 16.

(a) This text has direct reference to Jesus Christ and not to the Father.
   1 Tim. 6:14-16.

(b) Jesus Christ is King of kings and Lord of lords.
   Rev. 17:14

Rev. 19:16.

(c) To take this text in an exclusive unqualified sense would deny the immortality of the Father and of angels.

Mat. 22:29, 30.

(d) We yet inhabit mortal flesh, mortal bodies, which are subject to physical death; while Christ has already receiveed his immortal, resurrected body, and death hath no more dominion over him. In this sense he only hath attained immortality. Rom. 6:9.

(e) This text referring to the resurrection of these bodies has not a feathers weight of evidence against the immortality of the soul.

2. Seek for immortality.

Rom. 2:7.

(a) We are mortal in body.

Rom. 6:12; 2 Cor. 4:11.

(b) Our soul or spirit is immortal.

Mat. 10:28.

Rev. 6:9-11; 1 Pet. 3:3, 4.

(c) Our bodies are the only part of us that will put on immortality in the resurrection.

Phil.3:20, 21..

1 Cor. 15: 42-44.

(d) To seek for immortality is to so live that we may have a glorious resurrection in an immortal and glorified body to eternal rewards in heaven. Again, this proves nothing against the immortality of the soul.

I Cor. 15:51-55

3. The dead know not anything.

Eccl. 9:5, 6

(a) This applies to the outer man — the body —that part of us which returns to dust.

Gen. 3:19. Psa. 104:29

Dan. 12:2

(b) It can not apply to the real inner man —the soul — for that remains conscious after death.

Luke 16: 19-31

2 Cor. 5:1-9,

1 Thes. 5:40

Rev. 6: 9, 10

4. In the day of death our thoughts perish.

Psa. 146:4

(a) The mind is one thing and its thoughts, schemes, purposes, and intentions, quite another.

Isa. 59:7

Jer. 4:14

Mark 7:21.

(b) While the schemes, plans, and thoughts of worldly hearts are cut off by death, and perish,

Psa. 146:4.
Psa. 22:26.

II. Against Eternal Punishment.

Rom. 8:6.

1. The wages of sin is death.

Rom. 6:22
Ezek. 18:4

(a) Sin produces death to the soul the very day that man transgresses God's law.

Gen. 2:17.
Rom. 7:9.

(b) Sin separates from God now.

Isa. 59:1.

(c) All sinners are now dead, yet have a conscious existence.

Eph. 2:1
Rom. 8:6.
1 John 3:14.
1 Tim. 5:6

These scriptures plainly show that the death of the soul is incurred by sin is not the destrutcion of its consciousness.

The sinner still lives. It is the forefiture of the bliss of divine favor. Not a cessation of conscious existence, but an alienation from God, whose favor is the normal sphere of the soul's happiness. Sinners are now dead yet live. They are cut off from God's favor. Just so in the future. They will be cut off from union with God eternally—dead—yet have a conscious existence and be tormented forever and ever in the lake of fire, which is the second death.

Rev. 21:8.
Rev. 20:10.

2. Eternal life is only promised to the righteous through Jesus Christ.

Dom. 6:22.
Rom. 6:22.

(a) Eternal life is not only eternal conscious existence, but a blessed union with God, enjoyment in his service and favor without end. A blessed knowledge of his salvation.

John 17:3.

(b) Eternal life given by the word and Spirit of God reunites the soul to God and makes it alive to his glory. This blessed life is now attainable in this life.

Eph. 2:1, 5, 6.
1 John 3:14.
John 5:24.
John 6:47.
1 John 6:47.
1 John 5:11, 13.

(c) If we prove faithful until death, the

same blessed union with God and eternatl life we here enjoy in the world to come.
Mark 10:30.

(d) At the second coming coming of Christ, death, will be destroyed, the righteeous will be raised to eternal life, and the wicked to shame and everlasting contempt.
1 Cor. 15:22-26.
John 5:28, 29. Dan. 12:2.

3. The wicked shall be destroyed.
2 Thes. 1:7-10.
Psa. 37:38.

(a) Destroy does not always necessarily mean to annihilate. It also means to ruin, to render utterly useless for the purpose for which it was made. Floods may destroy cities and not annihilate them. Storms may destroy crops and not annihilate them.

(b) Examples of its use in the Scripture.

1. Israel destroyed herself, but not blotted out of existence as a nation.
Hos. 13:9.
2. A hypocrite with his mouth destroyeth his neighbor, but does not annihilate him.
Prov. 11:9.
3. We may destroy our brother by eating meat, yet he will have a living existence.
Rom. 14:15.
4. Destroy—to trouble.
Psa. 78:45.
5. Destroy – to pervert.
Eccl. 7:7.
6. Paul destroyed God's people by putting them in prison. They were not annilated.
Acts 9:21. Acts 8:3.
7. Faith was destroyed, yet lived.
Gal. 1:23.
8. Moral destruction, but conscious existence.
2 Chr. 26:16.
9. Destroy—to spoil.
Jer. 4:20.

(c) From all these scripture texts we learn that destroy does not imply anhihilation. So with the destruction of the wicked. It will not be a blotting out of existence as the heathen vainly hope; but an eternal separation from God, a depriviation of his approving smile and favor. Since man was created to enjoy God, live and serve him when etrnally disqualified by sin for that lofty end, he is ruined, destroyed, from the fact that he will never answer the exalted object of his creation. Being still conscious he will suffer an endless punishment.

Rev. 20:10

4. The wicked shall perish
   Luke 13:1-5.
   (a) The word perish not imply annhiliation for the following resons.
   1. The righteous perish as well as the wicked.
      Eccl. 7:15
      Isa. 57: 1; Mich. 1:2
   2. Truth may perish but still live.
      Jer. 7:28.
   (b) The sense in which the wicked shall perish is that their doom is inredeemable, and eternal, and there will be no hope of recovery from the state of torment.

THE STATE OF MAN BETWEEN DEATH AND THE JUDGEMENT

I. Natural Death
   1. Separates the soul from the body.
      Gen. 35:18
      Luke 12:20
   2. Is the time when the soul leaves the body.
      Gen. 35:18
   3. Does not involve the soul in its ruin
      2 Cor. 4:16
      Mat. 10:28

II. At Natural Death
   1. The body returns to dust
      Gen. 3:19.
      Psa. 104:29.
      Eccl. 12:7.
   (a) It sleeps.
      Dan. 12:2.
      Mat. 7:52.
   (b) It knows nothing.
      Eccl. 9:5, 6.
   2. The spirit goes to God.
      Eccl. 12:7.
      Act 7:59.
      Luke 23:46.

III. The State of the Soul After Death.
   1. The righteous
   (a) Are in a heavenly realm called
   1. Paradise.

FUTURE STATE

1. Man will not receive his full reward and punishment until after the Resurrection, beyond the Judgment.
   2 Tim. 4:1, 8.
   Eccl. 12:14.
   Rev. 20:11-15.
   2 Cor. 5:10.
   Rom. 14:10-12.
   2 Pet. 2:9

Mat. 16:26, 27.
2 Thes. 1:7-10.
Mat. 25:31-46.

II. The Reward of the Righteous.

1. Will be in heaven.
   Mat. 5:11, 12
   Mat. 6:19, 20.
   Mat. 19:21.
   Luke 6:22, 23.
2. Heaven will be our future and eternal home.
   Heb. 10:34.
   1 Pet. 1:4, 5. Col. 1:5.
   2 Tim. 4:18.
3. Heaven is a prepared place. John 14:2, 3.
   2 Cor. 5:1.
   (a) Like the "Lamb slain from the foundation of the world," heaven was prepared in the mind of God, in his divine plan, from the beginning.
   Rev. 13:8. Mat. 25:34.
   (b) Christ in reality had to be slain, also went and really prepared our future place of abode.
   John 14:2, 3.
   Rev. 7:9-17.
4. Heaven is termed
   (a) A city.
   Heb. 13:14.
   Rev. 22:14.
   (b) A country.
   Heb. 11:16.
   (c) New heavens and new earth.
   2 Pet. 3:7-13.
   Rev. 20:11-15.
   Rev. 21:1.

III. The Punishment of the Wicked.

1. The future punishment of the wicked will be in hell, which is a place prepared for the everlasting punishment of demons. Matt. 25:41.
   2 Pet. 2:4, 9. Jude 6.
   (a) Hell is a place.
   Luke 12:4, 5.
   (b) Hell is a place prepared. Mat. 25:41.
   (c) The wicked shall
   Psa. 9:17.
2. The place and state of future punishment is termed outer darkness, and in that darkness the wicked shall weep, wail, and gnash their teeth forever.
   (a) Outer darkness.
   Mat. 8:11, 12.
   Mat. 25:30.
   (b) There shall be wailing and gnashing of teeth.
   Mat. 24:50, 51.
   (c) The wicked shall remain there forever.
   2 Pet. 2:9, 13-17.
   Jude 13.
3. The place and state of future punishment is termed a lake of fire, which will be everlasting fire, and in this everlasting fire the wicked will suffer an everlasting punishment.
   (a) A lake of fire.
   Rev. 20:15.

Rev. 21:8.
(b) Hell fire.
Mat. 18:19.
Mark 9:47.
(c) Fire that never shall be quenched.
Mark 9:43-48.
(d) Everlasting fire.
Mat. 18:8. Mat. 25:41.
(e) Suffering the vengeance of etrnal fire.
Jude 7.
(f) Everlasting punishment.
Mat. 25:46. Rev. 20:10.

4. The future punishment of the wicked consists in torment and that torment will last forever and ever.
(a) Torment.
Mat. 8:28, 29.
Rev. 14:10.
(b) Forever and ever.
Rev. 14:10, 11.
Rev. 20:10.

5. The future punishment of the wicked consists in damnation.

GOD

I. Is a Spirit.
John 4:24.
2 Cor. 3:17.

II. Is declased to be
1. Invisible.
Job 23:8, 9.
John 1:18.
John 5:37.
(Invisible.)
Col. 1:15.
1 Tim. 1:17.
1 Tim. 6:16.
2. Eternal.
Deut. 33:27.
Psa. 90:2.
Rev. 4:8-10.
3. Immortal.
1 Tim. 1:17.
4. Incorruptible.
Rom. 1:23.
5. Omnipotent.
Gen. 17:1.
Rev. 19:6.
6. Omnipresent.
Psa. 139:7-10.
Jer. 23:23.
7. Omniscient.
Psa. 139:1-6.
Prov. 5:21.
8. Immutable.
Psa. 102:2, 6, 27.
Jas. 1:17.
9. Only-wise.
Rom. 16:27.
1 Tim. 1:17.
10. Incomprehensible.
Job 36:26.
Job 37:5.
Isa. 40:18.
Micah 4:12.
11. Unsearchable.
Job 11:7.
Job 26:14
Job 37:23.
Isa. 40:28.
Rom. 11:33.
12. Most High.
Acts 7:48.
Psa. 83:18.
13. Love.
1 John 4:8, 16.
14. Perfect.
Mat. 5:48.
15. Holy.
Psa. 99:9.

Isa. 5:16.
16. Just.
Deut. 32:4.
Isa. 45:21.
17. True.
Jer. 10:10.
John 17:3.
18. Upright.
Psa. 25:8.
Psa. 92:15.
19. Righteous.
Ezra 9:15.
Psa. 145:17.
20. Good.
Psa. 25:8.
Psa. 119:68.
21. Great.
2 Chir. 2:5.
Psa. 86:10.
22. Gracious.
Ex. 34:6.
Psa. 116:5.
23. Faithful.
1 Cor. 10:13.
1 Pet. 4:19.
24. Merciful
Ex. 34:6, 7.
Psa. 86:5.

THE SAVED SOULS ARE AT REST

Luke 23:43.
2. Abraham's bosom.
Luke 16:22.
(b) Are dwelling with Christ.
Phil. 1:21-24.
(c) Are absent from the body and present with the Lord.
2 Cor. 5:19.
(d) Are dwelling with their people.
Gen. 49:33.
Gen. 50:1-13.
(e) Are in a state of blessedness.
Rev. 14:13.
(f) Are at rest.
Job 3:17.
(g) Are comforted.
Luke 16:25.
(h) Are conscious.
1 Thes. 5:10.
Rev. 6:9, 10.
Luke 16:22,25,26.
2. The wicked
(a) Are in conscious suffering.
Luke 16:22-24.
(b) Are reserved in chain of darkness unto the judgment day, when they will be punished.

THE NATURE OF MAN IN HIS PRESENT STATE.

I. When God Created Man.
1. He made him a little lower than the angels.
Psa. 8:4-7.
2. He made him in his own image and exact likeness.
Gen. 1:26, 27.
(a) God is a Spirit.
John 4:24.
(b) A spirit hath not flesh and bones.
Luke 24:39.
(c) God is invisible.
Col. 1:15.
1 Tim. 1:17.
Heb. 11:27.
(d) God is immortal.

I Tim. 1:17
(c) To create man in God's likeness and image would be to create him a spirit being, immortal, and immaterial.
Job. 32:8
Eccl. 12:7
3. He formed a spirit in. man.
Zech. 12:1

Our doctrine on Justification and Sanctification, as definite works of grace cannot be changed. Our work shall be carried on by conference as the Bishop shall appoint. No Conference shall have any power to change any of our Doctrines or revoke any of our Doctrines and General Rules. We shall have quarterly Conference and General Conferences.

THE LORD'S SUPPER NIGHT

On the Lord's Supper night or day. the minister may preach the Lord's Supper sermon and after he has preached the sermon, he can read 1 Cor. 11:23-32. to his people and give the supper. We always have the supper on Sunday night, and the Feet Washing on Thursday night before the Lord's Supper.

CONSECRATION AND ORDINATION OF OUR ELDERS AND BISHOPS

Elder and Bisho pare of the same rank, only differ in their office work.

(This service is not to be understood as an ordination to a higher Order in the Christian Ministry, beyond and above that of Elders or Presbyters, but as a solemn and fitting Consecration for the special and most sacred duties of Superintendency in the Church).

The Elder need not be confined to this prayer according to form, but let him pray it in the spirit.

CONSECRATION AND ORDINATIONS

The Form of Consecrating

The Collect

Almighty God, who by Thy Son Jesus Christ didst give the holy Apostles, Elders, and Evangelists many excellent gifts, and didst charge them to feed thy flock; give grace, we beseech thee, to all the Ministers and Pastors of the Church, that they may diligently preach thy word and duly administer the godly discipline thereof; and grant to the People that they may obediently follow the same, that all may receive the crown of everlasting glory, through Jesus Christ our Lord. Amen.

Then shall he read by one of the Elders: The Epistle. Acts xx, 17-35.

From Miletus Paul sent to Ephesus, and called the elders of the Church. And when they were come to him, he said unto them, Ye know, from the first day that I came to Asia, after what manner I have been with you at all seasons, serving the Lord with all humility of mind, and with many tears, and temptations, which befell me by the lying in wait of the Jews; and how I kept back nothing that was profitable unto you, but have showed you, and have taught you publicly, and from house to house, testifying both to the Jews, and also to the Greeks, repentance toward God, and faith toward our Lord Jesus Christ. And now, behold, I go bound in the spirit unto Jerusalem, not knowing the things that shall befall me there; save that the Holy Ghost witnesseth in every city, saying that bonds and afflictions abide me. But none of these things move me, neither count I my life dear unto myself, so that I might finish my course with joy, and the ministry, which I have received of the Lord Jesus, to testify the Gospel of the grace of God. And now, behold, I know that ye all, among whom I have gone preaching the kingdom of God, shall see my face no more. Wherefore I take you to record this day, that I am pure from the blood of all men. For I have not shunned to declare unto you all the counsel of God. Take heed therefore unto yourselves, and to all the flock, over the which Holy Ghost hath made you overseers, to feed the Church of God, which he hath purchased with his own blood. For I know this, that after my departing shall grievous wolves enter in among you, not sparing the flock. Also of your own selves shall men arise, speaking perverse things, to draw away disciples after them. Therefore watch, and remember, that by the space of three years I ceased not to warn everyone night and day with tears. And now, brethren, I commend you to God, and to the word of his grace, which is able to build you up, and give you an inheritance among all them which are sanctified. I have coveted no man's silver, or gold, or apparel. Yea, ye yourselves know, that these hands have ministered unto my necessities, and to them that were with me. I have showed you all things, how that so laboring ye ought to support the weak, and to remember the words of the Lord Jesus, how he said, It is more blessed to give than to receive.

Then another shall read:

The Gospel. St John xxi, 15-17.

Jesus saith to Simon Peter, Simon, son of Jonas, lovest thou me more than these? He saith unto him, Yea, Lord; thou knowest that I love Thee. He saith unto him, Feed my lambs. He saith to him again the second time, Simon, son of Jonas, lovest thou me? He saith unto him, Yea, Lord; thou knowest that I love thee. He saith unto him, Feed my sheep. He saith unto him the third time, Simon, son of Jonas, lovest thou me? Peter was grieved because he said unto him the third time, Lovest tmou me? And he said unto him, Lord, thou knowest all things; Thou knowest that I love thee. Jesus saith unto him, Feed my sheep.

Or this, St. Matthew xxviii,18-20.

Jesus came and spake unto them, saying, All power is given unto me in heaven and in earth. Go ye therefore, and teach all nations, baptizing them in the name of the Father, and of the Son, and of the Holy Ghost: teaching them to observe all things whatsoever I have commanded you: and, lo, I am with you always, even unto the end of the world.

After the Gospel and the Sermon are ended, the Electer Person shall be presented by two Elders unto the Bishop, saying,

We present unto you this holy man to be consecrated a Bishop.

Then the Bishop shall move the Congregation present to pray, saying thus to them:

Brethren, it is written in the Gospel of Saint Luke that our Saviour Christ continued the whole night in prayer before he did choose and send forth his twelve Apostles. It is written also in the Acts of the Apostles that the disciples who were at Antioch did fast and pray before they laid hands on Paul and Barnabas, and sent forth on their first mission to the Gentiles. Let us therefore, following the example of our Saviour Christ, and his Apostles, first fall to prayer before we admit and send forth this person presented to us to the work whereunto we trust the Holy Ghost hath called him.

As the Holy Spirit shall move to Pray then shall the following prayer be offered:

Almighty God, Giver of all good things, who by Thy Holy Spirit hast appointed divers Offices in thy Church: mercifully behold this thy servant now called to the Work and Ministry of a Bishop, and replenish him so with the truth of thy doctrine, and adorn him with innocency of life, that both by word and deed he may faithfully serve thee in this Office, to the glory of thy name, and the edifying and well governing of thy Church, through the merits of our Saviour Jesus Christ, who liveth and reigneth with thee and the Holy Ghost, world without end. Amen.

Then the Bishop shall say to him that is to be Consecrated:

Brother, forasmuch as the Holy Scriptures command that we shall not be hasty in laying on hands and admitting any person to government in the Church of Christ, which he hath purchased with no less price than the sedding of his own blood;

before you are admitted to this administration, you will, in the fear of God, give answer to the questions which I now propound:

Are you persuaded that you are truly called to this Ministration, according to the will of our Lord Jesus Christ?

Ans. I am so persuaded.

The Bishop: Are you persuaded that the holy scriptures contain sufficiently all doctrines required of necessity for eternal salvation, through faith in Jesus Christ? And are you determined out of the same Holy Scriptures to instruct the people committed to your charge, and to teach or maintain nothing as required of necessity to eternal salvation but that which you shall be persuaded may be concluded and proved by the same?

Ans.: I am so persuaded and determined, by God's grace.

The Bishop: Will you then faithfully exercise yourself in the same Holy Scriptures, and call upon God by prayer for the true understanding of the same, so that you may be able by them to teach and exhort with wholesome doctrine, and to withstand and convince the gainsayers? Titus 1:9.

Ans.: I will do so, by the help of God.

The Bishop: Are you ready with faithful diligence to banish and drive away all erroneous and strange doctrines contrary to God's word, and both privately and openly to call upon and encourage others to the same?

Ans.: I am ready, The Lord being my helper.

The Bishop: Will you deny all ungodliness and worldly lust, and live soberly, righteously, and godly in this present world, that you may show yourself in all things an example of good works unto others, that the adversary may be ashamed, having nothing to say against you?

Ans.: I will do so, the Lord being my helper.

The Bishop: Will you maintain and set forward, as much as shall lie in you, quietness, love, and peace among all men; and such as shall be unjust, disobedient, and criminal, correct and punish according to such authority as you have by God's word, and as shall be committed unto you?

Ans.: I will do so, by the help of God.

The Bishop: Will you be faithful in Ordaining, or laying hands upon and sending others, and in all the other duties of your office?

Ans.: I will so be, by the help of God.

The Bishop: Will you show yourself gentle, and be merciful, for Christ's sake, to poor and needy people, and to all strangers destitute of help?

Ans.: I will so show myself, by God's help.

The the bishop shall say:

Almighty God, our heavenly Father, who hath given you a good will to do all these things, grant also unto you strength and power to perform the same, that he accomplishing in you the good work which he has begun, you may be found blameless at the last day, through Jesus Christ our Lord. Amen.

That ended, the Bishop shall say:

Lord, hear our Prayer.

Ans.: And let our cry come unto thee.

The Bishop shall then say:

Let us pray.

Almighty and Most Merciful Father, who of thine infinite goodness has given thine only and dearly beloved Son Jesus Christ to be our Redeemer, and the author of everlasting life; who, after he had made perfect our redemption by his death, and was ascended into heaven, pouring down his gifts abundantly upon men, making some Apostles, some Prophets, some Evangelists, some Pastors and Teachers, to the edifying and making perfect of his Church: grant, we beseech thee, to this thy servant, such grace that he may evermore be ready to spend abroad thy Gospel, the glad tidings of reconciliation with thee, and use the authority given him, not to destruction, but to salvation; not to hurt, but to help; so that as a wise and faithful servant, giving to the family their portion in due season, he may at last be received into everlasting joy, through Jesus Christ our Lord, who, with thee and the Holy Ghost, liveth and reigneth, one God, world without end. Amen.

Then the Bishop and Elders present shall lay their hands upon the head of the Elected Person, kneeling before them, the Bishop saying:

The Lord pour upon thee the Holy Ghost for the Office and Work of a Bishop or Elder in the Church of God now committed unto thee by the authority of the Church through the imposition of our hands, in the name of the Father, and of the Son, and of the Holy Grost. Amen. And remember that thou stir up the grace of God which is in thee; for God hath not given us the spirit of fear, but of power, and love, and of a sound mind.

Then shall the Bishop deliver to him the Bible, saying,

Give heed unto reading, exhortation, and doctrine. Think upon the things contained in this book. Be diligent in them, that the increase coming thereby may be manifest unto all men. Take heed unto thyself, and to thy doctrine; for by so doing thou shalt both save thyself and them that hear thee. Be to the flock of Christ a shepherd, not a wolf; feed them, devour them not. Hold up the weak, heal the sick, bind up the broken, bring again the outcast, seek the lost; be so merciful that you may not be too remiss; so minister discipline that you forget not mercy; that when the chief Shepherd shall appear, you may receive the never-fading crown of glory, through Jesus Christ our Lord. Amen.

(Then the Bishop shall administer the Lord's Supper to the newly Consecrated Bishop and other persons present.)

Then shall be offered the following Prayers:

Most Merciful Father, we beseech thee to send down upon this thy servant the heavenly blessing, and to so endow him with thy Holy Spirit that he, preaching thy word, and exercising authority in thy Church, may not only be earnest to reprove, beseech, and rebuke with all patience and doctrine, but also may be, to such as believe, a wholesome example in word, in conversation, in love, in faith, and in purity; that faithfully fulfilling his course, at the last day he may receive the crown of righteousness laid up by the Lord, the righteous Judge, who liveth and reigneth, one God with the Father and the Holy Ghost, world without end. Amen.

Prevent us, O Lord, in all our doings with thy most gracious favor, and further us with thy continual help, that in all our works, begun, continued, and ended in thee, we may gloify thy holy name; and finally, by thy mercy, obtain everlasting life, through Jesus Christ our Lord. Amen.

The peace of God, which passeth all understanding, keep your hearts and minds in the knowledge and love of God, and of his Son Jesus Christ our Lord: and the blessing of God Almighty, the Father, the Son, and the Holy Ghost, be among you, and remain with you always. Amen.

The Form of Ordaining Elders

(When the day appointed by the Bishop is come, there shall be a Sermon or Exhortation, declaring the Duty and Office of such as come to be admitted Elders; how necessary that Order is in the Church of Christ, and also how the People ought to esteem the Elders in their Office.)

After which, one of the Elders shall present unto the Bishop all them that are to be Ordained, and say;

I present unto you these persons to be ordained as Elders.

Then their names being read aloud, the Bishop shall to the people,

Brethren, these are they whom we purpose, God willing, this day to ordain Elders. For after due examination, we find not to the contrary, but that they are lawfully called to this function and ministry, and that they are persons meet for the same. But, if there be any of you who knoweth any crime or impediment in any of them, for the which he ought not to be received into this holy Ministry let him come forth in the name of God, and show what the crime or impediment is.

(If any crime or impediment be objected, the Bishop shall surcease from ordaining that person until such time as the party accused shall be found clear of the same.)

ORDINATION OF ELDERS

Then shall be said the Collect, Epistle, and Gospel, as followeth:

Now prayer can be offered as the spirit give utterance in the Holy Spirit.

The Collect.

Almighty God, Giver of all good things, who by thy Holy Spirit hast appointed divers Orders of Ministers in thy Church; mercifully behold these thy servants now called to the Office of Elders, and replenish them so with the truth of thy doctrine, and adorn them with innocency of life, that both by word and good example they may faithfully serve thee in this Office, to the glory of thy name, and the edification of the Church, through the merits of our Saviour Jesus Christ, who liveth and reigneth with thee and the Holy Ghost, world without end. Amen.

The Epistle; Ephesians iv, 7-13.

Unto every one of us is given grace according to the measure of the gift of Christ. Wherefore he saith. When he ascended up on high, he led captivity captive, and gave gifts unto men. Now that he ascended, what is it but that he also descended first into the lower parts of the earth? He that descended is the same also that ascended up far above all heavens, that he might fill all things. And he gave some, Apostles; and some, Prophets; and some, Evangelists; and some, Pastors and Teachers; for the perfecting of the saints, for the work of the ministry, for the edifying of the body of Christ; till we all come in the unity of the faith, and of the knowledge of the Son of God, unto a perfect man, unto the measure of the stature of the fullness of Christ.

After this shall be read for the gospel part of the tenth chapter of St. John: St. John 10:1-16.

Verily, verily, I say unto you, He that entereth not by the door into the sheepfold, but climbeth up some other way, the same is a thief and a robber. But he that entereth in by the door is the Shepherd of the sheep. To him the porter openeth; and the sheep hear his voice; and he calleth his own sheep by name, and leadeth them out. And when he putteth forth his own sheep, he goeth before them, and the sheep follow him; for they know his voice. And a stranger will they not follow, but will flee from him; for they know not the voice of strangers. This parable spake Jesus unto them; but they understood not what things they were which he spake unto them. Then said Jesus unto them again. Verily, verily, I say unto you, I am the door of the sheep. All that ever came before me are thieves and robbers; but the sheep did not hear them. I am the door; by me if any man enter in, he shall be saved, and shall go in and out, and find pasture. The thief cometh not but for to steal, and to kill, and to destroy: I am come that they might have life, and that they might have it more abundantly. I am the good shepherd: the good shepherd giveth his life for the sheep. But he that is a hiireling, and not the shepherd, whose own the sheep are not, seeth the wolf coming, and leaveth the sheep, and fleeth; and the wolf catcheth them, and scattereth the sheep. The hireling fleeth, because he is a hireling, and careth not for the sheep. I am the good shepherd, and know my sheep, and am known of mine. As the Father knoweth me, even so know I the Father: and I lay down my life for the sheep. And other sheep I have, which are not of this fold: them also I must bring, and they shall hear my voice; and there shall be one fold and one shepherd.

And that done, the Bishop shall say unto the Persons to be Ordained Elders:

You have heard, brethren, in your private examination, and in the holy lessons taken out of the Gospel and the writings of the Apostles, of what dignity and of how great importance this Office is whereunto ye are called. And now again we exhort you, in the name of our Lord Jesus Christ, that ye have in remembrance into how high a dignity and to how weighty an Office ye are called; that is to say, to be Messengers, Watchmen, and Stewards of the Lord; to teach and to permonish, to feed and provide for, the Lord's family; to gather the outcasts, to seek the lost, and to be ever ready to spread abroad the Gospel, the glad tidings of reconciliation with God.

Have always therefore printed in your remembrance how great a treasure is committed to your charge. For they are the sheep of Christ, which he bought with his body. And if it shall happen, the same Church, or any member tereof, do take any hurt or hindrance by reason of your negligence, ye know the greatness of the fault, and also the fearful punishment that will ensue. Wherefore consider with yourselves the end of the ministry toward the children of God, toward the spouse and body of Christ; and see that you never cease your labor, your care and diligence, until you have done all that lieth in you, according to your bounden duty, to bring all such as are or, shall be committed to your charge unto that agreement in the faith and knowledge of God, and to that ripeness and perfectness of age in Christ, that there be no place left among you either for error in religion or for viciousness in life.

Forasmuch then as your Office is both of so great excellency and of so great difficulty, ye see with how great care and study ye ought to apply yourselves, as well that ye may show yourselves dutiful and thankful unto that Lord who hath placed you in so high a dignity; as also to beware that neither you yourselves offend, nor be occasion that others offend. Howbeit ye cannot have a mind and will thereto of yourselves, for that will and ability are given of God alone; therefore ye ought, and have need, to pray earnestly for his Holy Spirit. And seeing that ye cannot by any other means compass the doing of so weighty a work, pertaining to the salvation of man, but with doctrine and exhortation taken out of the Holy Scriptures, and with a life agreeable to the same; consider how studious ye ought to be in reading and learning the Scriptures, and in framing the manners, both of yourselves and of them that specially pertain unto you, according to the rule of the same Scriptures; and for this selfsame cause, how ye ought to forsake and set aside, as much as you may, all worldly cares and studies.

We have good hope that you have all weighed and pondered these things with yourselves long before this time; and that you have clearly determined, by God's grace, to give yourselves wholly to this Office, whereunto it has pleased God to call you: so that, as much as lieth in you, you will apply yourselves wholly to this one thing, and draw all your cares and studies this way, and that you will continually pray to God the Father, by the meditation of our only Saviour Jesus Christ, for the heavenly assistance of the Holy Ghost: that by daily reading and weighing of the Scriptures ye may wax riper and stronger in your ministry; and that ye may so endeavor to sanctify the lives of you and yours, and to fashion them after the rule and doctrine of Christ, that ye may be wholesome and godly examples and patterns for the people to follow.

And now, that this present Congregation of Christ here assembled may also understand youd minds and wills in thes things, and that this your promise may the more move you to do your duties, ye shall answer plainly to these things which we, in the name of God and his Church, shall demand of you touching the same:

Do you think in your heart that you are truly called, according to the will of our Lord Jesus Christ, to the Order of Elders?

Ans.: I think so.

The Bishop: Are you persuaded that the Holy Scriptures contain sufficiently all doctrine required of necessity for eternal salvation through faith in Jesus Christ? And, are you determined out of the said Scriptures to instruct the people committed to your charge, and to teach nothing as required of necessity to eternal salvation but that which you shall be persuaded may be concluded and proved by the Scriptures?

Ans.: I am so persuaded, and have so determined, by God's grace.

The Bishop: Will you then give your faithful diligence always so to minister the Doctrine, and Sacraments and Discipline of Christ, as the Lord hath commanded?

Ans.: I will so do, by the help of the Lord.

The Bishop: Will you be ready with all faithful diligence to banish and drive away all erroneous and strange doctrines contrary to God's word, and to use both public and private monitions and exhortations, as well to the sick as to the whole within your charge, as need shall require and occasion shall be given?

Ans.: I will, the Lord being my helper.

The Bishop: Will you be diligent in Prayers, and in reading of the Holy Scriptures, and in such studies as help to the knowledge of the same, laying aside the study of the world and the flesh?

Ans.: I will nedeavor so to do, the Lord being my helper.

The Bishop: Will you be diligent to frame and fashion yourselves, and your families, according to the doctrine of Christ; and to make both yourselves and them, as much as in you lieth, wholesome examples and patterns to the flock of Christ?

Ans.: I will apply myself thereto, the Lord being my helper.

The Bishop: Will you maintain and set forward, as much as lieth in you, quietness, peace, and love, among all Christian people, and especially among them that are or shall be committed to your charge?

Ans.: I will so do, the Lord being my helper

The Bishop: Will you reverently obey your chief Ministers, unto whom is committed the charge and government over you, following with a glad mind and will their godly admonitions, submitting yourselves to their godly judgments?

Ans.: I will so do, the Lord being my helper.

Then shall the Bishop, standing up, say:

Almight God, who hath given you this will to do all these

things, grant also unto you strength and power to perform the same that He may accomplish his work which he hath begun in you, through Jesus Christ our Lord. Amen.

(After this the Congregation shall be desired secretly in secretly in their Prayers to make their humble supplications to God for all these things; for the which Prayers there shall be silence kept for a space.)

After which shall be said by the Bishop, the Persons to be ordained Elders, all kneeling, the Bishop beginning, and the Elders and others that are present answering by verse, as followeth:

Come, Holy Ghost, our souls inspire,
And lighten with celestial fire.
Thou the anointing Spirit art,
Who dost thy sevenfold gifts impart.
Thy blessed unction from above
Is comfort, life, and fire of love.
Enable with perpetual light
The dullness of our blinded sight;
Anoint and cheer our soiled face
With the abundance of thy grace;
Keep far our foes, give peace at home;
Where thou art Guide, no ill can come.
Teach us to know the Father, Son,
And Thee of both to be but ONE;
That through the ages all along
This may be our endless song:
Praise to thy eternal merit,
Father, Son, and Holy Spirit.

That done, the Bishop shall pray in this wise, and say:

Let us pray.

Pray in the Holy Spirit.

Almighty God and heavenly Father who of thine infinite love and goodnes stoward us hast given to us thine only and most dearly beloved Son Jesus Christ to be our Redeemer, and the author of everlasting life; who, after he had made Perfect our redemption by his death, and was ascended into heaven, sent abroad into the world his Apostles, Prophets, Evangelists, Teachers, and Pastors, by whose labor and ministry he gathered together a great flock in all parts of the world, to set forth the eternal praise of thy holy name: for these so great benefits of thy eternal goodness, and for that thou has vouchsafed to call these thy servants here present to the same office and ministry appointed for the salvation of mankind, we render unto thee most hearty thanks; we praise and worship thee; and we humbly beseech thee by the same, thy blessed Son, to grant unto all who either here or elsewhere call upon thy name, that we may continue to show ourselves thankful unto thee for these, and all other thy benefits, and that we may daily increase and go forward in the knowledge and faith of thee and thy Son, by the Holy Spirit. So that as well by these thy Ministers, as by them over whom they shall be appointed thy Ministers, thy holy name may be forever glorified, and thy blessed kingdom enlarged, through the same, thy Son Jesus Christ our Lord, who liveth and reigneth with thee in the unity of the same Holy Spirit, world without end. Amen.

When this Prayer is done, the Bishop and the Elders present shall lay their hands severally upon the head of every one that receiveth the Order of Elders; the Receivers humbly kneeling, and the Bishop saying:

The Lord pour upon thee the Holy Ghost for the Office and Work of an Elder in the Church of God, now committed unto thee by the authority of the Church, through the imposition of our hands. And be thou a faithful dispenser of the word of God, and of his Holy Sacraments; in the name of the Father, and of the Son, and of the Holy Ghost. Amen.

Then the Bishop shall deliver to every one of them, kneeling, the Bible into his hands, saying:

Take thou authority as an Elder in the Church to preach the word of God, and to administer the Holy Sacraments in the Congregation.

These prayers are good let God lead. It must be from the heart and through the Holy Spirit.

Then the Bishop shall offer the following Prayer:

Most Merciful Father, we beseech thee to send upon these thy servants thy heavenly blessings, that they may be clothed with righteousness, and that thy word spoken by their mouths may have such success that it may never be spoken in vain. Grant alos that we may have grace to hear and receive what they shall deliver out of thy most holy word, or agreeably to the same, as the means of our salvation; and that in all our words and deeds we may seek thy glory, and the increase of thy kingdom, through Jesus Christ our Lord. Amen.

Prevent us, O Lord, in all our doings, with thy most gracious favor, and further us by thy continual help; that in all our works, begun, continued, and ended in thee, we may glorify thy holy name, and finally, by thy mercy, obtain everlasting life through Jesus Christ our Lord. Amen.

The peace of God, which passeth all understanding, keep your hearts and minds in the knowledge and love of God, and of his Son Jesus Christ our Lord: and the blessing of God

Almighty, the Father, the Son, and the Holy Ghost, be among you, and remain with you always. Amen.

*** (If on the same day the Order of Deacons be given to some ,and that of Elders to others, the Deacons shall be first presented, and then the Elders. The Collect shall both be used; first that for Deacons, then that for Elders. The Epistle shall be Ephesians iv, 7-13, as before in this Office: immediately after which, they who are to be ordained Deacons shall be examined and ordained as is below prescribed. Then one of them having read the Gospel, which shall be St. John x, 1-16, as before in this Office, they who are to be ordained Elders shall likewise be examined and ordained, as in this office before appointed.)

The Form of Ordaining Deacons.

When the day appointed by the Bishop is come, there shall be a Sermon or Exhortation, declaring the Duty and Office of such as come to be admitted to the Order of Deacons.)

After which one of the Elders shall present unto the Bishop the Persons to be ordained Deacons, and their names being read aloud the Bishop shall say unto the People:

Brethren, if there be any of you who knoweth any crime of impediment in any of these persons presented to be ordained Dacons, for the which he ought not to be admitted to that Office, let him come forth in the name of God, and show what the crime or impediment is.

The Elder can use the Prayer or let the Lord give him one as he may be led.

(If any crime of impediment be objected, the Bishop shall surcease from ordaninig that persons unti such time as the party accused shall be found clear of the same.)

Then shall be read the following Collect and Epistle: The Collect.

Almighty God, who by thy divine providence hast appointed divers Orders of Ministers in thy Church, and dist inspire thy Apostles to chose into the Order of Deacons thy first martyr, Saint Stephen, with others; mercifully behold these thy servants, now called to the like Office and Administration; replenish them so with the truth of thy doctrine, and adorn them with innocency of life, that both by word and good example they may faithfully serve thee in this Office to thc glory of thy name, and the edification of thy Church, through the merits of our Saviour Jesus Christ, who liveth and reigneth with thee and the Holy Ghost, now and forever. Amen.

The Epistle: I Timothy iii, 8-13.

Likewise must the Deacons be grave, not double-tongued, not given to much wine, not greedy of filthy lucre; holding the mystery of the faith in a pure conscience. And let these also first be proved; then let them use the Office of a Deacon, being found blameless. Even so must their wives be grave, not slanderers, sober, faithful in all things. Let the Deacons be the husbands of one wife, ruling their children and their own houses well. For they that have used the Office of a Deacon well purchase to themselves a good degree, and great boldness in the faith which is in Christ Jesus.

Then shall the Bishop, in the presence of the People, examine every one of those who are to be ordained, after this manner following:

Do you trust that you are inwardly moved by the Holy Ghost to take upon you the Office of the Ministry in the Church of Christ, to serve God for the promoting of his glory and the edifying of His people?

Ans.: I trust so.

The Bishop: Do you unfeignedly believe all the canonical Scriptures of the Old and New Testaments?

Ans.: I do believe them.

The Bishop: Will you diligently read or expound the same unto the people whom you shall be appointed to serve?

Ans.: I will.

The Bishop: It appertaineth to the Office of a Deacon to assist the Elder in divine service, and especially when he ministereth the Holy Communion, to help him in the distribution thereof; to read and expound the Holy Scriptures; to instruct the youth; and to baptize. And furthermore, it is his office to search for the sick, poor, and impotent, that they may be visited and relieved. Will you do this gladly and willingly?

Ans.: I do so, by the help of God.

The BIshop: Will you apply all your diligence to frame and fashion your own lives and the lives of your families according to the doctrine of Christ; and to make both yourselves and them, as much as in you lieth, wholesome examples of the flock of Christ?

Ans.: I will do so, the Lord being my helper.

The Bishop: Will you reverently obey them to whom the charge and government over you is committed, following with a glad mind and will their godly admonitions?

Ans.: I will endeavor so to do, the Lord being my helper.

Then the Bishop, laying his hands severally upon the head of every one of them, shall say:

Take thou authority to execute the office of a Deacon in

the Church of God: in the name of the Father, and of the Son, and of the Holy Ghost Amen.

Then shall the Bishop deliver to every one of them the Holy Bible, saying:

Take thou authority to read the Holy Scriptures in the Church of God, and to preach the same.

Then one appointed by the Bishop shall read the Gospel:

Luke xii, 35-38.

Let your loins be girded about, and your lights burning; and ye yourselves like unto men that wait for their lord, when he will return from the wedding; that, when he cometh and knocketh, they may open unto him immediately. Blessed are those servants, whom the Lord when he cometh shall find watching: verily I say unto you, that he shall gird himself, and make them to sit down to meat, and will come forth and serve them. And if he shall come in the second watch, or come in the third watch, and find them so, blessed are those servants.

The Elder may use this prayer if he desire, or pray as the Holy Spirit move him.

Immediately before the Benediction shall be said these Collects following:

Almighty God, Giver of all good things, who of thy great goodness has vouchsafed to accept and take these thy servants into the Office of Deacons in thy Church; make them, we beseech thee, O Lord, to be modest, humble, and constant in their ministration, and to have a ready will to observe all spiritual discipline; that they, have always the testimony of a good conscience, and continuing every stable and strong in thy Son Christ, may so well behave themselves in this inferior office that they may be found worthy to be called, into the higher Ministries in thy Church, through the same, thy Son our Saviour Jesus Christ; to whom be glory and honor, world without end. Amen.

Prevent us, O Lord, in all our doings, with thy most gracious favor, and further us with thy continnal help; that in all our works, begun, continued, and ended in thee, we may glorify the holy name, and finally, by thy mercy, obtain everlasting life, through Jesus Christ our Lord. Amen.

The peace of God, which passeth all understanding, keep your hearts and minds in the knowledge and love of God, and of his Son Jesus Christ our Lord; and the blessing of God Almighty, the Father, the Son, and the Holy Ghost, be among you, and remain with you always Amen.

CHAPTER VII

SOLEMNIZATION OF MATRIMONY.

First, the bans of all that are to be married together, must be published in the congregation three several Sundays in the time of divine service, unless they be otherwise qualified according to law, the minister saying, after the accustomed manner:

I publish these bans of marriage between M of_________and N of __________. If any of you know just cause or impediment why these two persons should not be joined in holy matrimony, you are to declare it. This is the first, (second, or third) time of asking.

At the day and time appointed for the solemnization, the persons to be married standing together, the man on the right side and the woman on the left, the minister shall say:

Dearly beloved, we are gathered together here in the sight of God, and in the presence of these witnesses, to join together this man and this woman in holy matrimony; which is an honorable estate, instituted by God in the time of man's innocency, signifying unto us the mystical union which is between Christ and his Church; which holy estate Christ adorned and beautified with his presence, and first miracle that he wrought at Cana of Galilee, list, and is commended of St. Paul to be honorable among all men, and therefore not by any to be entered upon or taken in hand unadvisedly, but reverently, discreetly, advisedly, and in the fear of God.

Into which holy estate these persons come now to be joined. Therefore if any can show any just cause why they may not lawfully be joined together, let him now speak, or else hereafter forever hold his peace.

And also speaking to the persons that are to be married, he shall say:

I require and charge you both, as you will answer at the dreadful day of judgment, when the secrets of all hearts shall be disclosed that if either of you know any impediment why you may not be lawfully joined together in matrimony, you do now confess it; for be ye well assured that so many as are coupled together otherwise than God's word shall allow, are not joined together by God, neither is their matrimony lawful in the sight of God. For God's word forbids marrying to another while the first party of the first covenant are living. Malachi 2:14-16; Mark 10:11-12; Luke 16:18; Rom. 7: l-3.

If no impediment shall be alleged, then shall the minister say unto the man:

M Wilt thou have this woman to be thy wedded wife, to

live together after God's ordinance, in the holy state of matrimony? Wilt thou love her and cherish her and nurse her? Wilt thou love her, comfort her, honor and keep her, in sickness and in health, and forsaking all others, keep thee only unto her, as long as ye both shall live?

The man shall answer, I will.

Then shall the minister say unto the woman:

N Wilt thou have this man to be thy wedded husband, to live together after God's ordinance in the holy state of matrimony? Wilt thou obey him, serve him, love him, and honor him, and reverence him and keep him, in sickness and in health; and forsaking all others, keep thee only unto him so long as ye both shall live? The woman shall answer, I will.

I, M, take thee N, to be my wedded wife, to have and to hold, from this day forward, for better, or for worse, for richer, for poorer, in sickness and in health, to love and to cherish till death do us part, according to God's holy ordinance; and thereto I plight thee my faith.

Then they shall loose their hands, and the woman with her right hand, taking the man by his right hand, shall likewise say after the minister:

I, N, take thee M, to be my wedded husband, to have and to hold, from this day forward, for better, for worse, for richer, for poorer, in sickness and in health, to love. cherish and to obey, till death do us part, according to God's holy ordinance; and thereto I plight thee my faith.

Then shall the minister say, Let us pray.

O, Eternal God, Creator, Preserver of all mankind, giver of all spiritual grace, the author of everlasting life; send thy blessing upon these thy servants, this man and this woman, whom we bless in thy name; that as Isaac and Rebecca lived faithfully together, so these persons may surely perform and keep the vow and covenent betwixt them made, and may ever remain in perfect love and peace together, and live according to thy laws, through Jesus Christ our Lord. Amen.

If the parties desire it, the man shall here hand a ring to the minister, who shall return it to him and direct him to place it on the third finger of the woman's left hand. And the man shall say to the woman, repeating after the minister:

With this ring I thee wed, and with my worldly goods I thee endow, in the name of the Father, and of the Son, and of the Holy Ghost. Amen.

Then shall the minister join their right hands together and say:

Those whom God hath joined together, let no man put asunder.

Forasmuch as M and N have consented to live together in holy wedlock and have witnessed the same before God and this company, and thereto have pledged their faith to each other, and have declared the same by joining hands: I pronounce that they are man and wife together, in the name of the Father, and of the Son, and of the Holy Ghost. Amen.

And the minister shall add this blessing.

God the Father, God the Son, and God the Holy Ghost, bless, preserve and keep you; the Lord mercifully with his favor look upon you and so fill you with all spiritual benediction and grace, that you may so live together in this live, that in the world to come ye may have life everlasting. Amen.

Then shall the minister say:

Our Father, who art in heaven, hallowed be thy name. Thy kingdom come. Thy will be done on earth, as it is in heaven. Give us this day our daily bread. And forgive us our trespasses, as we forgive those who trespass against us. And lead us not into temptation; but deliver us from evil: for thine is the kingdom, the power, and the glory, forever. Amen.

Then shall the minister say:

O God of Abraham, God of Isaac, God of Jacob, bless this man and woman, and sow the seeds of eternal life in their hearts, that whatsoever in thy holy word they shall profitably learn, they may indeed fulfill the same. Look, O Lord, mercifully upon them from heaven and bless them. And as thou didst send thy blessings upon Abraham and Sarah, to their great comfort, so vouchsafe to send thy blessings upon this man and this woman, that they obeying thy will, and always being in safety under thy protection, may abide in thy love unto their lives' end, through Jesus Christ our Lord. Amen.

O God, who by thy mighty power hast made all things of nothing who also (after other things set in order). didst appoint that out of man (created after thine own image and similitude,) woman should take her beginning; and knitting them together, didst teach that it should never be lawful to put asunder those whom thou, by matrimony, hast made one; O God who has consecrated the state of matrimony to such an excellant mystery, that in it is signified and represented the spiritual marriage and union betwixt Christ and his Church,—look mercifully upon this man and this woman; that both this man may love his wife according to thy word (as Christ did love his spouse, the Church, who gave himself for it, loving and cherishing it even as his own flesh,) and also that this woman may be loving and obedient to her husband; and in all quietness, sobriety and peace, be a follower of holy and godly matrons. O Lord, bless them both, and grant them to inherit thy everlasting kingdom, through Jesus Christ our Lord. Amen.

Then shall the minister say:

Almighty God, who at the beginning didst create our first parents, Adam and Eve, and didst sanctify and join them together in marriage, pour upon you the riches of his grace, sanctify and bless you that ye may please him both in body and soul, and live together in holy love unto your lives' end. Amen.

BURIAL OF THE DEAD

(We will on no account whatever make a charge for burying the dead.)

448. Form for the Burial of the Dead

Any of these Scriptures may be taken for the occasion.

The Minister, going before the Corpse, shall say:

I am the resurrection, and the life; he that believeth in me, though he were dead, yet shall he live; and whosoever liveth and believeth in me shall never die John xi, 25, 26).

I know that my Redeemer liveth, and that he shall stand at the later day upon the earth: and though after my skin worms destroy this body, yet in my flesh shall I see God: whom I shall see for myself, and mine eyes shall behold, and not another. Job: xix(25-27.

We brought nothing into this world, and it is certain we can carry nothing out. The Lord gave, and the Lord hath taken away; blessed be the name of the Lord. 1Tim. vi, 7; Job i, 21.

In the House or Church may be read one or both of the following Psalms, or some other suitable portion of the Holy Scriptures:

We may read this at the unsaved but not at the saved.

I said, I will take heed to my ways ,that I sin not with my tongue: I will keep my mouth with a bridle, while the wicked is before me. I was dumb with silence. I held my peace, even from good; and my sorrow was stirred. My heart was hot within me; while I was musing the fire burned: then spake I with my tongue, Lord, make me to know mine end, and the measure of my days, what it is; that I may know how frail I am. Behold, thou hast made my days as a handbreadth; and mine age is as nothing before thee; verily every man at his best state is altogether vanity. Surely every man walketh in a vain show: surely they are disquieted in vain: he heapeth up riches, and knoweth not who shall gather them. And now, Lord, what wait I for? my hope is in Thee. Deliver me from all my transgressions: make me not the reproach of the foolish. I was dumb, I opened not my mouth; because thou didst it. Remove thy stroke away from me; I am consumed by the blow of thine hand. When thou with rebukes does correct man for iniquity, thou makest his beauty to consume away like a moth: surely every man is vanity. Hear my prayer, O Lord, and give ear unto my cry; hold not thy peace at my tears; for I am a stranger with thee, and a sojourner, as all my fathers were. O spare me, that I may recover strength, before I go hence, and be no more.

Psalm xc:

Lord, thou has been our dwelling-place in all generations. Before the mountains were brought forth, or ever thou hadst formed the earth and the world, even from everlasting to everlasting, thou art God. Thou turnest man to destruction; and sayest, Return, ye children of men. For a thousand years in thy sight are but as yesterday when it is past, and as a watch in the night Thou carriest them away as with a flood; they are as a sleep; in the morning they are like grass which groweth up. In the morning it flourisheth, and groweth up; in the evening it is cut down, and withereth. For we are consumed by thine anger, and by thy wrath are we troubled. Thou hast set our iniquities before thee, our secret sins in the light of thy countenance. For all our days are passed away in thy wrath; we spend our years as a tale that is told. The days of our years are threescore years and ten; and if by reason of strength they be four score years, yet is their strength labor and sorrow; for it is soon cut off, and we fly away. Who knoweth the power of thine anger? even according to thy fear, that we may apply our hearts unto wisdom. Return, O Lord, how long? and let it repent thee concerning thy servants. O satisfy us early with thy mercy; that we may rejoice and be glad all our days Make us glad according to the days wherein thou hast afflicted us, and the years wherein we have seen evil. Let thy work appear unto thy servants, and thy glory unto their children. And let the beauty of the Lord our God be upon us; and establish thou the work of our hands upon us; yea, the work of our hands establish thou it.

Then may follow the reading of the Epistle, as follows:

1 Corinthians xv, 41-58:

There is one glory of the sun, and another glory of the moon, and another glory of the stars; for one star differeth from another star in glory. So also is the resurrection of the dead. It is sown in corruption, it is raised in incorruption: it is sown in dishonor,it is raised in glory; it is sown in weakness, it is raised in power; it is sown a natural body, and is raised a spiritual body. And so it is written, The first man Adam was made a living soul; the last Adam was made a quickening spirit. Howbeit that was not first which is spiritual, but that which is natural; and afterward that which is spiritual. The first man is of the earth, earthy; the second man is the Lord from heaven. As is the earthy, such are they also that are earthy, and as is the heavenly, such are they also that are heavenly. And as we have borne the image of the earthy, we shall also bear the image of the heavenly. Now this I say, brethren, that flesh and blood cannot inherit the kingdom of God; neither doth corruption inherit incorruption. Behold, I show you a mystery; We shall not all sleep, but we shall all be changed, in a moment, in the twinkling of an eye, at the last trump: for the trumpet shall sound, and the dead shall be raised incorruptible, and we shall be changed. For this corruptible must put on incorruption, and this mortal must put on immortality, then shall be brought to pass the saying that is written, Death is swallowed up in victory. O death, where is thy sting? O grave, where is thy victory? The sting of death is sin; and the strength of sin is the law. But thanks be to God, which giveth us the victory through our Lord Jesus Christ. Therefore, my beloved brethren, be ye steadfast, unmovable, always abounding in the work of the Lord, forasmuch as ye know that your labor is not in vain in the Lord.

At the grave, when the Corpse is laid in the Earth, the Minister shall say:

Man that is born of a woman hath but a short time to live, and is full of misery. He cometh up, and is cut down like a flower: he fleeth as it were a shadow, and never continueth in one stay.

In the midst of life we are in death; of whom may we seek for succor, but of thee, O Lord, who for our sins are justly displeased?

Yet, O Lord God most holy, O Lord most mighty, O holy and most merciful Saviour, deliver us not into the bitter pains of eternal death.

Thou knowest, Lord, the secrets of our hearts; shut not thy merciful ears to our prayers, but spare us, Lord most holy; O God most mighty, O holy and merciful Saviour, thou most worthy Judge eternal, suffer us not at our last hour for any pains of death to fall from thee.

Then, while the Earth shall be cast upon the Body by some standing by, the Minister shall say:

Forasmuch as it hath pleased Almighty God, in his wise

providence, to take out of the world the soul of the departed, we therefore commit his body to the ground, earth to earth; ashes to ashes; dust to dust; looking for the general resurrection in the last day, and the life of the world to come, through our Lord Jesus Christ; at whose second coming in glorious majesty to judge the world, the earth, and the sea shall give up their dead; and the corruptible bodies of those who sleep in him shall be changed and made like unto his own glorious body; according to the mighty working whereby he is able to subdue all things unto himself.

Then shall be said:

I heard a voice from heaven saying unto me, Write, From henceforth blessed are the dead who die in the Lord: Even so, saith the Spirit, for they rest from their labors.

Then shall the Minister say:
Lord, have mercy upon us.
Christ, have mercy upon us.
Lord, have mercy upon us.

This prayer only can be prayed at the save grave.

Then the Minister may offer this Prayer:

Almighty God, with whom do live the spirits of those who depart hence in the Lord, and with whom the souls of the faithful, after they are delivered from the burden of the flesh, are in joy and felicity: we give thee hearty thanks for the good examples of all those thy servants, who, having finished their course in faith, do now rest from their labors. And we beseech thee, that we, with all those who are departed in the true faith of thy holy name, may have our perfect consummation and bliss, both in body and soul, in thy eternal and everlasting glory, through Jesus Christ our Lord. Amen.

The Collect.

O Merciful God, the Father of our Lord Jesus Christ, who is the resurrection and the life; in whom whosoever believeth shall live, though he die, and whosoever liveth and believeth in him shall not die eternally; we meekly beseech thee, O Father, to raise us from the death of sin unto the life of righteousness; that when we shall depart this life we may rest in him; and at the general resurrection on the last day may be found acceptable in thy sight, and receive that blessing which thy well-beloved Son shall then pronounce to all that love and fear thee, saying, Come, ye blessed children of my Father, receive the kingdom prepared for you from the beginning of the world. Grant this, we beseech thee, O merciful Father, through Jesus Christ our Mediator and Redeemer. Amen.

Our Father who are in heaven, hallowed be thy name. Thy kingdom come. Thy will be done on earth, as it is in heaven. Give us this day our daily bread: and forgive us our trespasses, as we forgive them that traspass against us; and lead us not into temptation, but deliver us from evil; for thine is the kingdom, and the power, and the glory, forever. Amen.

The grace of our Lord Jesus Christ, and the love of God, and the fellowship of the Holy Ghost, be with us all evermore. Amen.

Article V, as an additional piece to the Constitution, covering doctrinal points and articles of faith.

The Apostolic Faith Mission, 312 Azusa Street, stands for the following Scriptural Doctrines, ordinances, and truths, to-wit:

First, as amended: "Justification by faith, which we interpret as being the 'Forgiveness of Sins,' which is the 'New Birth,' spoken of in John 3:1-13; also Acts 10:42-43; Rom. 3:25. The Doctrine of Justification shall not be changed."

Second, as amended: "Sanctification by faith as a second definite work of Grace upon the heart, which represents entire cleansing, made Holy in heart" John 17:15-17; 1 Thess. 4:3-5; Thess. 4:3; Heb. 2:11-13; Heb.10:10; Heb. 13:12. The doctrine of Sanctification cannot be changed.

Third, as amended: "The Baptism with the Holy Ghost as a gift of power upon the sanctified life, an anointing for service and work" Acts 2:1-4; Acts 10:45-46; Acts 19:6; 1 Cor. 4:21.

Fourth, as amended: "The speaking in tongues being one of the 'signs following' the baptised believers and other evidences of the Bible casting out devils, healing the sick and with the fruits of spirit accompanying the signs" 1 Cor. 13; Mark 16:16-19; Acts 2:23; Acts 10:44-45-46; Acts 19:6.

Fifth, as amended: "We believe and teach that God intended and Jesus taught that there could be no Holy union between man and woman after divorcement for any cause, so long as both parties to the first covenant lives" Mal. 2:14-17; Matt. 5:32; Matt. 19:3-9; Mark 10:11-12; Luke 16:18; Rom. 7:1-4; 1 Cor. 7:39.

Sixth, as amended: "We believe in the ordinance of 'Water Baptism,' and teach that immersian is the only mode, in the name of the Father and of the Son, and of the Holy Ghost, only one dip, in the name of the Trinity."

Seventh, as amended: "We believe in the ordinance of the Lord's Supper as insttiuted by Jesus and followed by the Apostles, and teach that it, should be frequently observed in holy reverence."

We do not believe in Baptizing babies or children before they come to the age oc accountability. A little child cannot believe.

Eighth, as amended: "We believe in feet washing as an ordinance, as it was established by our Master before the Lord's Supper, according to John 13:4-18, and believe it was practiced by the Apostles and disciples through the First Century." I Tim, 5:10.

To belong to this faith they must obey its teachings.

MARRIAGE.

* 1. We do not prohibit our people from marrying persons who are not of our Church, provided such persons have the New Birth, and are seeking the power, of godliness; but we are determined to discourage their marrying persons who do not come up to this description. Many of our Members have married **unawakened** persons. This has produced bad effects; they have been either hindered for life, or have turned back to perdition.

* 2. To discourage such marriages, 1. Let every Minister publicly enforce the Apostle's caution. "Be ye not unequally yoked together with unbelievers" (2 Cor. vi. 14). 2. Let all be exhorted to take no step in so weighty a matter without advising with the more serious of their brethren.

* 3. In general a woman ought not to marry without the consent of her pearents. Yet there may be exceptions. For if, 1. A woman believe it to be her duty to marry; if, 2. Her parents absolutely refuse to let her marry any Christian; then she may, nay ought to marry to marry without their consent. Yet even then a Minister ought not to be married to her.

SLAVERY.

We declare that we are as much as ever convinced of the great evil of Slavery. We believe that the buying, selling, or holding of human beings, to be used as chattles, is contrary to the laws of God and nature, and inconsistent with the Golden Rule, and with that Rule in our Discipline which requires all who desire to continue among us to "do no harm," and to "avoid evil of every kind." We therefore affectionately admonish all our Ministers and people to keep themselves pure from this great evil, and to seek its extirpation by all lawful and Christian means.

EDUCATIONAL INSTITUTIONS

Our preachers must take a caurse of studies as the Bishop shall prescribe later on.

* I. The educational institutions under the patronage of the Church shall be classified as follows:

1. Primary Schools,
2. Secondary Schools,
3. Colleges,
4. Universities,
5. Schools of Theology,
6. Apostolic Faith or Bible Schools,

In mission fields and other localities where inadequate provision has been made for elementary instruction, primary schools may be established.

THE ORDINANCE OF FEET WASHING

Then shall the minister say on the night or day when they gather to wash feet: Dear Beloved Brethren; We have gathered here in the name of our Lord Jesus Christ to partake in this holy and sacred Ordinance of Foot Washing which our Lord instituted on the same night he instituted the Lord's Supper, so we count it a happy night or day to carry it out. For our Lord said (John 13:13-17): "Ye call me master and Lord, and ye say well; for so I am. If I am then, your Lord and master have washed your feet; ye also ought to wash one another's feet. For I have given you an example that ye should do as I have done to you. Verily, verily, I say unto you: The servant is not greater than his Lord; neither he that is sent greater than he that sent him. If ye know these things, happy are ye if ye do them." Then the minister shall say to his people this is the Master's saying, so we will obey it. Then shall he say Christ so loved the church, that he gave himself for it, that he might sanctify by the washing of water by the word, that he might present unto himself a glorious Church without spots or wrinkle, or any such thing; but that it should be Holy and without blemish. So when we wash each other feet we acknowledge that we are washed in the Blood of Jesus, and have pure hearts, and love each other. So Foot Washing gives every member a chance to examine himself before taking the Lord's Supper. So he can wash all the stripe like the Phil Jailer (Acts 16:21), that is to say if we wrong any we will be willing to Humble ourselves. The minister can read St. John 13 and comment on it as the Lord gave words to say in Harmony with the ordinance.

THE CHURCH AND ITS MISSION

The mission of the Church is to "Go Ye therefore and teach all nations, baptize them in the name of the Father, and of the Son, and the Holy Ghost. Teaching them to observe all things whatsoever I have commanded you: and lo, I am with you always, even unto the end of the world. Amen."

Now the church is to teach all that the Saviour commanded it to teach. Matt 28:19-20; Matt. 10:1-14; Luke 9:1-6; Luke 10:1-20; Luke 22:35-37.

So the Church is to hold fast to Christ's teaching till he comes. Our children are to be instructed in their homes; the little babes are to be blessed by the church. Christ commanded to bring the little children to the church and have them blessed. And they brought young children to him, that he should touch them; and his disciples rebuked those that brought them.

But when Jesus saw it, he was much displeased, and said unto them, Suffer the little children to come unto me, and forbid them not: for of such is the kingdom of God.

Verily I say unto you, Whatsoever shall not receive the kingdom of God as a little child, he shall not enter therein.

And he took them up in his arms, put his hands upon them, and blessed them.

DUTY OF PARENTS

I. The duty of parents to their children.
  1. They should love them.
     Titus 2:4.
  2. They should train them up for God.
     Prov. 22:6.
     Eph. 6:4.
  3. They should instruct instruct them in God's word.
     Deut. 4:9.
     Deut. 11:19.
     Isa. 38:19
  4. They should rule them.
     1 Tim. 3:4, 12.
  5. They should correct them.
     Prov. 13:24.
     Prov. 19:18.
     Prov. 23:13.
     Prov. 12:7.

II. Good parents.
  1. Pity their children.
     Psa. 103:13.
  2. Provide for their children.
     2 Cor. 12:14
     1 Tim. 5:8.
  3. Pray for their children.
     1 Chr. 29:19.
     Job 1:5.
     John 4:46-49.

DUTY TO CHILDREN

I Children are
  1. A blessing
     Prov. 10:1
     Prov. 15:20

Prov. 17:6.
Psa. 128:1-4.
2. A gift from God.
Psa. 127:3.
Gen. 33:5.
II. The duty of children.
1. They should obey God.
Deut. 30:2.
2. They should seek God early.
Eccl. 12:1.
3. They should attend to parental teaching.
Prov. 1:8, 9.
4. They should honor their parents.
Heb. 12:9.
5. They should obey their parents.
Prov. 6:20-23.
Eph. 6:1-3.
6. They should take care of their parents.
1 Tim. 5:4.
III. Good children.
1. Observe the law of God.
Prov. 28:7.
2. Shall be blessed.
Prov. 3:1-6.
3. Show love to their parents.
Gen. 46:29.

A CHRISTIAN HOME

A christian home is one of the sweetest places on God's green earth. It is a place where God is honored: a place where the Christ of God is worshipped! O how blessed it is to enter a Christian home where God is honored! God is mindful of our homes for we read in Gen. 18:17 and 19, God said, "Shall I hide from Abraham the destruction of Sodom and Gomorrah? Shall I hide from Abraham that thing which I do, seeing that Abraham shall surely become a great nation and all the nations of the earth shall be blessed in him: for I know him." Praise the Lord! God knows us. He knows our hearts, praise his name! Just listen to what God said about Abraham? Can he say that about every home? This is a standard for us to go by. I know him that he will command his children and his household. Everything followed him: that is to say that the whole family would follow the example of Abraham in holiness and obedience to God's word. It is so blessed when you can find a home saved. The father takes his place at the head of the home. Eph. 5:23. He rules it according to the word of God. Again God says, "And they shall keep the way of the Lord to do justice and judgment: that the Lord may bring upon Abraham that which he has spoken of him. We read again in 1 Tim. 3-4, To be a bishop he must have a home that will measure up to the word, he must be one that ruleth well his own house, having his children in subjection with all gravity, for if a man know not how to rule his own house how shall he take care of the Church of God. 1 Tim. 3, 4, 5. We read again in the Old Testament,

Joshua 24:15. Joshua could speak for his whole family. When the Israelites were going astray after other gods Joshua brought them together, and he said: "If it seem evil unto you to serve the Lord, choose you this day whom you will serve whether the gods which your fathers serve when you were on the other side of the flood, or the Gods of the Amorites in whose land ye dwelt, but, as for me and my house, we will serve the Lord." And the people answered and said, "God forbid that we should forsake the Lord, to serve other Gods." We can see that Joshua's home was a home for God. The promise is to you and your children. Act 2:39. We see in another place in the word where God saves a whole home in one night. The Philippian jailer was saved and his whole household. Acts 16:32. This was a wonderful time in the prison. O how sweet it is to be a servant of God! We see that they had been beaten for this Gospel. But they were not discouraged. They prayed and sang at midnight and Heaven and Earth met together in that jail and God shook all those locks open so that they could carry on the meeting for souls. God awoke the jailer out of his sleep and he was saved that night and all his house was saved. Home is a place where characters are fashioned. If the Lord rules the home, all will be right. Home is a place where father and mother are found; where children are born and reared. It is a community of persons, self-governed, or a kingdom within itself. It is an organization formed by God himself. The home is a sacred place which should be godly. Our preachers, statesmen, governors, and president comes from the home. When Moses was found, Pharaoh's daughter said, "Take this child away and nurse it for me and I will give thee thy wages." The woman took the child and nursed it. Ex.2:9. This was the great leader of Israel. O how sweet these words are! "Take this child away and nurse it for me and I will give thee thy wages." This is God's word to every mother. "Take this child and raise it for God" and he will pay us in glory, for we don't know what he will be for God. We should be more careful in rearing our children. Although many homes have not children, they should be Christian homes just the same so that God would make them blessings to those who enter in them.

THE SOUL OF MAN

The soul is the real man. Matt. 16:26. For what is a man profited if he gain the whole world and lose his own soul or what shall a man give in exchange for his soul? And fear not them that kill the body but are not able to kill the soul;

but rather fear him which is able to destroy both soul and body in hell. Matt. 10:28. The soul stands for the whole man. It is immortal and immaterial. But yet man himself is a trinity. He is a trinity like his maker. Consisting of spirit, soul and body. 1 Thes. 5:23. And the very God of peace sanctify you wholly; and I pray God your whole spirit and soul and body be preserved blameless unto the coming of our Lord Jesus Christ. Faithful is he that calleth you, who also will do it. So we see that we are spirit and soul and body.

The soul stands for the whole man because it will be required at the judgment. Thou fool, this night thy soul shall be required of thee. Luke 12:20.

Since man fell he has a perfect salvation granted him through Jesus Christ for spirit, soul and body. 1 Thes. 5:23. So, when speaking about the eternal existence of man, we say his soul.

The spirit, the higher nature of man is that which knows God. John 3:5-6. Jesus answered, "Verily, verily I say unto thee, Except a man be born of water and of the Spirit, he cannot enter into the Kingdom of God. That which is born of the flesh is flesh; and that which is born of the Spirit is Spirit." Therefore it is through the Spirit that we know God. St. John 4:24. God is a spirit and they that worship him must worship him in Spirit and in truth. The Spirit is man's higher nature which knoweth God and commune with God by the Spirit. Before we can know God we must repent of our sins and accept Jesus and be born of the Spirit. Then we can know God for we have his Spirit to witness with our Spirit that we are the sons of God. The Spirit itself beareth witness with our Spirit, that we are children of God. Rom. 8:16. The Spirit is the higher nature of man which knows God, distinguishes between right and wrong and is capable of religious affections, emotions and exercises. This is Spiritual life.

MAN A TRINITY

The highest life a man can live is to commune with God, being born again and being filled with God's spirit.

Man, according to the Bible philosophy, is a trinity like his creator, consisting of spirit, soul and body. 1 Thes. 5:23. And the very God of peace sanctify you wholly; and I pray God your whole spirit, and soul and body be preserved blameless unto the coming of our Lord Jesus Christ.

Faith is he that calleth you, who also will do it. Heb. 4:12.

The word of God is quick and powerful, and sharper than any two-edged sword, piercing even to the dividing asunder of soul and spirit and the joints and marrow, and is discerner of the thoughts and intents of the heart. Neither is there any creature that is not manifest in his sight. Heb. 4:12, 13. Man is a trinity. The spirit is his higher nature, that which knows God and distinguisnes between right and wrong. Adam knew right from wrong because as soon as he did wrong he hid himself from the presence of God. Gen. 2:17; Gen. 3:7.

The spirit is the higher nature of man, capable of religious affections, emotions and exercise. The physical is the other extreme. It is the earthy part of man, material organism indewlt by the soul. They are tied together with spirit and the instrument of its desires, purposes and operations. Intermediate between these is the soul, the rational mind, the seat of the affections, the understanding, that which loves and hates, that which can discriminate, that which thinks, that which can be cultivated and which has at once its lower passion and its fined tastes.

The physical man is the man that is controlled by the physical nature. There are three conditions in which we may live. First, we may be controlled by our lower nature, our animal life or existence—our body and its gross appetites. This is pure sensuality, the real flesh life, the fruit of the flesh. Gal. 5:19-21.

Secondly, by our intellectual department, our tastes; by our intelligence and our affections and passions; the proud and haughty physical nature. If a man is controlled by his intelligence, it makes him proud many times. If he is controlled by his mind alone, he will be heady and high minded. He will be nice but in his heart he will be proud. Nothing can atone for him but the blood of Jesus Christ, the Son of God.

Thirdly, he may be controlled by his spiritual nature. This will be quite different. The man that is controlled by his intellect will be worldly minded. His mind must be fed. How? By the material things—shows, picnics, card parties, dances, and big dinners. The natural man is controlled by his natural mind. He cannot help it because he was born after the fallen Adam. He must be born again. St. John 3:3. Behold I was shapen in iniquity and in sin did my mother conceive me. Psalms 51:5; Psalms 58:3.

Since all three departments of man's nature are fallen and under the curse, he needs the blood of Jesus Christ. When a man is born again he is a new cerature. 2 Cor. 5:17. Old things are passed away, all things have become new.

Since the three departments are fallen we need to turn the whole man over to God. 1 Thes. 5:23. All of these departments are tied together by the almighty God. His body is mortal, his spirit and soul are immortal.

It seems that the soul stands for the entire man or the whole of man. Heb. 10:39.

Believing to the saving of the soul. "What will it profit a man if he gain the whole world and lose his own soul."

Temptations are great but the blood is sufficient for every trial. If we yield to the bodily appetites, we become sensual; if we yield to those of the mind, we become worldly-minded, and if we yield to an evil spirit we become devilish. May God help us to become strong and arm ourselves against the flesh. Eph. 6:10, 11.

We must remember that every man that is born in the world is lame in his intellect, will and affections. He must be born again and get sanctified and get filled with the Holy Ghost and go on to perfection. Heb. 6:1-4. That is the only safeguard for Christians.

Many churches today get a physical preacher to preach about Christ and many of them know nothing about Christ because they have not been born again. The Bible teaches that a man must be born again. St. John 3:3.

We learn from the Bible that a man must be holy to see God. Matt. 5:8. In Christ's first sermon on the mount, he preached holiness. Matt. 5:8; Matt. 5:20; Matt. 5:48; Heb. 12:14. Holiness, without which no man shall see the Lord. Many people today go to church and just hear a physical sermon and come back no better in their soul than they were before going. God help us. Amen.

PLAN OF SALVATION

The plan of salvation is already laid, so we can do nothing to improve it. It is fixed for all eternity. We are to accept it as it is. When we set up our own standard of holiness for God to work by, we dishonor God and set up an idol in our hearts. When we do this, also we tell God in the way we act that we won't hear his word without him coming to our terms. God wants us to have faith to take him at his word. So many people have made shipwreck of their faith by setting up a standard for God to respect or come to. When we set up tongues to be, the Bible evidence of Baptism in the Holy Ghost and fire only. We have left the divine word of God and have instituted our own teaching. But if we will take the divine word of God, it will lead us right. Ezekiel 14, says when a man set up any idols in his heart and seek the Lord, and if the prophet be deceived. He says he is the one that deceive the prophet. Ezekiel 14:9.

While tongues is one of the signs that follows God's spirit filled children, they will have to know the truth and de- the truth. If not, grievious wolves will enter in among the flock and tear asunder the sheep. How will he get in? They will come in through the sign gift of speaking in tongues, and if God's children did not know anything more than that to be the evidence, they would not have no hard time to enter in among them and scatter them. The Holy Ghost gives men and women wisdom to execute the power of his word. 1 Cor. 4:20.

All ordination must be done by men not women. Women may be ministers but not to Baptize and ordain in this work.

THE APOSTOLIC FAITH

Stands for the restoration of the faith once delivered to the saints—the old-time religion, of camp meetings, revivals, missions, street and mission work and Christian unity everywhere. According to God's word. John 17:21-22.

Teaching on Repentance. Mark 1:14, 15.

Godly Sorrow for Sins—Examples: Matt. 9:13; 2 Cor. 7:9, 11; Acts 3:19; Acts 17:30.

Confession of Sin. Luke 15:21; Luke 18:13.

Forsaking Sinful Ways. Isa. 55:7; Jonah 3:8; Prov. 28:13.

Restitution. Ezek. 33:15; Luke 19:18 ,and Faith in Jesus Christ.

Jesus died for our sins and arose for our Justification

Rom. 4:25.

First Work: Justification is that act of God's free grace by which we receive remission of sins Rom. 3:25; Acts 10:42, 43; Rom. 5:1,10; John 3:3,14; 2 Cor. 5:17.

The Holy Ghost call the second work the second benefit. The margin read second grace. And the Syriac read that you might receive the grace doubly. 2 Cor. 1:15.

Second Work: Sanctification is the second work of grace and is that act of God's grace by which He makes us holy in Doctrine and life. John 17:15, 17; Heb. 13:12; 2:11; Heb. 12:14. Jesus opened the Bibye to his disciples before He went back to Heaven. Luke 24:24-50. He taught his doctrine to them well before He went to Heaven so when we get sanctified Jesus will teach us the Bible also, bless the Lord.

Sanctification is cleansing to make holy. The disciples were sanctified before the day of Pentecost. By careful study of Scripture, you will find it is so now. "Ye are clean through the word which I have spoken unto you" John 15:3; John 13:10; and Jesus had breathed on them the Holy Ghost. John 20:21, 22. You know that they could not receive the Spirit if they were not all clean. Jesus cleansed and got all doubt out of His church before He went back to glory. The Disciples had the grace of the Spirit before the day of Pentecost. The Disciples had an infilling of the spirit before the day of Pentecost. For Jesus had cleansed the Sanctuary and they had the witness in their hearts that he was their risen Lord and Savior and continually in the temple praising and blessing God. Luke 24:51, 53.

The baptism in the Holy Ghost and fire means to be flooded with the love of God and Power for Service, and a love for the truth as it is in God's word. So when we receive it we have the same signs to follow as the disciples received on the day of Pentecost. For the Holy Spirit gives us a sound mind, faith, love and power. 2 Tim. 1:7. This is the standard Jesus gave to the Church.

The greatest evidence of the Holy Spirit abiding in the believer is what Jesus Christ promised he would do. Jesus promised he would teach us all things, and bring all things to your remembrance, whatsoever I have said unto you, so he means what he says, whatsoever I have said so he means what he says. John 14:17-26. Also John 16:7-15. So when he comes he does that in the believer, for he does it for me.

Seeking Healing. We must believe that God is able to heal. Exodus 15:26, "I am the Lord that healeth thee." Jas. 5:14; Psa. 103:3; 2 Kings 20:5; Matt. 8:16, 17; Mark 16:16-18. "Behold I am the Lord, the God of all flesh; is there anything too hard for me?" Jer. 32:27; Luke 24:52, 53. With great joy.

God, Spirit and Word goes together. They are the two witnesses spoken of in Zech. 4:3-14; Rev. 11:3. When these two witnesses are not recognized all kinds of confusion will be manifested in the Church.

Too many have confused the grace of Sanctification with the Enduement of Power, or the Baptism with the Holy Ghost; others have taken "the annointing" (John 20:21-24) which we receive after we are santified for the Baptism and failed to reach the glory and power of a true Pentecost. Acts 2:3, 4.

We read in the second chapter of Colossians, "Beware lest any man spoil you through philosophy and vain deceit, after the tradition of men, after the rudiments of the world, and not after Christ" This chapter tells us about Christ blotting out the handwriting of ordinances that were against, and contrary to us, and I am glad he did nail these ordinances to the cross with Him, took them out of the way, nailing it to His cross. Bless the Lord. These were the old Jewish ordinances of divers washings, Sabbath days, new moons, circumcision and the passover supper, and so on. But Jesus has ordinances in His church. Bless His dear Name.

Three ordinances Christ Himself instituted in His Church. First—He commands His ministers to baptise in water in the name of the Father and the Son and the Holy Ghost. Matt. 28:19; and it was practiced by the Apostles. Acts 2:38; Acts 22:16; Acts 8:12, 17. The enuch Acts 8:35,38. The Apostle Paul was baptised. So many cases we can find in Acts where it was practiced after John the Baptist had died. Second—Foot washing is an ordinance that Jesus Himself instituted in His Church, and we, His followers, should observe it. For He has commanded us to observe all things that He has commanded us to teach. So we find we will have to recognize these three ordinances.

We believe in the feet washing; we, believe it to be an ordinance, John 13: Jesus said, in the 13th verse of the 13th Chapter of John: "Ye call me Master and Lord, and ye say well, for so I am." Verse 14th: "If I then, your Lord and Master, have washed your feet, ye also ought to wash one another's feet." Verse 15: "Says, for I have given you an example, that ye should do as I have done to you. Verily, verily I say unto you, the servant is not greater than his Lord: neither is he that is sent greater than he that sent him. If ye know these things, happy are ye if ye do them. John 13:13-17.

We believe in the ordinance of the Lord's supper, as it is set forth in 1 Cor. 11:2, 23-34; and Matt. 26:26-29. We believe in taking unfermented wine and unleavened bread.

We believe in water baptism. Our mode is immersion only, and single, in the name of the Father, and of the Son, and of the Holy Ghost. Matt. 28:19,20; 2 Cor. 13:13; and as much light as the Holy Ghost will reveal to us by His word. We, the ministers, must be the husbands of one wife, 1 Tim. 3:2; Tit. 1:6-9. We do not believe in unscriptural marriage. Rom. 7; 2-4; 1 Cor. 7:39.

In Matt. 19:3-9; Matt. 5:32, and Mark 10:5-11, Jesus restored marriage back to the Edenic standard. Many are confused over the meaning of these passages. If either the husband or wife have defiled themselves in the sins mentioned Jesus does not give either recognition as being legally married, while the first husband or wife is still living. They must repent to God and be reconciled to each other (1 Cor. 7:11) "for as Christ forgives so must we forgive." If a man or woman marry and either one has a living husband or wife their continuing to live together as a committing of fornication or adultery and the party who has a living husband or wife should be put away by the other, leaving the man or woman who has no living companion free to marry again to someone who is also free. 1 Cor. 7:2; Matt. 19:9.

We do not believe in making a hobby of this doctrine of divorce, but we believe in the truth by comparing Scripture with Scripture, that no one in this work can marry the second husband or the second wife, while the first one is living. Rom.

7:2,3,4; 1 Cor. 7:10, 11; 1 Cor. 7:39; 1 Tim. 3:9; Matt. 5:32; Luke 16:18; Mark 10:2-12.

Bishop Hurst says, in his Church History, that the gift of tongues has appeared in communities under powerful religious stimulus, as among the Carnisards, early Quakers, Lasare in Sweden in 1841-43, in the Irish Revival in 1859, and in the Catholic Apostolic (Irvingite) Church. (Vol. 1, page 90.)

I can say, through the power of the Spirit, that wherever God can get a people that will come together in one accord and one mind in the Word of God, the baptism of the Holy Ghost will fall upon them, like as a Cornelius' house (Acts 10:45, 46). It means, to be in one accord, as the Word says, Acts 2:42, 47.

The Blood of Jesus will never blot out any sin between man and man they can make right; but if we can't make wrongs right, the blood graciously covers. Matt. 5:24; Matt. 6:15; Matt. 18:35; 1 John 1:7-9.

Dear Loved Ones: God's promises are true. We read in Exodus 12:3, God commanded Moses to take a lamb for a house and a house for a lamb when he was about to bring the children out of Egypt. Bless His Holy Name, amen! They were to kill the lamb and take its blood and sprinkle it over the door overhead and the sides to save them from the destroyer. But in the very house they were instructed to eat the body. The blood saved them from the destroyer, but the body of the lamb saved them from disease and sickness. Glory to His Name! May we obey God's word and voice and we shall be saved through Jesus from sins and feast on His perfect body. Jesus is founder of His Church, the Christian Church, by His own precious Blood. Hallelujah! so Jesus is the Christian passover? So when the Jews eat the passover they remember God bringing them out of Egypt, and point to His coming. So we eat the Christian passover and remember Calvary, how Jesus died and saved us, and we look forward to His coming again.

Moses' lamb was a type of Christ, the true Lamb, so Christ is our Lamb, bringing health to our imperfect body. Moses was founder of the Jewis Church by God through the paschal lamb by the blood and body of the lamb. But Jesus is the Lamb of God, the founder of the Christian Church.

WILLIAM JOSEPH SEYMOUR.
Azusa Mission, 312 Azusa St., Los Angeles, Cal.
U.S.A.